...me shudder she is very ...nty indeed. Eternal love your ...lated houseboy.

, you are my Bristol Massive, ...yousweetie, the Hackster.

BE MINE ALL mine for all your greatest fan.

SY, WAITING for a bit of your Little miss patient.

B. When the boys are ...ed and the animals fed ...e the curtains hung and a ...e washing done. ...e there with a hug and a ...ket of love 'til the alarm ...sk goes and you pull on your clothes. All my Love P.B

BUCHI I love you crazy mad

E, I'M OFF my trolley, about ...Happy sixteenth, love Chaz.

US FOUR YEARS on and still ...gling to top the pizza. I love ...Nicola.

AFTER 5 YEARS I still have ...feeling I love you so much ...e you do all the cleaning.

THANKS! It just keeps get-...better. Love from MTM.

ER WOLFIE: LOVE you lots! ...(oh no!) mister badger

E PLUS ONE sends love to ...y dad

RLING PHILIP I love you for-...and forever. M. XXX

IN, MR TICKLE wants green ...and ham!

AIGE IS ABOUT sharing, ...g, understanding and being ...ul Dilu

CHERI: Just to let you know ... much you mean to me ... is our next cruise? Love ...ne.

YOU ARE my bonnie Prince ...lie, more than you will ever ... Lets do lunch love Lissa

LASHINGS of love from ...ghana banana! Sx

E PLUS ONE sends love to ...y dad

BUCHI I love you crazy mad

E, I'M OFF my trolley, about ...Happy sixteenth, love Chaz.

US FOUR YEARS on and still ...gling to top the pizza. I love ...Nicola.

AFTER 5 YEARS I still have ...feeling I love you so much ...e you do all the cleaning.

NGTREE PETE meet me in ...for tea and toast my treat! ...honeybun and buster ...ghter! Happy Anniversary.

OTTISH THISTLE- love you ...all my heart - Husb

KON, I see you at work every ...I want you to be my little sol-...ove Bilco.

NEIL I love you though I say ...enough, Mrs O'Neill

YOU'VE SUNVI me your flo-...ce admiral.

THAN WORDS can say. ...ever you say I love you, a ...Heart says you care.

WAITS UNDER amber lights ...de Odeon

N GA'I PLIS dwi isio gwneud ...sh? taten.

JPPET, MEET me in front of ...fire tonight, I will bring the ...o! I love you Doris.

LENTINE RISTIC for ever. ...Andy.

MOISELLE CLOCHE, WEAR ...umpers, borrow my car, but ...se come whale spotting with ...oon, love Bambi

MATT
All you did was ...alk into a bar in ...'C - changing my ...life forever. ...e my Valentine ...always. **APRIL**

---

ood, especially tonight. With love from slow Doris X.

POPPET, (C"O"CHARTERS"). Lets cuddle up in bed tonight...and read our Peter Rabbit stories! Love you more than Noddy! Pick-lexxx

P. I WILL love you until you are grey. L.

POOHY AFTER 25 years, what is there left tosay except love you. Pigs.

PAUL GSOH VGIB EIEO WITC WLYF Your Lee

PAINTED LADY. YOUR love asleep nomore fills me with wonder and joy and has made me whole again.

PETER DO YOU believe in mira-cles? I know that I do NOW! love Tink xxx

PERRO CANNOT WAIT for pup in Summer Hammie

POOH LOVES PIGLET and little woozle even more than hunnie.

PUSS, CHESTNUT TREE awaits us. love always, Lamb x

POOCH THE MONKEY's back again! love ratbag xxx

PRINCESS HOBBIT, LOVE to the prettiest of the species.

PETER LOSING LOVE is like a win-dow in your heart, ghosts and empty sockets, Pat

PIN UP A Gold Heart and show the world you care.

PARKS, PICNICS, PATRICIA- love them all but adore you.

PRACTICE CUPID'S CODE today - wear your heart on your sleeve - left sleeve if you're looking for love - right sleeve if you're in love.

PETRINA my favourite contempo-rary artist with love Simon.

PEACHY, PUMPKIN, Porcupine, Petit Pois, Pineapple, Princess. I love you. xxx

PETE let me be your Juliet and I'll prove more true than those that have more cunning to be strange. I love you.

POCAHONTAS I STILL love you with all of my heart. george

PSYCHIC FORCES FROM the vas-cular bundles of extrasecnsory mystical fibres lodged in the lower region of the pingala (and upper left ventriloquial) signal movement of fandopodistic pro-portions towards shantockolous and altogether rather pantock-olous times. You'd be a fool not to give that girl a chance. URI Geller

Q LOVES XXX. xxx loves q. quack

Quentin
Happy 1st Valentine Day I love you Now and Forever lots of love Wonder

RUTH THANKYOU FOR mmsh ily mamam 4e be my valentine Tone xxx.

ROSE YOUR MY bobbie kall my love and happy VD. I miss you lots

RETIRING ROK ROCK with me

RABBIT, MUTCH WARM, straw set-tled love you. Big Bunny

RUDE WIFE LOVES blues fan xxx.

RACHEL 4 MARCUS: I will never alter nor bend.

ROD- TIME OUT was the best place to meet. Love always Fi

ROBERT LONG BEFOR... kiss my life was neat t... spectacular. Miss swe...

ROSES ARE RED, violet... you're black and whi... brown.

ROCKVILLE ROMEO- old etcetera JTA.

ROB. TU M'AS fiance d... dresse

M.A.F!

SCHMALISON, LUBRICOUS LINEUIST sets cerebral cbe sali-uatine

SAM: It's me or the Nintendo! Looking forward to the sixth. Love Jo xxx

SCRUMPY, LET'S CRUISE off-piste in our own little boat

SUITS YOU LORD battersby eternal fluffy hearts pumpkinhead

S. COME AND go with me to the Allegheny. A.

SQUEEZE ME BUCKETS Janna! Love you

SUNSHINE THANKS FOR every-thing. I will always love you Nik.

SHAILA, YOU STILL have one book overdue... Dominic

SQUIRREL, YOU HAVE my heart until the end of time. Your'e all I need. My love, my valentine. K.

SLIPPY are you still awake, forever yours the stable girl.

SHOW YOU CARE, buy a Gold Heart and help The Variety Club

SARAH YOU ARE still what I love. flowers.

STROKED LIKE CATS? I love you always. B.

SYMPHONIC C BEAT the clock vir-tuoso. Love classic lady.

SWEET SAINT DORMOUSE still my valentine little owl.

SCHOOL LAUNDRY ROOMS, French barns, wood in Barcelona too??

SUPALUMP LOVE YOU more now than twenty years ago

SARAH,
I love you more than my hair colour.
Dino

SHARON ROSES ARE red the leaves are green, I'm in love with you, I hope you're still keen! Scott.

SARAH, LIQUEURS?

T O SUE, I love you more than yesterday, miss you, Phil.

TE QUIERO MUCHISIMO Virginia! Thanks for a wonderful past two years. Happy valentines day. All my love, from Adam. xxx

TO MY PUSSY, love you forever, purry monster.

TERTIUS ET AL will you marry me M.

TOLERANT: 4, YOU must be joking! love you anyway. Bald Eagle.

TO PEAS I love you forever love from carrots.

TO MY GRIZZLY bear, with love from your lovely Lion. V xxx

TITIN IS VERY loved from the old acro.

TO MY PRINCE charles, love always your Queen B

TO MY SEXY tons, keep smiling, from Big Hairy D.

TO THE IRISH chef with all the right ingredients I'm yours forever from this brown eyed girl.

To my Darling Caroline, I am sure that 1998 will be our best year ever. Love Mark xxx

TOM JE VEUX recommencer tes cours de francais- can you "elp me?"

TO THE GUY with a tunefull tonefull soul.

"THERESA, I LOVE you more each day, Piero"

To the captain of my heart, masses of love from your land locked tart.

To my Prince Charles, love you always your Queen B.

To Pudding, all my love as always Poo! xxx

TO "RRR" MAYBE we can get back together love "TT" xxx

TIFFANY SORRY I missed you on Monday. See you soon lots of love David

TOM IT'S NOT felt this good since Micky Thomas scored against Liverpool to win the title in 1989 - lots of love Emily xxx

TOM . ROSES ARE red, your Play Stations white lets see if we can make level one tonight. Love and kisses Emma.

TRYFAN BORNEO AND Elan. Hell and high water but still together.

TO MY BEAUTIFUL wife Alison, I am so happy to have as the sexy and exciting focus of my life. There is no more lovely a lady to grow old with! Truly in love, Philxxx. P.S. The footie is on tomorrow...

THETA REMEMBERING J.

TESSA ROSES ARE red & very prickly. I'm 'gonna make you laugh 'cause I know you're tickly. M.A.

TO BERT LOVE you loads Emma.

TO THE BODY BEAUTIFUL
with thighs of steel. You left me breathless in Cuego and overheated in the Galapagos! WHAT NEXT? **I CAN'T WAIT**

The Heart-Shaped Bullet

KATHRYN FLETT

WE TWO WERE one now three in five, with laughter our love multi-plies.

WITH LOVE FROM a badger to his ferret

WICKED HUSSY- BEAR loves you all his muches. Blue skies!

WHATEVER IT TAKES lapped sax-ophonist willingly wears double sash for sushi loving chef.

WEAR YOUR HEART on your sleeve...a Variety Club Gold Heart.

WISHING YOU A long and happy marriage to me! Love always your R.C.P. p.s nervous yet?

WILL AUNTIE MARY'S canary be happier in drawers than a back-wards FF in JL

WISHING AND MISSING my little "Giblet" a happy valentines day. Lots of love Baa-Lamb

WELCOME BACK CYNTHIA Got, please be my mistress love from an absolute bastard.

WITH LOTS OF love fron Nicol to Sooty Norah and Smudge-all the very best for 1998+.

WE TWO WERE one now three in five, with laughter our love multi-plies.

WITH LOVE FROM a badger to his ferret

WICKED HUSSY- BEAR loves you all his muches. Blue skies!

WSJJM2T THANKS FOR the best year of my life marry me. Gor-geous girl.

WHATEVER IT TAKES lapped sax-ophonist willingly wears double sash for sushi loving chef.

WEAR YOUR HEART on your sleeve...a Variety Club Gold Heart.

WHEN I'M WITH YOU life is never a bore, on holiday we were chased by hippo's, elephants and more. but I still can't wait till our next trip in May, even though you'll annoy me 24 hours a day.

YRRAB BBOC
I will be your pusher, love from your Nº1 fan YlleK xxx

YOU ARE MY debris who taught piaget and will always be the skoolie for me.

YOU PUT THE kettle on

YOU FILL UP my senses 7.7.77

YOU WON'T BELIEVE it, you'll say "It's not true!" Dawn It's just my way, to say "I love you"

YOU CHEEKY! now you've found me. your raskyroodler's holding on tight - weyhey!

YVONNE LET THE 14th be the start of something special in our hearts love Aldo, peewee pen-quin

YOU ONLY WANTED a gesture today. Happy valentines day, Lynne

YVONNE LET THE 14th be the start of something special in our hearts. Love Aldo Piwi and Pen-guin.

YOU FILL UP my senses 7.7.77 9.00pm.

YOU WON'T BELIEVE it, you'll say "It's not true!" Dawn It's just my way, to say "I love you"

YOU CHEEKY! now you've found me. your raskyroodler's holding on tight - weyhey!

YVONNE LET THE 14th be the start of something special in our hearts love Aldo, peewee pen-quin

ZOE, FOLLOW YOU, follow me, love, your Neil.

30,000 FT UP I stir my coffee and think of you. move? sometime?

ZEB MAKE THE earth move a phew more times-love always. 188 4 168

MARION, AS USUAL better late than never. I'll have a cheese sandwich, all my love Alan xxx

The
Heart-Shaped
Bullet

Kathryn Flett started her career as a staff writer on *i-D* magazine before moving to *The Face*, as Features Editor and Fashion Editor. Between 1992 and 1995 she was the Editor of the men's magazine *Arena*, and also launched the bi-annual *Arena Homme Plus*, Britain's first 100 per cent fashion magazine for men. She currently writes for the *Observer* and lives (with a Battersea rescue dog called Possum) in West London.

KATHRYN FLETT

The Heart-Shaped Bullet

PICADOR

First published 1999 by Picador

an imprint of Macmillan Publishers Ltd
25 Eccleston Place, London SW1W 9NF
Basingstoke and Oxford

Associated companies throughout the world

ISBN 0 330 37037 5

Copyright © Kathryn Flett 1999

The right of Kathryn Flett to be identified as the
author of this work has been asserted by her in accordance
with the Copyright, Designs and Patents Act 1988.

1 3 5 7 9 8 6 4 2

A CIP catalogue record for this book is available from
the British Library.

Typeset by SetSystems Ltd, Saffron Walden, Essex
Printed and bound in Great Britain by
Mackays of Chatham plc, Chatham, Kent

To my best friend, Debra Bourne,
with inexpressible love and gratitude.

'There they sat, those two happy ones, grown up and yet children – children in heart, while all around them glowed bright summer – warm, glorious summer.'

Hans Andersen, 'The Snow Queen'

The
Heart-Shaped
Bullet

contents

one

souls, bodies, thoughts, words and deeds

I was eight or nine when I designed my first wedding dress: a frothy cliché with a nipped-in waist (a waist I didn't yet possess, although I was optimistic) and an enormous bell jar of a skirt – 'Bridal Barbie' kitsch, made of something highly flammable. But I didn't actually start asserting any kind of design sensibility on this important process until I was about thirteen, rejecting enormous Cinders-you-shall-go-to-the-ball-in-polyester gowns in favour of a frankly Bianca Jagger-esque (this was, after all, the seventies) cream trouser suit with coordinating silk waistcoat. I still have the sketch, on the inside back cover of an old school exercise book.

When it came to making decisions about the real thing, though, I floundered. Having been a fashion journalist for the past ten years didn't help at all; in fact it made it worse. I was so paralysed with indecision that it was just as well I had two opportunities to crack the wedding dress conundrum: there was one outfit for the register office and another for the church blessing the following day. I had originally wanted to get married in church but my fiancé was a divorcee, and the C of E vicar couldn't be persuaded to marry me to a divorced Catholic. A disappointment, then, but one tempered by the realization that at least I would have two opportunities to dress up.

I spent the evening before I got married alone, waiting for dress number one. It arrived very late, at about eleven, accompanied by the flustered girl who had only just finished stitching it together. She hung it on the back of the living room door and left soon after, refusing my offer of tea, I think, because even the most down-to-earth prospective bride is quite dauntingly untouchable and Other. I sat on what passed for my sofa and stared at the frock, chain-smoking, for about an hour. I wasn't nervous, just introspective during the last hours of a single life.

Then I roamed the flat collecting accessories and arranging them around the dress, like fetishes at a pagan altar: a pair of cream forty-denier tights, because stockings would have ruined the line; under-wear – resolutely, perhaps shockingly, unsexy garments designed to push my premenstrual stomach in and my bust out in a very businesslike sort of way; shoes – a pair of cream fabric kitten-heeled slingbacks with pointed toes purchased in desperation the previous day (I don't know why I left it quite so late); a frilly waterproof parasol as the weather promised to be predictably autumnal; and jewellery – Victorian white sapphire drop earrings and a diamond fleur-de-lis pendant, 'something borrowed' from my mother who used to deal in antique jewellery and kept some of the best pieces when she gave it up.

The shapeless form hanging limply under polythene on the back of the living-room door was a compromise. I was actually still quite keen on the Bianca look, which was making a bit of a comeback in 1995, but I hadn't been one of those newly engaged women who spend the months leading up to the wedding starving themselves, and Bianca had never been a size fourteen, so I ended up with something that was certainly bridal, but not remotely sexy, hip, urbane or sophisticated. This dress – Empire-line cream viscose with a sweeping fishtail skirt, which I dubbed 'Pride and Prejudice' – was not really very me. I am neither delicate nor waifish, don't really do demure and would make a lousy Austen heroine. It was helped out a bit, however, by the addition of a big cream coat the designer had given to me as an afterthought, in case of the weather.

Too late now, though, to worry about my nuptial drag. At eleven the next morning, Friday 8 September 1995, at Chelsea Register Office in London's King's Road, I would not be playing Bianca to my fiancé's Mick, Grace to his Rainier or Diana to his Charles, but I would be a proud, unprejudiced, viscose-clad

Lizzie Bennet to his dashing Savile Row Darcy. Fictional characters, then, both of us.

I can't remember whether I spoke to my fiancé before I went to bed (he was staying on a friend's sofa half a mile away), but I slept a deep, untroubled seven-hour sleep with no dreams – or at least none that I could remember – and woke, uncharacteristically unfazed, to louring skies and steady drizzle. Soon after I got up, George arrived. Even if there had been the space in my tiny rented flat, I hadn't wanted a crowd in my home on the morning of my marriage, just one girlfriend whom I knew I could rely on to keep me calm, escort me around the corner to the hairdresser, pick up my bouquet, hand me over to my father, who was coming to collect me later, and, I suppose, be the sister I don't have. In the event George sort of selected herself and appeared at my door wearing a cream wool suit which effortlessly encapsulated the essence of Bianca Jagger. She cooed and fussed soothingly before we set off to get me some grown-up hair.

I'd read my share of bridal periodicals in the last few months and so I knew that this sort of thing needed to be taken very seriously. I hadn't had a trial run, hadn't even thought very specifically about how I wanted to look, but I felt sure that my long hair had to go up because the dress seemed to demand it, even though my fiancé much preferred my hair down. In the local trendy hairdressers, the owner and the 'hair-up' specialist discussed 'concepts' while I sat mute and thoughtful, and George went to collect my bouquet (pink and white roses) from the posh florist opposite, plus gratuitous amounts of *pain au chocolat* and cappuccino from the nearby deli.

I struggled to describe the dress to hair-up.

'Well, it's a bit *Pride and Prejudice* – but maybe as if they'd made it into a film in the Sixties, starring Britt Ekland,' I said, helpfully.

'Uh-huh . . .' said hair-up vaguely and started pulling me about a bit. Which is how, rather to my surprise, I was married wearing a mini-beehive.

It was raining properly and the sky was parchment white as George and I darted the couple of hundred yards back to the flat. I got dressed, slowly – there were innumerable layers and hooks and tiny buttons to negotiate. The diamond fleur-de-lis, which I planned to wear as a choker, didn't have a chain, so George sewed it onto some spare ribbon that had been used to trim my dress and then stitched the ribbon around my neck. Etiquette allegedly decrees that diamonds should never be worn before dark. Sod etiquette – this was probably going to be my only opportunity ever to wear diamonds.

I was just sponging on blobs of a slightly too pink foundation I'd impulse bought in Selfridge's a couple of days previously when the phone rang.

'Hello, darling!' said my father. 'Do you have a number for a cab company?'

This was disappointing. I had entrusted my father with organizing our transport to Chelsea ages ago, and he'd evidently left it about as late as he could. And while I had said that a taxi would be fine, I hadn't really meant it. It was, suffice to say, a very short conversation, and when I put the phone down I felt nervous for the first time.

I couldn't stop my hands from shaking, which made drawing the lipstick line a bit like that game we always had at the school fête, where you have to pass a hook along an electrified wire without touching it. By the time my father rang the doorbell, half an hour later, I might as well have been in the advanced stages of Parkinson's. George left to meet her boyfriend, BJ, and try to beat us to Chelsea. Her job was done, and anyway, the mood had changed.

My father told me I looked beautiful, of course. And, because brides in their regalia are even more spectacularly untouchable than they are the night before their wedding, he kept a bit of distance between us, occasionally glancing at me with a broad, slightly self-conscious smile.

As it turned out, I had brushed up OK. The quasi-beehive gave 'Pride and Prejudice' a welcome contemporary edge and the big white coat was not only sweepingly romantic but necessarily warming. I picked up my keys, cigarettes, the bouquet, the parasol and a small silk evening bag that had belonged to my father's mother, and then we went down in the lift to the cab, which was scab-red and not very clean. I could have been any old Friday morning fare (the driver didn't say a word) and so my father and I were driven to Chelsea. We didn't speak much, but he carried on smiling and occasionally squeezed my hand as he steeled himself to give away his only child.

Even the grandest register offices reek of civic pettiness, and Chelsea is no different. A reception room would be a nice addition. As it was, the guests hovered around in the Pledge-scented hallways, waiting for something to happen. I don't remember if I arrived before or after my fiancé, but I sought a few minutes alone in the loo with the lipliner and a Consulate and when I emerged, very matte and slightly menthol, my mother and little brother had arrived. She was a tiny silver-haired vision in a little black dress. She has always worn clothes enviably well, and I doubt that anybody would have guessed her Jackie Kennedy look came courtesy of M&S.

We were asked to sign some paperwork and pay for the marriage licence but, because neither my fiancé nor I had thought to bring any money, it fell to my soon-to-be brother-in-law to pay for it. I made a joke about whether this meant I was actually going to be married to Joe.

By this time all the thirty or so guests had arrived and filed into the Jif-lemon coloured marriage room (my best friend, Debra, was last, but not technically late). I stood outside with my father, who having been denied the opportunity to escort me down an aisle was nonetheless determined to give me away, even if it involved steering me the mere ten feet between a pair of double doors and a desk. I don't remember much after that, but it's all on the video.

Snobbish, I know, but I had hoped to be married by a man with both gravitas and received pronunciation. In the event we got John, whose sing-song, nasal, estuary accent made our union sound like the imminent departure of the 18.30 from King's Cross. In the video John exists only as a disembodied voice, while my fiancé and I try to look ... well, what, precisely? I spend most of the time either staring at the floor or at the registrar, while hopping from foot to foot and jiggling my left arm. My fiancé, on the other hand, is calm incarnate, trying to catch my eye and seek out my non-jiggling hand. We giggle quietly during the exchange of the rings (I have trouble with his), and we laugh when John pronounces us 'man and wife' before correcting himself – 'Sorry. Husband and wife.' And then, of course, we kiss and it's all over.

I've been to several register office weddings recently, and they have become increasingly personalized. I have heard 'Wonderwall' played when the bride enters, and wilfully contemporary poetry read before an outbreak of idiosyncratic vows. We had none of this. Nondescript, council-issue classical music twiddled and parped in the background, and our vows were of the bog-standard solemn and legally binding variety. This was partly because I had much more invested in the church service than I did in the legal bit; I knew I wouldn't really feel married until I'd had it resoundingly Hallelujah-ed and Amen-ed by a choir at full throttle. But it was also partly because neither of us had known we could customize the proceedings.

After the signing of the register, congratulations from the throng and some rather stiff family group shots taken behind the registrar's desk, we went and stood on the steps for more pictures. It had stopped raining, and the sun was attempting to break through the torn parchment. While it was Friday morning business as usual in the King's Road, we were married, and nothing could ever be the same again.

We walked to the small reception at the Chelsea Arts Club. In the bar a handful of bemused members played snooker, while the wedding party assembled in the garden to drink champagne. There was lunch in the conservatory, followed by rambling speeches from the Best Man, Joe, the Father of the Bride and the Groom. I don't know what I'd expected from these speeches, but they were a considerable surprise. Joe kicked off with 'Having known Kate for, um, not that long really...' and then told the circuitous tale of how, in the summer of the previous year, his brother had come to spend some time sleeping on his floor (omitting, of course, the detail that he had just emerged from a long relationship and was temporarily homeless). Joe said that he had looked forward to spending more time with his brother, but that lo and behold if he hadn't straight away found himself a girlfriend and, blimey, look where we all are today! Then my father started his speech and the video reveals that I spent the whole of it staring at my plate.

'It behoves me to name just a few guests and special friends. Patsi – Katie's mother – and her brother, Jonathan, have travelled twelve thousand miles to be here today. Had they not, I doubt if the occasion would have taken place. (*applause*)

'The Flett clan has had a very, very bad day. It's akin to the Highland Clearances. Since cockcrow this morning the clan has been halved. It has, in fact, been completely decimated . . . (*laughter*)

'It is perfectly clear to Patsi and me that Eric is a man of impeccable taste and discernment. He is clearly astute and profoundly wise. I have known him for less than a year but I have to say that I think he is a wonderful young man. And I congratulate his parents on whatever potions – actually I have written down "alchemical devices" – they used in nurturing their son. Perhaps the most important ingredient was one of love. I'm thrilled, and I know Patsi is, to welcome you into our little family, Eric. I think it was last Easter when Eric was in France, in his previous incarnation as a teacher of children with special needs, when I mentioned to Kathryn that I observed in Eric a particularly fine and all too rare quality – that of compassion.' My father and my husband glance bondingly at each other. 'I am thrilled for Kathryn and I am thrilled for Eric.'

Then my father thanks various guests for coming and manages to refer to Eric's brother, Joe, as Jim.

'We nearly called him Jim but we changed our minds,' responds his father in a flash (*much laughter*).

'Well,' says my father recovering successfully, 'I look forward to getting to know you and learning your name. What are you doing on Monday? (*laughter*)

'Kathryn's nearest and dearest are gathered around her today and we are all mindful of the love she has for us and' – very fast – 'of the depth of love and affection we hold for her.

'I know Kathryn's girlfriends have been tremendously caring and supportive of her recently, and I know all you girls had a wonderful weekend last weekend and I thank you for that. Patsi and I are very proud of our lovely and talented daughter, her qualities and achievements, and we are thrilled that she has found Eric, who clearly loves her very much. We feel sure that they will love and cherish one another, whatever fortune brings. And now ... (*patently relieved*) ... finally, we get to the good stuff!'

And my father reads from Kahlil Gibran's *The Prophet*:

'Then Almitra spoke again and said, "And what of marriage, master?" ... And he answered, saying:

"You were born together and together you shall be for evermore. You shall be together when the white wings of death scatter your days ... But let there be spaces in your togetherness, and let the winds of the heavens dance between you. Love one another, but make not a bond of love ... Give your hearts, but not into each other's keeping. For only the hands of life can contain your hearts. And stand together, yet not too near together. For the pillars of the temple stand apart, and the oak tree and the cypress grow not in each other's shadow ..."

(*a pause: silence*)

'So, may their love be great and enduring and constantly renewed. A toast to Kathryn and Eric!'

And the video records a roomful of people raising their glasses of pink champagne and muttering 'Wonderful, wonderful!' while I smile up at my father. But all the time I was thinking, *Aren't fathers of the bride meant to talk about the bride more than they talk about the groom? 'Proud of our lovely and talented daughter, her qualities and achievements?' Is that as intimate as it's going to get?* Then my new husband made his speech, which was groundbreakingly concise and to the point: 'This is a fantastic day and I'll remember it for ever ... (*tears welling, a catch in his throat*) ... and, um, we love each other, and ... we're married!' There were cheers, lots of aaah!s, a kiss from the bride followed by the cutting of the single-storey heart-shaped cake.

Hours later, at our hotel on Piccadilly, there was

one gerbera – 'our' flower – from my husband sitting in a vase on the desk. We drank some champagne and then Eric cut the ribbon of the fleur-de-lis pendant with a pair of nail scissors. Shortly after that the marriage was consummated, giggling self-consciously. There was plenty of time for a good night's sleep.

No rain the following day, but the warm last gasp of summer. I suppose the newly-weds had an enormous breakfast in bed, perhaps we made love. My husband left me in the late morning while I waited for the hair and make-up artist and some girlfriends and the designers of my second wedding dress, who were bringing their creation to the hotel at the last minute. Eric, I found out later, walked across Hyde Park in his Savile Row suit (being a bloke, he had only one outfit for both occasions) and ate some lunch on his own before meeting up with his family.

This felt much more like a wedding day. It was a Saturday, the weather was perfect, and there was the fact of having someone else to wield the make-up sponge and apply the correct-coloured foundation (week-old gold top milk, rather than yesterday's Barbie-polyurethane). It was, indeed, just as well that I had a professional in attendance because something unnervingly unattractive was starting to happen to those bits of my dermis that had been brutally waxed a few days previously. For instance, where once I had sported a daintily feminine but inescapably evident moustache, the hint of hair had been replaced by a kind of blistering effect. Still, I brushed up OK again. Yesterday's beehive was reconfigured into three looping sausage rolls at the back of my head, fiercely pinned to withstand up to a dozen hours of scrutiny, and interwoven with black silk flowers which echoed the monochromatic theme of my dress.

This was an extraordinary dress. I don't know what to make of it now and I don't quite know how it came to be the way that it did but, whatever it was and however it happened, it was a long way from anything I could ever have conceived on the back of an exercise book during double chemistry.

Created in collaboration with two dress-designer friends, the frock was a collision between a Singer Sargent painting and a Mexican fiesta, via something Holly Hunter might have worn if she'd ever had a vaguely cheerful moment during *The Piano*: a thigh-length single-breasted fitted-and-flared jacket in crisp white self-striped silk, trimmed with black-and-white tartan ribbon; a cravat of white chiffon and black silk roses at the neck; and a long sweeping bias-cut asymmetrical black silk skirt, with a pleated frill at the hem, trimmed with black ribbon which, I was assured, was made by aged widows in a remote French village and retailed at something absurd like £150 a metre. The designers had also created a secret pocket in the skirt, so that I might become one of, presumably, a very tiny minority of brides ever to walk up the aisle with a packet of Consulate and a lighter secreted on her person.

This was a Best Friend moment and so Debra turned up, as did Kelly. Kelly was, by now, my sister-in-law – but only technically, since she was in the process of divorcing my brother-in-law, Joe. Joe and Kelly remained extraordinarily close, however, to the point where Joe's new fiancée, Barbi, and Kelly were on the fast track to best friend-dom themselves. It was all very modern and complicated. My husband's ex-wife, Sue, had also been invited to the blessing, so I would be meeting her for the first time later.

Debra, a brunette pocket Venus, looked bodaciously curvaceous in a midnight-blue velvet floor-length frock; Kelly, equally dark-haired and olive-skinned, was ectomorphically dramatic in a black silk trouser suit. I was, I suppose, something in between. After I had been shoehorned into my finery and had selected the accessories (which included yet more 'something borrowed' from my mother – Victorian ruby earrings and a matching brooch), I felt quite extraordinarily conspicuous. Pale, dramatic (although perhaps more of the Arts Council grant-assisted repertory variety than, say, my friends' *films noir*) and now clad in something which prompted a friend, several hours later, to ask, 'So, Kate, do you ride side-saddle?' Staring at myself in the full-length mirror, I tried to imagine my husband's response to this incredible get-up which had bypassed fashion entirely, and I couldn't, apart from having a sudden, instinctive and nagging sense that it was something he – an avowed modernist minimalist – might loathe.

The service was at 3 p.m. I was chauffeured by Debra's boyfriend, David, who owned an impressively photogenic sixties convertible Mustang. I sat in the back and we drove slowly, to preserve my coiffure, up Park Lane and along the Bayswater Road to Notting Hill, then up Ladbroke Grove to St John's, a solid Gothic-revival Victorian church which stands in a glorified traffic island on the brow of the hill. While my friends went in to get their seats and my father, beaming, took some snaps, the vicar gave the Happy Couple a small pep talk. I don't remember Eric saying anything about how I looked, although he did seem appropriately pleased to see me. Then we were on.

If there was one bit of my marriage I wish had been captured on video, it was the service. As it is, Gorecki's 'Olden Style Piece No. 1' and 'Amen', the hymns 'Dear Lord and Father of Mankind' and 'God is Love', Fauré's 'Sanctus' and Widor's 'Toccata', Joe's reading from 1 Corinthians xiii and my oldest friend Jonathan's reading from Thomas à Kempis's *The Imitation of Christ*, not to mention the 'I have given you this ring as a sign of our marriage. With my body I honour you, all that I am I give to you, and all that I have I share with you, within the love of God,

Father, Son and Holy Spirit...' live on only in the ethereal plane. Gone, all of it.

Memories, then. Walking into the packed church, dazed (people turned up!). Getting to the end of the aisle and turning to see, in the front right-hand pew, my god-daughter, Rachel, seated next to her father, Peter. Blonde and five years old, Rachel appeared to me (and I remember the impact of this more, perhaps, than I remember anything else about the service) to be, unnervingly, a perfect miniature of her mother Susannah – my funny, warm, wild and clever Susannah, who had taken her own life six months earlier. When I saw her tiny daughter resplendent in the deep red velvet dress I had bought her, it was if my friend had turned up at my wedding. I remembered Rachel at her mother's funeral, in the front left-hand pew, next to Peter, singing 'All Things Bright and Beautiful' and had a moment of panic, in case this big strange room full of people and flowers reminded her of any of that. I wanted to pick her up and hold her very, very tight.

I remember the choir (some colleagues of Eric's from the school where he taught) going a bit wobbly during the Gorecki but doing rather better with Fauré; I remember my oldest friend Jonathan, a former actor, staring right at me while he read, passionately. I remember remembering how I had to turn away from the vicar so that I wouldn't get my skirt in a knot and trip over. I remember walking back down the aisle in some kind of suspended animation, while everyone clapped and cheered. I remember emerging, blinking, into the warm sun. I remember the chaos of the photographs, and my astonishment at the number of people who were there – the majority of them my friends rather than my husband's – and how most of them kept their distance, smiling the sort of uncynical smiles reserved exclusively for brides.

The reception, at the elegantly kitsch Polish Hearth Club in Princes' Gate, was crowded and informal. There was a buffet (paella) but no placement, so our 150 guests sat where they liked, in their cliques. There was no cake and no speech-making, but there was a toast during which Eric reprised his 'we're in love . . .' from the day before, but slightly less tearfully. Then there was dancing for hours and hours. Our first dance was to Van Morrison's 'Queen of the Slipstream' but the one that got everybody going (cue post-ironic air guitars, and lighters aloft) was Boston's 'More Than A Feeling'.

Eric and I didn't get to spend a lot of time together, but that's quite normal, apparently. My friends monopolized me and his friends monopolized him and so we both worked the room, occasionally making brief, unblinking, starry eye contact over other people's shoulders. I tried to hang on to these moments and all the other odd, disjointed snippets of conversation, with Eric and others. I was enjoying it all but conscious, too, of being swept along; of not having enough time to feel all the things I wanted to feel, or say all the things I wanted to say.

At one point Eric and I crept away into the garden and sat on a bench and, for just a few minutes, watched our wedding party happening over there, without us. I doubt if we were even missed (which is probably the sign of a good party), but if we were there would have been nudging and winking, although there was nothing to nudge or wink about because we just sat and held hands and looked up at the bright gold harvest full moon, smiling at each other. What was there to say? We were simply here, now, in the moment, together, at the beginning of it all.

Later, when it came time to throw the bouquet (I'd brought yesterday's flowers for the job – today's black roses were going to be a souvenir for Rachel) I knew exactly in which direction I wanted it to go. When she caught it, George feigned surprise, but I knew she knew it was a set-up. I wanted her to have my flowers, though, because I knew how much she wanted to marry BJ.

We left sometime around midnight. Despite my best efforts to get drunk, adrenalin had kept me sober, but my husband – *my husband!* – was, having availed himself of a great deal of the exotic Polish vodka that the (by now extremely relaxed and generously munificent) father of the bride had encouraged everyone to drink, on the house. But even if I wasn't drunk, I was high. As we were driven back to the hotel, I don't remember anything other than the sense of wanting, somehow, to relive it all. Still, it was over, we were married and that was that, for ever and ever, till death did us part. I didn't mind. As weddings went, it was the best I'd ever had.

I found out much later that at the reception a lot of people had been indulging in Class A pharmaceuticals. I'd had no idea because nobody offered me any, but then who is going to offer coke to an untouchable fairytale princess?

'Out of the nine weddings I went to last year,' said my friend Fiona, months later, 'yours was the best. You could *feel* all the love.' And I'm pretty sure she wasn't attributing it to the drugs. For some of us, at least, love was its own drug.

two

a bucketful of
oven gloves

I was thirty-and-a-half when I met my husband, and
I was more than ready.

At the start of my fourth decade I was a cliché, a
tail-end baby-boomer ten years into a career which
seemed to be on an upward trajectory and two years
into editing a glossy magazine. Although I loved it I
recognized that, increasingly, I also needed it. I was
wholly identified with my job, and entirely out of
synch with any idea of who I might be outside of that
job. My sixteenth birthday fell at the very start of the
eighties, and while I hadn't earned anything like
enough to qualify as a yuppie, that decade had been
good to me. I wasn't exactly what you'd call Political
and hadn't ever described myself as 'a feminist' but I
didn't lose much sleep about the possibility of being
able to compete with men (or win, come to that); it
was simply a given. Obviously I had to have a career
in place before I even thought about marriage. And
as for children, well, there was an infinite amount of

time before I need consider shopping around for the perfect gene pool and accessorizing myself with an ankle-biter. Children I thought about (if I thought about them at all) only with the arrogance and ignorance of peachy-skinned and oestrogen-blessed youth. I was a product of the times. Biology was not my destiny, it was simply recreation.

When I hit thirty, though, something shifted. Some kind of reappraisal was called for. Although the business of editing a magazine involves more than enough frenetic extra-curricular activity (openings, closings, reopenings, revampings, the launch of a new kind of napkin) to keep a fluffy fashion bunny abreast of the Zeitgeist, there was no escaping the fact that I hadn't stumbled across anything that resembled romance, much less a relationship, since I'd started the job two years earlier. If I wasn't exactly on the shelf, I could picture the damn shelf. Maybe from the Conran Shop, it was slightly dusty and decorated with pictures of cats and godchildren and invitations to dinner parties where 'there will just be the seven of us, hope that's OK?! . . .'. Recently, the friends who had said things like 'Well! there's obviously one thing you're not going to be short of! . . .', when I'd first told them I'd landed a job editing a men's magazine had long since stopped enquiring about my love life. I remembered the 1970s copies of *Cosmo* that had belonged to my mother. *You've Come A Long Way, Baby!* they hollered, and a career seemed to be defined mostly by one's ability to wear snappy trouser suits and have taxi drivers wolf-whistle while you jay-walked nonchalantly through the Manhattan canyons swinging a darling little calfskin briefcase containing a bottle of Charlie, a diaphragm, Marilyn French's *The Women's Room* and the *Wall Street Journal*. When I eventually got around to trying the nineties version, I twisted an ankle in a pothole. It wouldn't have happened to Lauren Hutton.

So How Far Do You Think You've Really Come, Baby? Magazines still reassured me that the Right Man was bound to stride around the next corner and head straight for my G-spot and my heart. But if he didn't that was OK, too. I could simply beat my head against the glass ceiling in a bid to distract myself from the fact that I had emotional needs that couldn't be met by either a lunch hour in Harvey Nichols or some supportive girlfriends – and probably in that order.

Why did I feel I *deserved* something more, actually *believe* that the noxious concept of Having It All was a divine right? What I sought – a successful career, a wonderful man, perfect children, a beautiful home, inner peace, intellectual stimulation, exotic travel and knees like Princess Diana – was, I knew, at least in part an agglomeration of powerful but pernicious glossy magazine fantasies, but the fantasies were too powerful to be resisted, even by a woman who helped peddle them.

Working alongside men while editing a men's magazine, constantly trying to second-guess their needs and desires and fears and then wrap all that up in a shiny package and sell it to them, meant that men were, at least in theory, my *Mastermind* specialist subject. But theory wasn't practice.

Though An Expert, by 1994 I had forgotten how to think of men as anything other than interesting items for objectified discussion, cool theorizing and raw material for fashion-page makeovers. I'd split up with my previous love, and former fiancé, Daniel (who, ironically, was also the previous editor of the magazine I now edited – our careers had been entwined for a decade), in early 1991 after six years together. It had been my decision because we seemed to be heading towards an unscratchable seven-year itch, a result of the fact that, after a year of mystifying and surreal illness, I had been diagnosed as having ME in 1989. After that our relationship, fuelled by an exhilaratingly 1980s cocktail of love, nightclubs and competitiveness, never stood a chance.

Getting the illness was the closest I came to being a yuppie. After a particularly virulent bout of flu, in 1988, my ability to cope with any mental or physical stress was undermined to the extent that just making a phone call or doing the shopping could reduce me to a wobbly, perspiring, weeping wreck. I was then working as an editor on *The Face*, and keeping on top of my work took up all my time, with weekends spent sleeping to conserve energy. But, ostrich-like, I refused to admit that something could be seriously wrong and did self-flagellatory things like joining a gym and forcing myself to do circuits at lunchtimes. Inevitably, I just succeeded in making myself ill to the point of collapse, as well as confusing and alienating those close to me with mood swings that redefined the description unpredictable.

Discovering that I was no longer able to hold down my job was the first major body-blow. After several months of going through the motions it became painfully obvious to both me and those around me that things were not exactly going according to plan. I piled self-loathing on top of self-pity on top of hopelessness and resentment ... If I wasn't capable of holding down a job I loved then just what *was* I capable of? How could I have failed?

In an attempt to rationalize, I persuaded myself that perhaps I just wasn't the aggressive career woman I'd always thought I was. I quit my job that spring and applied to do a full-time degree in philosophy the following autumn. I spent most of the year that Communism collapsed in bed, staring at the ceiling and continuing to deny the obvious, even when I was forced to shrink the world to fit within the narrow confines of a one-bed first-floor flat in Shepherd's Bush. On the worst days, when I woke to find my limbs had apparently been replaced with second-hand Eastern Bloc concrete and my brain with borscht and potatoes, I would set myself only the tiniest tasks: making a cup of tea, running a bath or grappling with the monumental concept of walking to the end of the road to buy a pint of semi-skimmed and a newspaper with large type and lots of pictures. On a bad day it would take me eight hours to accomplish this, punctuated by hot tears of frustration. On a really bad day it would remain a concept.

ME was an introduction to a parallel universe, a bad-trip world where the twenty-five-foot journey from bed to bathroom and back again would be interrupted by half an hour spent sitting on the hall floor desperately trying to remember why I'd got out of bed in the first place. When the bath overflowed I'd usually remember. On better days I could functional fairly normally but by grasping at energy resources I inevitably overdid it and would spend the next three days in bed recovering, back in the vacuum. Still, I refused to confide in those closest to me, including Daniel. I'd sleep all day if that was what it took to appear completely normal in front of other people in the evening, even if a quiet night spent watching TV was a challenge I quite often failed to meet. In this warped world, screen-boy met screen-girl and screen-boy lost screen-girl and long before he found her again I had lost them both, muttering things like 'So why are they in Paris now?', fuddled and furious, like an old woman with senile dementia.

Throughout all of this I was aware of ME. I'd

read quite a bit about it, but for some reason couldn't make the connection between the words on the page and my own experience. But eventually, after months of enforced disengagement from both the rest of the world and my relationship with Daniel, I finally read a small piece about ME in *Time Out* magazine. There was a checklist of symptoms accompanying the piece and with a combination of both relief and horror I noted that I had them all. Scared of having to speak about any of this, I vividly recall Daniel arriving home from work and me urging him to sit down before handing him a lengthy, typed missive (writing by hand was too tiring and usually looked like the work of a five-year-old with Attention Deficit Disorder). He cried. And so, relieved, did I.

I'd owned up, then, but I still refused to be an invalid. When I started my degree all the old insecurities resurfaced – I had to succeed, I had to prove to myself that I could succeed – and so I was soon caught up in an internal battle between my ego and my depleted reserves of energy. Inevitably, perhaps, my ego lost. After just a month at college I realized that things, yet again, were not going according to plan. I didn't feel quite as intellectually inadequate as I'd expected. But soon enough the work started to slip from my tentative grasp. Some days the lectures fell into place, on others they were just a meaningless jumble of words and so, after establishing that I was never going to get to grips with logic when I hadn't even got to grips with a maths CSE (but that this wasn't necessarily the fault of the lecturers), I felt myself slipping back into the vacuum. One day I collapsed in a tutorial on Descartes. 'Why didn't you tell us?' they asked. 'I think, therefore I am not going to think about it,' I said – i.e., it was the usual combination of pride and stubbornness.

It was the end of philosophy, then, and pretty much the beginning of the end for Daniel and me, although it was another two years before I was strong enough to leave. In May 1991, I moved into my friend Debra's spare room in Crouch End, taking a single bed, a stack of clothes and books and a word-processor. I was twenty-seven, I felt seventeen. I was starting again from scratch.

I can't be sure, of course, because other people's relationships are, ultimately, wholly mysterious, but I'd long had a suspicion that I didn't have relation-ships in quite the same way that most other people I knew seemed to have relationships. While my closest girlfriends had, on the whole, met people, gone out with them for a while and then, eventually, decided to live together and/or marry, I had always felt that this well-trodden (and, frankly, highly attractive) route was not on my map. Virtually all my relation-ships were defined by their speed, intensity and a powerful, chaotic, filmic quality, but they never lasted. Daniel was the exception; otherwise the pattern had been identical: I met someone, cue passion and drama;

we flew along for a bit, caught up in the romance of it all; then, sooner or later, we crashed and burned. After the first year of living with Debra, during which I had readjusted to life as a Single Person, with particular emphasis on hoovering, fat paperbacks and soap operas, there followed a triumvirate of romances that all followed a predictably farcical, doomed course.

I met Adrian, briefly, at a club, shortly after returning from a month in Mexico with Debra over Christmas and the New Year. I was tanned, I was relaxed, I was below ten stone and, after a year without so much as a snog, frankly very enthusiastic. Adrian was twenty-one, looked like Clark Kent and had once had a trial with Arsenal. We flirted at the bar and then didn't speak again until, several weeks later, I bumped into him at a fashion trade fair. I knew he worked in the theatre, so I was surprised to see him.

'I thought you'd probably be here,' he said. 'I did some research.'

This was seriously impressive in one so young and while Adrian proceeded to woo me in heart-pounding fashion I decided that my underwear drawer needed the kind of overhaul commensurate with my new-found status as a comparatively mature and sophisticated sex symbol.

I lived a long way from both his home and his office but he turned up on my doorstep a few weeks later, early on the morning of my twenty-eighth

birthday, bearing roses, croissants and the newspapers. After several weeks spent investigating the
hurly-burly of our respective chaise longues, Adrian
impetuously asked me if I'd like to swap it for the
deep, deep peace of a happy-ever-after double bed. I
took his proposal with the proverbial pinch of salt,
but was flattered. And then, just as quickly and
dramatically as it had started, it stopped. It was Easter
Sunday morning when he announced, coolly, unequivocally, that 'it's over. That's it. I can't carry on.' No
explanations, nothing.

After trying and failing to persuade him to
explain, I retreated to lick my wounds which, given
the brief amount of time we'd been together, were
surprisingly deep. Adrian and I eventually became
friends but I never found out why he'd reacted so
suddenly in the way he had. When I invited him to
my wedding, three years later, he sent me a note: 'I
just don't think I could bear to come. I'm sure you
understand.' I didn't, actually.

Then the musician resurfaced. He was an old
flame for whom I had carried one of my impressive
selection of guttering Olympic torches ever since we
had met eight years previously. Shortly after Adrian
went AWOL, it turned out that the musician had
also recently split up with a girlfriend, so he invited
me away for a mutually sorrow-drowning weekend
in a country house hotel. We shared a four-poster,

chastely, and laughed a lot and then, slowly, we started seeing each other.

'I should marry you . . .' he said one perfect midsummer Sunday, most of which had been spent staring at the sky while lying in a Somerset field dotted with those hay stacks that look like Swiss rolls. I laughed. It wasn't a proposal (which I would have taken only marginally more seriously than I had Adrian's), but it felt very fine. A month later he went abroad but, after he returned, the atmosphere changed. He had previously called me every day, often several times, but now he was suddenly elusive. I gave it a couple of weeks and then demanded an explanation. We met on neutral territory.

'I'm sorry, Kate. I can't give you what you want. I can't make you happy. And, um, anyway, I've met someone else.'

Ho-hum. I retreated with, I like to think, dignity before driving, with splashy, girly tears clouding my vision, straight round the corner to see my conveniently situated friend Susannah, who had been very taken with the idea of this latest 'relationship'. We sat in her garden, ate figs straight from her tree and while her small daughter, Rachel, played at our feet I spent an entire afternoon whingeing and wondering why the hell I was so dumpable when it seemed that *they* were always the ones who did all the running. Was it normal to have two men mentioning the M-word, albeit largely in jest, within the space of a few months, and then for them to bale out so fast? Susannah didn't have answers – she was married, after all – but she made the right noises.

Within days I had started writing poetry. It was Susannah who, perhaps alarmed by the poetry-writing (clearly a benchmark of desperation in anyone who isn't a) a poet, or b) under the age of eighteen), suggested there might be something to be gained by contacting an astrologer who had recently produced a birth chart for her. I was casting around for the nearest clutchable straw and because Susannah, a journalist herself, was very switched on to all this stuff and even harboured a fantasy of some day, when she was old and grey, opening a fusty tea-shop-cum-witch's emporium, specializing in pink string and sealing wax, candles, tarot, seances and gossip, I took her advice.

At first the astrologer and I spoke on the phone, and he agreed to do my chart. Within a few days, however, I received a letter in a loping copperplate script that looked as though it might have signed the Magna Carta. It was short and to the point. On reflection he had decided that I had been a little too 'fierce' during our earlier conversation, when I had outlined a few things I had hoped to discover via the chart while also making it plain that I wasn't simply looking to 'cope' my way through life. The astrologer felt that I was asking too much of him – all any of us could be expected to do was 'cope' with life – and said he was sorry but he wouldn't be able to help.

Now I knew that he had the right to decide whom he was prepared to help and whom he wasn't but nonetheless I hadn't expected an out-and-out rejection. Another rejection, dammit, on the heels of two recent romantic rejections that I was, by contacting him, partly attempting to understand. I called immediately and, trying very hard to sound less 'fierce', managed to talk him round. I explained that I wasn't expecting him to solve my problems, that they were clearly my responsibility alone, but that I was simply feeling stuck. Eventually he agreed to do the chart and a fortnight or so later I received a dozen sheets of A4 paper covered edge-to-edge in the distinctive loping script. He preferred, he said, to write in longhand.

Far beyond simply telling me my rising sign (I'm an Aries, for the record, with Libra rising) or fobbing me off with flattery and a wishy-washy wish-fulfilment life where the possibility of tall dark strangers and major Lottery jackpot wins perpetually hover somewhere off in the wide blue yonder, the astrologer wasn't afraid to go down to my basement and shine a torch into its gloomy recesses.

Astrology isn't for everyone, of course. What I got was a character analysis which was so incontrovertibly me that it would have tested the skills of even the most acutely attuned psychoanalyst but, at the same

time, my wary, if fascinated, voyage around it proved
to be quite messy and at times untrustworthy. It is
sometimes wise not to ask too many questions if what
one fears the most is answers.

I wasn't learning the lessons, either, because, in
the autumn of 1992, I met the third Man of the Year.
I hardly need describe how that panned out, except to
say it followed the pattern (although it should be
noted, in his defence, that I was perhaps more the
pursuer and he the pursued). The by now rather
familiar blow of rejection was, however, cushioned by
the fact that at last I stopped faffing about with a
thesaurus trying to find new ways to tell people that
wearing this summer's essential free-n-easy, crumple-
free, drip-dry hot-pants in directional shades of camel
and fuchsia would ensure they got both a shag and a
pay-rise. In short, I got myself a proper job.

Daniel had informed me several weeks earlier that
he was leaving *Arena*, the magazine he edited, and so
we mused about who might be his successor. The job
wasn't in his gift, but he was obviously going to be
taking an interest.

'Well,' he said after a bit, 'would you want to do
it?'

'Me?!' I came over all modest. 'No. Oh, *no way*!
Besides, I'm so far out of the loop these days that I
shouldn't think they'd want me.'

Weeks went by and there had been no appointment even as Daniel was preparing to leave. I boarded

the rumour train occasionally. This name or that name cropped up and I thought, *Yeah, they could probably do it.* Then, suddenly, I heard a particular name that made me, quite involuntarily, sit up and think, *Bloody hell, I don't want him editing my magazine . . .*

'Thank God you called,' said my old boss (whose magazine it actually was) about twenty minutes later. 'Get me something down on paper and then we'll talk . . .'

By the middle of November I had a desk, an office, a (small) staff and an empty magazine. I was very rusty and indescribably nervous (which I attempted to mask with stroppiness), but I was also as excited as hell. I stopped thinking about men (or, rather, I stopped thinking about men personally, in relation to me) and started thinking about men in just about every other context possible. What were men, anyway – and how was I going to make more of them buy my magazine? Shortly after landing the job I was interviewed for the women's page of the *Guardian* and quoted, cringingly, as saying, 'Well, I may not understand the offside rule, but I'm sure I know a man who does.' Now there's post-feminism for you.

1993 was a blast. On the day that Clinton was inaugurated as leader of the free world, David Bowie – with whom we were collaborating on an upcoming issue – poured me coffee and asked my advice about the choice of shots for the cover of his new LP. I knew it was just a smart ice-breaking ruse but I didn't care – this was a grown-up *Jim'll Fix It* moment. While Debra had, by this time, more or less vacated her flat to move in with her new boyfriend, the nights of unrelentingly dull predictability were leavened by the fact that having people like Bowie to chat with over breakfast, however rarely, actually constituted *work*. Bowie, incidentally, went with my choice for his LP cover.

Soon enough the magazine's sales were up and so, at that point, for a woman who hadn't been entirely convinced that she'd ever have one again, the realization that I had reclaimed my career was its own reward. Work was perfect for distracting me from just about everything else in my life, but I still kept in occasional touch with the astrologer – conscious even while I was abandoning my interior world that it might come back to haunt me.

At some point in 1993 the astrologer recommended a therapist (who had herself recovered from ME) whom he thought might be helpful, if I ever felt the need. I wrote down the name and phone number and carried it around in my wallet, next to my RAC membership card. You could, I reasoned, never anticipate a breakdown.

Eighteen months later, I was still passionate about my job, although it had become less of a novelty, more of a distraction and increasingly seemed to highlight the gaps in other areas of my life. Then I went to interview a pop star and after the tape was switched off he started talking more freely about the lessons he had learned in the three or four years since he had become famous. At one point he mentioned a therapist whom he credited with keeping him sane.

'Hang on a minute . . .' I said, fishing in my wallet and unearthing a very crumpled bit of paper, 'I *knew* I knew that name. I've been carrying her number around with me for months!'

'Ha! Perhaps you should call her . . .' he suggested. And I took it as a Sign, because I still believed in Signs in 1994.

I made the phone call about a week later. She was initially wary, largely because a good therapist will rarely take on anyone they think might be intimately involved with another client (much later I was to discover why).

After a few weeks, when she'd got to grips with the idea of my job being about a woman working in a man's world, not just figuratively (after all, most of us do) but literally, she started to pinpoint one of my problems. The crunch probably came around about the time that I admitted I hadn't bought a skirt or a dress, just trousers and suits, for the past two years. You can't get away with making jokes like that to a therapist: it was time, she said, for me to get in touch with my feminine side.

She wasn't wrong. Far too much of my professional life was spent poring over photographs of large-breasted blondes, saying 'Yes, yes, that's fine, but can't we find something a bit, y'know, *sexier*?' before knocking off and downing a few pints at the Spanner and Sprocket Set. One day, at work, a male contributor to the magazine pitched me an idea for a story.

'Hmm. Yes, I'd be very interested to read about that and I think most other men would be too . . .'

The therapist suggested that I might like to join a weekly women's group that met informally at her house. Initially I resisted because I've always been a lousy joiner. As a kid my idea of the perfect club was the Puffin Club. I was never a Brownie or a Guide and my Pony Club membership was notable for a much greater interest in receiving the magazine than ever going to camp. Typical only kid. Typical magazine editor manqué, come to that. Then there was the fact that I'd always considered myself blessed by having the finest female friends in the world and didn't see the point of paying for more. Nonetheless me and my baggage of sad prejudices were successfully persuaded to pitch up somewhere in north London for a wary bid at bonding. We introduced ourselves.

'Hi, my name's Kate. I'm the honorary bloke.'

Even though I was several years younger than the other women (who had all been meeting regularly for many months) and I was slightly ill at ease with the touchy-feeliness of it all, I enjoyed that first meeting. It happened to coincide with me being asked to write a column in the *Observer* magazine and I thought this was potentially good material for my first piece.

'So, will we be seeing you next week, then, Kate?'

I ummed, I aahed, I shrugged. Ho-hum. I capitulated. To hell with the Monday night poker game. The following day I wrote about joining the group in order to locate my inner woman.

I preferred the second meeting because the person I had liked the least wasn't there. This woman had, in fact, irritated me hugely – a squeaky-voiced, skinny, nervy type, wearing a floral-print frock, she was the archetypal feminine girlie-woman and therefore pretty much my complete opposite. It was interesting that it was she who became the catalyst for my relationship with the group, simply because she was the embodiment of an idea of femininity that I despised so much I didn't even want to share a room with it, much less get in touch with the bit of it that might be hidden inside me. In the event I had to miss the following week, but I turned up, enthusiastic, for the next meeting.

My reception was grim. It transpired that Floral had read my column and, though neither she nor any of the other women involved had been mentioned even obliquely, she had taken it upon herself to get angry on everyone's behalf. I knew nothing about any of this until I arrived when, to my considerable surprise, they took it in turns to make the kind of judgements about me that I would never have presumed to make about any of them. Apparently this piece had been some kind of betrayal, although I failed to see how, and so the previous week's meeting had evolved into a cauldron-stirring plot for revenge, fuelled both by the insecurity of this one particular member and the others' keenness to protect her.

I stuck it out though, because, however inaccurate, I wanted to hear all they had to say, but stunned into a defensive silence I didn't try to put across my side of the story. After the best part of an hour I left, and that might have been the end of it, except that by the time I got home I had stopped feeling sorry for myself and started getting angry, indignant. *How dare they foist their own paranoia on to me.* I immediately sat down and wrote a long open letter to the group which, for a few days, I considered passing on to them via the therapist (after initial doubts I had decided to continue seeing her one-on-one simply because, until this episode, we had made great strides), but then I knew what I had to do. Anything less would have meant unfinished business.

The following week, nervous as hell, I went back to the group and, despite the inevitably frosty reception, stayed long enough to read out the letter. Then, having got the last word (which, to a card-carrying control freak, felt important) I folded up the sheets of paper, put them in my bag, wished everybody a very pleasant life and left, deciding there and then that if I needed to get in touch with my feminine side I would do it the way I had been doing it for the last decade – over a bottle of wine with my loyal (and, goddamit, genuinely sisterly) gang of girlfriends.

Although I'd brazened it out, I was actually quite shaken by the experience and so the following week I made contact with the astrologer for the first time in ages, wondering if he had any insights – not specifically about this situation but about what I perceived to be a pattern of emotional dislocation and isolation. He did. Back came an immensely downbeat and difficult reading, revealing that, amongst other things, I was going to have an even rockier emotional ride for a few months, but that I would come through, eventually. He also advised me that if I was feeling emotionally volatile this was probably not the right time to embark on a relationship. *Yeah, right!* I thought. *Like there's any chance of that.*

A week later I was at a party, a mini-wedding reception for some friends of mine who lived in New York, had just got married in Scotland but wanted to celebrate with their London friends before returning to the Apple. I was having quite an intense conversation with a male acquaintance whom Debra, in matchmaking mood, thought I should probably get to know better, when a man appeared at our table, stared right at me, broke into an enormous grin and said, 'Hi!'

I appraised the face (which, though familiar, I couldn't place) and then the rest of him. His smile was large and wonky and generous, his features slightly Asiatic, and he was very good-looking in a sweet, stubbly, unkempt-around-the-edges kind of way. His hair was receding a little and, though short, was in need of a trim. He was slim but wearing baggy clothes that I recognized to be a version of the west London male uniform (MA1 flight jacket, combat trousers or jeans and designer trainers). The overall effect was, I thought rather horridly, as though he'd read a mid-1980s copy of *The Face* and tried to assemble a thirtysomething simulacrum of urban style with whatever he had to hand, but that it had all come out a bit wrong. He was also wearing a Tag Heuer wristwatch and a pair of ergonomic Birkenstock footgarments which, on him, bypassed potentially groovy and headed straight towards sociology lecturer. It was, I thought, a very big shame about the shoes. I noticed all this and I noticed it fast because, if nothing else, I was in the business of observing what men wore, but though more than capable of professional shallowness I was just about three-dimensional enough to notice his eyes, which were gentle, a deep dark brown and looked unhesitatingly, distractingly, straight into mine.

'Hi!' I said, grinning back. There was, I thought something gauche, almost childlike, about his smiling approach. Particularly as he didn't follow it up and disappeared straight back into the crowd. I was curious, if only because he didn't seem to fit in.

'Who's that?' I asked my companion.

'That's Joe's brother, Eric. He's staying with Joe for a while.'

I knew Joe but I hadn't known he had a brother. Glancing over at Eric I saw the physical similarities, but whereas Joe was all cheekbones, chutzpah and an unerring sense of style, his brother was softer, quieter, altogether warmer and smilier. I assumed he was a younger sibling, hanging out with his big brother's crowd and then I stopped wondering about him and carried on talking to my companion.

Several of us ended up having dinner together after the party. I sat next to the man I'd been talking to all evening, while Eric was on the other side of a large table. We didn't exchange a word all night but when he left he smiled me a goodbye. He cropped up in conversation a few days later though, when Debra, who had met him before, filled me in on the salient biographical details.

'He teaches – wait for it! – blind children ...' *Blimey*, I thought, *how fabulous is that?* '... and I had a long conversation with him once, at some party. He's very interesting. And ...' there was a discernible glint in my best friend's eye, 'he's just split up with his girlfriend. Maybe you should meet him ...' *Maybe I should*, I thought and then, *He'd be very good-looking with just a little bit of help.*

'So let me introduce you to Eric,' said Debra, a few weeks later, backstage at a fashion show. It turned out that Joe had produced the show and persuaded Eric to help out.

'Hi!' said Eric, smiling.

'Hi!' said I, smiling back.

We talked. I learned that he taught science and music to visually impaired children, some of them with other special needs, was in the final year of an Open University MBA and very interested in radical transatlantic management techniques (he mentioned a book called *The Seven Habits of Highly Effective People* and something else called Neuro-Linguistic Programming). After about half an hour of this, when the room was nearly empty and everyone was talking about getting something to eat, Eric asked what I was doing.

'I don't know. I'll probably go home and get changed then go out for dinner with this lot. What about you?'

He shrugged, said he had no plans. There was a pause, pregnant with possibilities. Quite uncharacteristically, I found myself saying:

'Well, if you're not doing anything, do you want to come back to mine and then maybe we can meet up with everybody later?'

Carpe diem. I liked this man, attracted by his intellect and his easiness. There was no overwhelming sexual frisson, partly because he had an unmacho, even slightly androgynous kind of energy. Though indubitably both male and very attractive he was also as easy to talk to as, well, a woman, and because I didn't meet many straight men where that was the case I suspected we would become, at the very least, friends. We snuck out of the tent, giggling, trying not to attract too much attention, and as we walked around the corner to my car in the balmy Indian summer evening light I remember feeling quite astonished at my boldness.

'I don't normally do this kind of thing!' I blurted. Well, I hadn't for a while.

'I'm very glad you did.' And there was that huge smile again. His top lip looked like a child's quick line-drawing of a bird in flight, a scrappy, elongated 'm'. Back at my flat, as the evening wore on, we both realized we weren't going anywhere other than on a sofa-bound journey with infinite horizons.

It was a strange, edgy, intimate and extraordinary evening. At some point, encouraged by Eric, who seemed unprecedentedly interested in hearing about me, I found myself opening up like a desert seedling that had lurked below the dunes for months and months, waiting for a brief passing cloudburst in order to bloom. As Eric kept on asking penetrating questions that were not about my work, but about how I felt about things, I couldn't stop talking. At some point, perhaps put off by my own garrulousness, the depth of my revelations and the fact that this

gentle, persuasive, compassionate and quietly charis-
matic man kept on pressing all the right buttons, I
retreated.

'I'm actually a bit of a mess at the moment,' I said,
both laughing and then suddenly sniffing, somewhere
on the edge of tears. But he didn't seem remotely put
off by this and how many men had I met who were
unlikely to be put off by a woman they barely knew
in tears? Precisely, I think, none, so I explained about
joining the lousy women's group and my rubbish love
life and how my job was starting to make me feel
like a sheep in wolf's clothing.

Eric was calm and practical and told me in greater
depth about his attraction to business techniques, like
Steven Covey's 'The Seven Habits', or Tom Peters'
Chaos Management, and how these 'tools' were just
as applicable to managing one's life as they were to
managing a business. He talked about them with the
zeal of a religious convert and though I wasn't sold
on the specifics, I listened intently because he made
life sound like something controllable, rather than
something that was capable of running away with
you.

It got very late and, perhaps because we knew by
then that our journey together had already started,
one or other of us raised the question of staying the
night. Eric, who didn't have his car, was at that point
sleeping on his brother's floor several miles away

while looking for a place to live, so he ended up staying and we shared my bed. But that was all. We could wait. In the morning I felt embarrassed about my behaviour the previous evening, but Eric wasn't fazed, so we exchanged phone numbers and he left, promising to call. I felt quite confused.

A couple of days later, I met Debra for Sunday brunch. She knew that Eric and I had disappeared together on the Friday night and, naturally, wanted to hear the rest. I didn't quite know what to say, if only because the events had already taken on a slightly dreamlike quality. And then there was the fact that, the following night, I was going out for dinner with the man who had monopolized me when I had first met Eric at the wedding reception. Eric and this man had known each other for years.

We had a great evening, then, about two-thirds of the way through the meal, he narrowed his eyes, smiled and said:

'So, Kate, what's going on with you and Eric?'

I was slightly thrown because he'd given no indication that he knew anything about it.

'Nothing!' I lied brightly. 'There's absolutely *nothing* going on.'

Eric called the next day.

Falling in love. Why do we never use any other word, only *falling*? For such a profound experience you'd think there would be a wider vocabulary. Who decided that we fall? Why can't we climb into love, or plough, or hurtle or walk or wobble, or wade, or run? Maybe this explains why every time one falls in love it is, somehow, exactly the same as it was the last time and the time before that, and the only thing that ever seems to change is the script, and sometimes not even that changes very much.

For me the process of falling in love with Eric involved all the half-remembered, visceral, hurtling-down-the-roller-coaster-with-solar-plexus-in-the-throat sensations; the near delirious, drugged detachment from the outside world and – *pinch me I must be dreaming* – a sense of having just discovered what was, perhaps, maybe, the missing piece of the big jigsaw. But despite the familiar, addictive high, I also felt as the ancient explorers must have felt when they threw away the old maps marked 'Here Be Dragons' and struck out into uncharted territory. I stumbled and, finally, fell hard and fast, but then it was never going to be any other way. And while I obviously needed him, he seemed to need me just as much. Soon we had 'Our Song' – 'Sense' by Terry Hall.

When we made love I found myself awed by what we could be, the places we could go, the things we learned about each other. Our physical love was like holding each other's hand *tight, tight, tight*, closing our eyes and jumping out of a plane into sharp, thin air, not knowing if we were wearing parachutes or what might lie below, or even if we could carry on breathing. For the first time, then, I had discovered the most exquisite abandonment, the ability to lose myself in someone else completely, to trust them utterly. But though this was extraordinarily powerful and liberating, each time we made love we also journeyed further, inextricably bound together. It scared me sometimes, this total love, this absolute need for the other.

I had, in fact, been strangely perturbed early on, after a fortnight of seeing each other, when Eric had called me from a phone box and, sounding almost desperate, told me he loved me.

'You can't say that! *Not yet . . .*' I replied.

And I didn't know if this was really because he'd said it so very soon, or because he'd said it on the phone or whether it was just because he'd said it at all. I think perhaps I felt slightly cheated out of having to wait, maybe even earn, the moment when he would tell me he loved me. Something he would do while making eye contact. But that was that. He'd done it.

And then there was a watershed night, after he'd told me he loved me but before we had got too much further, when I was out having dinner with a girl-friend. Eric and I had had a vague arrangement to meet later but the evening was characterized by deteriorating levels of sobriety, so by about eleven I realized I had better call Eric on his mobile.

'Hi,' I said. 'Sorry, but I haven't seen Fiona for so long and we're having a bit of a night. Maybe we can see each other tomorrow, if you're not busy?'

'Ah,' said Eric, 'that's a shame because I'm actually sitting on your doorstep.'

It was November. It was cold. I can't remember my exact words but, far from being thrilled by this spontaneous display of devotion, I was confused.

'Um . . .' I muttered, 'well, I suppose I'd better come back, then.' And part of me hoped he'd say no, not to worry, he'd go, but he didn't. I explained to Fiona.

'How wonderful! God, I wish somebody would sit on my doorstep waiting for me to come home.'

'Well, to be honest I don't know how I feel about it.' But I got in a cab and went home and there was Eric, smiling that big wonky smile, sitting on my doorstep with a huge bunch of gerberas.

'Oh well, you'd better come in, then,' I said ungraciously.

Eventually I relaxed. They were beautiful flowers and it had been an obviously romantic gesture. The next morning, fortunately, I had an appointment with the therapist, who had been receiving bite-sized bits of information about Eric and was, on the whole, enthusiastic. I told her about the previous evening and my reaction, which had surprised me. She listened and then, with just a few words, changed my perception entirely.

'Have you never thought, Kate, that you are a person for whom somebody might think it was worth sitting on a doorstep in the freezing cold in the middle of the night with a bunch of flowers?'

I was slightly shocked. No, since she'd asked, I never had thought that. Not in those terms, anyway. If anything, I'd perceived Eric's gesture as slightly cloying, even sentimental, and because of that I had reacted badly. The therapist talked to me gently about how to proceed. Told me about co-dependency, which I had heard of but didn't really think applied. (Dependent? Me? Oh, come on! I was Princess Independent. I even read the newspaper.) She also said that this needn't be, by any means, an insurmountable obstacle. My insecurity and neediness, coupled with fear, came from an understandable wariness about any kind of relationship; while Eric's came from . . . well, she didn't know where his came from, actually (I could offer hardly any biographical clues. Eric, as far as I could tell, was Mr Sane-and-Sorted-Thank-You-Very-Much), but if mine manifested as a kind of push-me-pull-you struggle for intimacy, his was different. He ran straight towards intimacy, arms wide open, eyes tight shut. None the less, we had every chance of overcoming all this stuff and moving towards something called interdependency, which was apparently healthier.

'Well, we talk. We talk all the time about everything,' I said.

'Good. Carry on talking!' and with that she had, I felt, finally given me permission (although I don't know why I thought I needed it) to fall completely in love, so I did. Later that night I told Eric everything that had happened at the session and he listened intently and smiled and said that that was good, that of course we would be fine.

'Have you ever thought about having therapy?' I wondered. 'I used to be so against the idea – which was probably the biggest sign that I needed it!'

Eric laughed.

'No,' he said. 'No, I don't think I need therapy!'

And I felt slightly foolish for having asked.

So, co-dependent or not, we were an 'us', then, sailing through our tides of loving madness like Ford Madox Ford's 'tall ships with white sails upon a blue sea . . . one of those things that seem the proudest and the safest of all the beautiful and safe things that God has permitted the mind of men to frame. Where better could one take refuge?' Where indeed?

This period, during which we bathed in each other's love, was of course, the part of a relationship that's meant to be perfect. Much later I described it to someone as 'Eric showing me what love could be . . .' ('Yes,' she said, sighing, 'I know exactly what you mean.') I had never been swept so far and so fast by my emotions (and I took being swept away as the norm, not the exception) while, for all his flow charts and stratagems, Eric was also patently a full-blown, flower-bearing, love-declaring, pedestal-building, all-or-nothing, now-or-never, from-here-to-eternity, hopeless romantic of the very first order. I felt privileged. Some people spent their entire lives just waiting for the possibility of feeling the way I was feeling now.

Still, as Eric and I built our little lovers' world, which, though uniquely ours, was for all its impenetrable codes and REST OF THE WORLD KEEP OUT defences and secrets and passwords probably just like every other happy couple's world, I still felt disarmed by the warp-speed of its trajectory. *If I had finally got what I'd always wanted, what did I do with it?*

Sure, I felt loved and treasured and beautiful and wanted, and all of these with an intensity I had never felt before: being with Eric was like coming home after a long and stressful journey; he was a hot bath and a crisp duvet made flesh; he eased my aching bones. And he was always so keen to accommodate me: the ergonomic sociology lecturer shoes were relegated to the back of the wardrobe, his hair was cut and the stubble shaved. And he was, too, more than happy to shop for new clothes under the guidance of a menswear guru – especially if that menswear guru was his one true love.

'He teaches blind children and he wears Comme des Garçons!' I told my girlfriends, who all sighed approvingly. He was happy to become the him he thought I wanted him to be. Interestingly he didn't seem to want me to change, seemed to love me just the way I was, so I climbed straight onto his pedestal. Occasionally, bizarrely, I even thought of this pedestal as a tangible object – white marble, with 'my darling Kate' engraved in an Eric Gill font.

Our relationship was, we firmly believed, founded as much on a celebration of our differences as it was on recognizing the things we had in common. Eric, for example, didn't read anything that wasn't either a textbook, a management manual or, of late, something written by me. He didn't have time, did he, with all that studying for his MBA – and then there was his eyesight, which wasn't great (he needed glasses for reading). Even when he told me that he wouldn't ever consider reading a novel for entertainment, that in fact he'd only read about four in his whole life, I thought that was kind of fascinating. Anyway, the four novels he had read included Joyce and Sartre, so he could hit heavy enough if he wanted to. Funny thing, but I started reading less.

For his part, Eric had me down as a social animal because of my job, and professed to be one himself, but it soon became clear that after a hard day at the office my idea of the perfect evening was a quiet meal out and then home in plenty of time for *ER*. He didn't seem to care. And I wasn't bothered that he never went out for nights with his friends because, obviously, this meant that I had much more of him all to myself. He didn't seem to have a best friend, either, aside from his brother, and in fact I didn't really know who his friends were. But obviously I'd find out.

And I didn't mind too much when I told him I'd had an abortion and he told me that, as a student, he'd been a rabid pro-lifer.

And he had never taken any drugs and had tried a cigarette only once, but he wasn't remotely concerned that I was a smoker. And, on top of all his other qualifications, he was also a qualified sports teacher, who loved playing football and tennis, skiing and (new fetish, this) snowboarding, and was good at all of them. I, on the other hand, would rather call a cab to take me to the nearest tube than walk there, and was quite intractably stubborn about the fact that I would never voluntarily interact with snow. Actually, I felt a bit guilty about my non-existent fitness levels, so I started working out. For a little while. Then on impulse we bought a couple of pairs of his-and-hers matching rollerblades and it turned out that he was rubbish at rollerblading. I'd roller- and ice-skated through my teens. I was great at rollerblading.

And I wasn't bothered that Eric had a boxed set of Yes CDs and waxed purple about numerous dirgy seventies synth-rockers (I loathed them); while I was still passionate about Steely Dan and Stevie Wonder's

'Songs in the Key of Life' (he didn't much like soul). This obviously didn't matter because we both liked Oasis.

And it didn't even matter that I earned much more than him. After all I was working in the media and everybody knows that pays far too well, while he worked in the public sector, which everybody knows doesn't. And the work he did was so much more important, in the global scheme of things, than mine. I mean, let's face it, he changed people's lives.

Oh, and he loved Bath Olivers (which he bought from Harrods), while I was a cheap Jaffa Cake date, but our differing tastes in dunking material were outweighed by the fact that both of us agreed we never wanted to see the other using the lavatory.

At this stage I didn't know too much about Eric's family background but I did learn that he and Joe had been born eighteen months apart and that Eric was the elder, although you wouldn't necessarily think so from their relationship. Both brothers spoke with very proper, rather old-fashioned BBC received pro-nunciation, although they were the products of a Singaporean mother and an Irish father, which exotic genetic cocktail accounted for their good looks. If they'd had a sister she would, I thought, have been beyond gorgeous. They had both been quite academic, had degrees in biology and were talented musicians, having spent most of their youth in the kind of bands where Edward Scissorhands haircuts and skinny leather ties were as important a statement as their middle eights. I only had Eric's word for the fact that he was a talented musician, but proof in the fact that Joe, formerly a model, now earned his living composing music for commercials. Eric and Joe were close siblings, but as personalities they were as different as they had appeared to be when I'd first seen them together.

They also both had failed marriages behind them. Eric had got married on the day of the Live Aid concert, in July 1985. 'Too young,' he said, 'at twenty-five.' It had lasted four years, there were no kids and the divorce had been a bit messy so they weren't exactly what you'd call close, though they spoke and met up occasionally. It was, he said, 'history' and so I didn't push for details. After all, I had failed relationships, too. He had, though, just emerged from another lengthy live-in relationship, about which I was a good deal more interested, but he didn't reveal a great deal about that one, either.

'She was always hoovering,' he once said. 'Eventually it drove me mad.' I was quite fetishistic about hoovering myself, but I laughed.

My friends loved both the idea and the fact of Eric, which was very important to me. He charmed everyone in my immediate circle, one by one. And two of my closest colleagues at work (who had, I suspect, been hoping for something like this to happen for ages, if only so that I would become a bit less of a hatchet-faced virago in the office) described him as 'the Gorgeous Boyfriend' after meeting him for the first time.

Within weeks Eric had moved in to my flat. He travelled very light, bringing only clothes, his Apple Macintosh, a designer lamp, some records, a pair of skis, his childhood cuddly toy, Bunny, a library of OU course texts and a small box containing a few documents, photos and bits of ephemera. He owned less than any other man I'd ever met but this was easily explained by the fact that almost immediately after he had started seeing his previous girlfriend (around about the time his marriage had ended – although he was quite vague about that) Eric had moved into her home, leaving both the marriage and its accoutrements behind. In his new relationship all the furniture had belonged to his girlfriend, and any joint purchases they had made in their four years together, he left with her when they split. He had had a car when we first met, but shortly afterwards he passed it on to his ex.

'It seems only fair, somehow,' he explained.

He was the one who had left her, but he didn't seem to suffer from guilt; was in fact very calm, pragmatic and generous, which I read as yet another sign of his emotional maturity. He didn't go into details about the demise of the relationship, just admitted that 'it has been over for a while . . .' and although when we started seeing each other they were both still in the process of extricating themselves, things seemed to be on more of a practical basis than an emotional one – at least if the one-sided mobile phone conversations I would occasionally overhear were anything to go by. Eric was impressively calm whenever I heard him speak to his ex, opting for a tone of voice that seemed to successfully straddle the chasm between warm intimacy and cool distance. I marvelled at this because I knew that, in a similar situation, I would never be capable of it. It was a very different tone to the one he used with me.

Once he was in my home (it was a tight fit; when I'd rented it I hadn't expected to be sharing), Eric made little secret of the fact that, had he not met me – which extraordinary event had, of course, tilted the axis of his world – he would probably be living on his own in a little studio flat, with just a bed and his computer. He had never lived on his own, he admitted, and I said that I found that pretty unusual in a man of thirty-five, which he acknowledged with a shrug. It was just the way things had turned out.

'Are you sure you wouldn't rather live on your own for a while now?' I wondered, seeking some reassurance that he was moving in with me for the right reasons; reasons which did not include, for example, convenience. He looked me in the eye and told me, unhesitatingly, that this was so obviously right that any previous plans were simply no longer an issue. I didn't push the point, after all I wanted him with me as much as he wanted to be there.

Just before Christmas, Eric invited me to the open day at his school.

The building smelt of bad plumbing. This was the first thing I noticed about it and I realized that I hadn't set foot in a school since I'd left my own, which was a rather different environment. When I arrived, Eric was busy organizing things, with a small posse of teenagers in tow. All were blind, or partially sighted, some also had Down's syndrome. Suddenly, in this place, Eric was 'sir', and it made me laugh.

A man who is good with kids is very seductive. Eric wasn't soppy with them or when he talked about them – apart from when he once told me a moving story about watching a firework display and trying to describe the images to the blind boy who was with him – but I could tell that the kids loved him, and he was fond of them. It was all a bit *Dead Poets Society*, and I thought that if I was a blind kid I'd definitely want a teacher like Eric.

He showed me his classroom and everywhere were vases and jars of tactile-looking bits of biology, plants and mosses, leaves and fungi, and his guitar leaned against a wall. I knew that he was a creative sort of teacher and that a biology lesson could easily accommodate a burst of live music or the creation of some spontaneous installation-cum-artwork in the playground (a pyramid of chairs once, he told me). I was already in love, of course, but I was completely sold at this point. I even went so far as to question what it was I was doing with my life. Was editing a glossy magazine really a worthwhile way to earn a living? On the other hand, what else could I do? And realistically, I knew I could never work in a place that smelt quite this bad.

I blame Steve Martin. If it hadn't been for a late-night TV screening of his film *LA Story*, Eric might not have asked me to marry him. Or at least he wouldn't have done it then. Each time 'Doo-Wah-Diddy-Diddy-Dum-Diddy-Doo, I'm Hers, She's Mine, Wedding Bells Are Gonna Chime...' was played during the film (which was often), I got giggly. Eventually Eric smiled his funny, wonky smile but he didn't really need to say anything because I knew.

In fact he waited until the following afternoon. I was in the living room when he walked in and knelt (which, because I was already lying on the floor, wasn't quite as effective as it might have been) and asked me to marry him. I said yes immediately. We had only been together for three and a half months, but that was OK. Time didn't enter into it.

It had been over twenty years since I'd started sketching wedding dresses on my exercise books and, frankly, twenty years felt like quite long enough to be in rehearsal. I couldn't have stopped it happening any more than the silent movie heroine, tied to the tracks, can stop the runaway train. But the big difference between me and her was that I wasn't scared of dying.

three

limitations are like
the clouds

Long before we were married, Eric and I were invited
to spend a weekend with one of his MBA course-
mates, whom I had never met. In his early thirties
and married, with one small child and another on the
way, this man lived in a neat modern house on a
small private estate within commuting distance of
central London. When we arrived he and his wife
welcomed us warmly, showed us to their spare room,
gave us some clean towels and asked if we'd like to
freshen up after the drive.

Afterwards, in the living room, we drank tea and
chatted for a while, before Eric's friend's wife rustled
up some dinner (politely refusing my offer of help).
Then we sat at the dining table and talked a bit more
and ate and drank a few beers and, after dinner, we
went back into the living room with the new leather
suite and the floral frieze around the faux-dado
and the African carvings and carried on talking.
Eventually, the wife, who was tired because she was

pregnant, went to bed, and the three of us stayed up late, Eric and his friend discussing their work and me mostly just listening. At one point, Eric's friend lamented the fact that he always got back from the office so late that he didn't get to see his daughter much – or his wife, come to that! *But, hey! That was work for you!*

This man was, I could tell, exceptionally proud of his great big grown-up workaholic breadwinning capacity, particularly the fact that he was now charged with the sole responsibility of providing for his family because his wife could only work part-time (as a primary school teacher) and soon, with a new baby, she wouldn't be working at all. But that was OK because, after all, he was in a good management position with plenty of scope for moving on up through the ranks of the huge multinational that employed him (especially as he'd soon have an MBA). They'd had a fantastic holiday in, I think, South Africa the previous Christmas and were planning to go to Disneyworld this Christmas. He hoped the new baby was a boy because then they would have one of each, so that would be that. Although if it was a girl (and of course that would be great, too) they might try for another one.

It went on like this until, eventually, we all called it a night and slept very soundly before getting up to a big cooked breakfast and more chat. Then we were asked if we wanted to stay for lunch. We didn't. And so we left, wending our way out of the little estate, where some smiling, waving young neighbours, wearing their Sunday-casual trainers and sweatshirts, were washing medium-sized family saloons, while small children learned to ride tiny bicycles with stabilizers, and slightly bigger children played football in the road, which was OK because it was a quiet cul-de-sac, and there were lots of sleeping policemen.

I felt a kind of nonspecific but none the less queasy dread about all of this.

'Please . . .' I said to Eric, 'can we never do that again?'

But I don't remember what he said. In truth I was surprised that Eric had friends like that, although it was obvious what they saw in him. Eric's friend had made all sorts of slightly blokey and gently joshing remarks about Eric's clothes and his former life as a struggling musician, for example, and I knew that he saw Eric as being connected to something which he was not, a kind of distant, urban, vaguely bohemian world.

I was amazed by this aspect of Eric, by his chameleon-like ability to enthuse about corporate middle-management strategy with people whose lives seemed, at least on the surface, to be untroubled by issues outside of their own traditional, neatly bordered, middle-class existence. But then, one of Eric's strengths, I had decided, was precisely this ability to get on with all kinds of people. I admired it, even slightly envied it, because I didn't have it myself. I'd lived my life only ever bothering to get on with the kind of people I wanted to get on with. I'd been (I hoped) polite to our hosts, but I honestly didn't care if I ever saw or spoke to them again. There was nothing about their lives or their ambitions that resonated with mine, to the point where I can no longer remember their names, or even the town where they lived.

Eric, I felt sure, was somehow better than this, although I also felt slightly guilty about the concept of 'better'. There was obviously so much more to Eric than there had been to this Mondeo-owning middle-management thirtysomething man with his predictable passions and prejudices – something more magical, more in touch with a bigger and wilder dream of what one's life could be. And yet, unlike any man I'd ever been involved with, Eric actually knew lots of these decent, upstanding, backbone-of-Britain types, whose lives appeared to me to be less than they might have been. It was like slipping into another generation in a parallel world. But maybe that was what being a grown-up was about? Perhaps when it came time to put away childish things, you really had no choice but to turn into your parents. Except that my parents weren't like that.

Over the months that followed I thought quite a bit about what being a cool, modern, Nineties wife might be like. When Eric and I discussed it, the conversation often involved flip-charts and marker pens (Eric's idea, obviously). I remember one in which Eric encouraged me to draw pictures of the things we wanted out of our life together. My indulgent, escapist drawings included an enormous country house with several wings, a huge circular drive, 'Capability' Brown-style landscaped gardens with fountains, topiary, a lake, and an island in the middle of the lake featuring, I think, both a weeping willow and a small folly. I was much better at drawing very large houses than I was at drawing something abstract like, say, 'respect', or 'togetherness' or 'mutual understanding' or 'maturity' or 'space' or 'communication' – or even something down-to-earth, like a nice flat in a pleasant part of London and a decent car.

I was certainly (if ambiguously) ambitious for us as 'a couple', a mutually satisfying sort of an arrangement, I thought, through which we both stood a better chance of realizing our ambitions, emotional and practical. We had talked about travelling, even about living abroad, but there were never any specific long-term plans, and although I knew children would come in to the equation at some point, that point was not quite yet. I thought we would (should) work hard and that then we would get somewhere – although quite where that somewhere was, I had no idea. I guessed it would reveal itself eventually.

I had a much better idea of what I didn't want marriage to be. While I was desperately scared of chaos, uncertainty and loneliness and craved the kind of safety and sense of purpose that I imagined a happy marriage could provide, I felt a degree of psychic terror at the thought of a life of the kind that had been embraced, seemingly unquestioningly, by some of his friends. Perversely, I also believed that, if I could only come to accept and understand it, within precisely that life there might be found a kind of peace, although any practical idea about how this easy contentment might be attained completely eluded me. I had absolutely no experience of that kind of life because I had not been a product of one (and didn't really know anyone who had). And then there was the fact that although I very much wanted to be married to Eric, I just couldn't quite see myself in a nice little home looking after the kids while he went out into the big bad world to kill the metaphorical woolly mammoth and drag it back to our cave.

But what was the alternative? And was it really any different if, instead of a neat modern home on an estate in the 'burbs, with a World of Leather three-piece suite, a copy of *TV Quick* on the IKEA coffee table, a Ford Probe in the drive, a Blockbuster video and a curry on Fridays, a nice M&S-catered dinner party on Saturdays with a few of your best friends, at which the men talked about Manchester United and the women talked about Princess Diana, you instead chose to live in an *Elle Decoration*-style loft in the centre of London, with a copy of *Blueprint* on the

Conran Shop coffee table, a 4WD in the residents' parking bay, an Indonesian takeaway and a video (with subtitles) on Fridays, a nice dinner party with a few of your best friends on Saturdays, catered by, say, the Real Food Store, at which the men talked about Arsenal and the women talked about Princess Diana's psychotherapy habit? These things were, when it came down to it, just a matter of style. And though my married life was likely to be a good deal closer to the latter than it was to the former, what if, despite the stylish trappings, the substance was exactly the same?

And then there was the other bit of me: the half-secret part whose earliest memories are potent snapshots of the year I spent in the Australian bush with my mother when I was three. This was the Kathryn who was not the Londoner born and bred, but her mother's daughter, who didn't want to be urban and cool but rural and messy, surrounded by kids and dogs and who might throw open the back door and walk out into an endless space with a big sky. This Kathryn craved to live somewhere that might feel like the edge of the world, where she could walk and be alone, if need be, or get on a horse and just ride.

Confused, then, I looked around for inspiring models for my upcoming role of cool modern Nineties urban rural full-time working career woman wife and mother.

I didn't have that many married friends of my own age: Lucy and Andrew, married for four years, with a baby boy, who were devoted to each other. Lisa and John, married for two years who also had a baby son, but I didn't see them often enough to know the state of their marriage. Mike and Cathy had been married for two years, had yet another boy child and their relationship was apparently pretty rocky. Meanwhile, Claudia and Simon, who had been married for four years with no children, had now split; as had Susannah and Peter, married for six years, with one daughter. Two of my close girlfriends had a daughter each, and only one of them was in a long-term relationship, though no longer with the father of her child.

Not much to go on. Apparently, Cool Modern – not to mention successful – Nineties Wifedom was, at least among the majority of my friends, pretty much a trail yet to be blazed, so I attempted a desperate bit of alchemy, tried to create a Frankenstein's monster of a CMNW from stray body-parts left lying around the pop-cultural sponge that passed for my brain:

HOPE FROM *THIRTYSOMETHING*: The smuggest-of-smug characters from that smuggest-of-smug 1980s TV shows used to really piss me off, but she looked great in 'no-make-up' make-up, Wash 'n' Go hair, artlessly sloppy jeans and baggy sweatshirts, while painting walls, cooking, hoisting toddlers onto her hips and talking earnestly to Michael.

PRINCESS DIANA: Her legs.

MY FRIEND CLAUDIA'S MOTHER, SHIRLEY: In the absence of my own mother, who had moved back to Australia when I was fifteen, I had adopted Shirley as the perfect surrogate. I was so besotted that in my late teens I moved in with the family without actually ever being invited. Shirley, and her husband, Jerrold, were very long-suffering.

JOANNE WOODWARD: Living proof – perhaps the only living proof – that it is possible to have it all.

COUPLES PHOTOGRAPHED AT THEIR COUNTRY HOMES FOR POSH GLOSSY MAGAZINES: Always had a Gloucestershire pile with mellow yellow brickwork and a walled kitchen garden, plus improbably beautiful children called Camellia and Charity, Beauregarde and Tyrone, Arab stallions, golden retrievers and pots of cash. Bliss.

THE SECOND MRS DE WINTER: Of particular interest to second wives-in-waiting.

MICHAEL DOUGLAS'S WIFE IN *FATAL ATTRACTION*: Of particular interest to would-be pet owners.

ROSALIND RUSSELL IN *HIS GIRL FRIDAY*: For her brains, beauty, one-liners, suits, legs ... and the moment when her character, Hildy Johnson, tells her ex-husband, Cary Grant as Walter Burns, that she's quitting journalism and getting married:

'You can't quit, Hildy – you're a newspaperman!'

'I know – I want to go someplace I can be a woman!'

No – the more I thought about my friends and my attempt at genetic engineering, the more I knew I'd have to make it all up as I went along, if only because nobody had volunteered any advice (and I was too embarrassed to ask). There was, though, one person whom I would very much have liked to have asked but I didn't get the chance.

When I think about Susannah – which I do nearly every day – I think about several things. In no particular order: her va-va-va-voom blonde voluptuousness; her wicked, take-no-prisoners sense of humour; her helter-skelter, oh-fuck-let's-just-go-for-it apparent lack of emotional fear, coupled with – of all things – a distinctly girlish coyness; her innate stylishness as a writer; her unstintingly generous and supportive friendship; her skill at being able to get you to spill the beans about the kind of things you wouldn't reveal to most people; and, if you did reveal them, her ability to keep schtum.

I told her one of my secrets in the summer of 1994, just before I met Eric. I was surprised by her response. Susannah's middle name was unshockable.

'Kate! I'm not sure about that *at all*!' she said with mock-horror and despite the tone, I felt slightly chastized (she could do judgemental, too).

'Ooh-er,' I said. 'You don't approve, do you?'

She was disarming that way, could easily do *tut-tut, now listen up to your big sister*, but this time there was something else, a kind of weariness. I thought I'd let her down a bit, confessing this tawdry little tale. I sensed I'd somehow disappointed her, so I changed the subject lightly.

'OK, so how tawdry are *you*?' And she disarmed me with her response.

'Well, actually, it's hard at the moment...' And she told me she was depressed. We arranged to meet because she hadn't been to my new flat and was keen to see it and so, the following week, we spent a long evening, well into the small hours, drinking, smoking, giggling, bitching ... girl stuff. A few days later she sent me a postcard. On the front was a naive painting of the top deck of a bus with smiling faces at the window and, above that, in the blue crayon sky, was a bird amid puffy clouds. Right at the top of the card there was a sun, moon and distant planets, plus the legend: *Limitations Are Like The Clouds, Just Thoughts Which When Allowed, Hide The Sun And The Infinite Beyond*.

On the back, in her distinctive, expressive hand, was a typical Susie note.

> Kate,
>
> What can I say? How about, bonding never felt so good! It was wonderful to see you. These are weird and hard times to be sure, but I felt so positive, so optimistic . . . Here's to us, the future; getting there in the end . . .!
>
> Love always, Susie X

This card is now framed and sitting on my desk, because from wherever it was that Susannah got to in the end, less than six months later, on 7 February 1995, she couldn't send me another one.

When I thought I should be crying I'd find myself, inexplicably, inappropriately, laughing; when I thought I should be awash with compassion and understanding I found myself feeling guilty or consumed by rage. In the few days after Susannah's death I went through a cycle of unexpected emotions and, it transpired, all of us who had been close to her were going through something similar. I had been dreading speaking to her husband and seeing Rachel, but when I did it was strangely, powerfully, healing, despite the fact that we were all (and nobody more so than they) floundering around in emotional quicksands, sometimes being sucked down and suffocated, other times emerging into the air and the light, breathing deeply and thinking clearly. Because Susannah had compartmentalized many of her relationships, I spent hours on the phone to some of her other girlfriends. All of us got to know each other a bit better in those early days and helped to fill in the pieces of the jigsaw that constituted her last weeks.

I was asked to write her obituary for a newspaper and felt overwhelmed by the responsibility, both to Susannah (who I knew straight off would not have appreciated anything gushing) and to the people she had left behind, particularly her daughter, who might, when she was older, want to read it. I felt like I couldn't begin to sum up Susannah for people who didn't know her, but I had a go. It was published the following week, on the day of her funeral, which I went to with Daniel.

In the days, weeks and months that followed, I needed a lot of support. Those of us close to Susannah helped each other as best we could, but we needed it from elsewhere, too. Unsurprisingly, I turned to Eric.

While I did not expect him to feel or demonstrate any pain himself – after all, they had never met, so she was largely abstract to him, starting to come truly alive, ironically, only as I talked about her endlessly in death – I did want him to both recognize and help me to deal with my loss. But pretty soon, I found myself uncomfortable talking to Eric about Susannah. While I felt it was OK for me, as somebody who had known her so very well, to be judgemental about her suicide, I felt it was wrong for him to do the same. It was selfish, but all I really wanted was for Eric to understand the pain and then listen to me bang on about it for as long as I needed. It didn't seem too much to ask because he'd always been so good at it before.

By April, I was drained, volatile and badly in need of a holiday, so I spontaneously booked us a fortnight in Crete. Eric didn't make any objections, didn't in fact seem bothered either way. Maybe he had mentioned it before we left (he later claimed he had) but, shortly after our arrival, he told me he had been to Crete with his ex-wife. I thought I would've remembered something like that.

I couldn't relax. It was too early in the season for Crete to be hot, and it was dark by six, so there were long, chilly evenings in our self-catering studio, mostly spent playing Scrabble for 'The Cretan Challenge Cup' – a bit of faux Graeco-Roman statuary we bought at Knossos (I won it). Eating out was a chore (precious little variation on the theme of lamb) and so there was a lot of reading beside the pool (fat, no-brainer paperbacks for me, big management tomes for Eric), engaging with the contents being unthinkably masochistic. And then, armed with Eric's birthday present to me, a Wilson 'Sting Hammer' racquet, there was tennis.

As a qualified coach, Eric took charge. He tackled my creaking backhand, helped me conjure topspin and backspin from no-spin and got me to serve and volley rather than cling to the baseline like chalk. I was alternately delighted and horrified at being coached by Eric – delighted because he slipped effortlessly into patient and painstaking teacher mode, horrified because I was a vile student. We spent a lot of time shouting at each other over the net (I had a startling propensity for McEnroe-esque bouts of petulance) but my game improved enormously – until I twisted my ankle.

After a few days of relentlessly attempting and failing to relax, I had a breakthrough. One night I dreamed a dream which didn't, in fact, feel remotely like a dream. I found myself in Susannah's flat and, when I walked into the living room, she was kneeling on the floor uncorking a bottle of wine. She looked up when I entered, and smiled.

'Susie!' I shouted. 'You're back. You're here! This is brilliant. Everybody will be so thrilled!'

'Yup,' she said, pouring us a glass of wine each and lighting a Silk Cut, 'but I'm not here for long. Just for a bit of a girly chat.'

We talked about the kind of stuff we'd always talked about, and we did it the way we always had, equal parts dark humour, jaded cynicism and bright-eyed optimism. We moaned and we giggled and I told her about being engaged to Eric (she was so excited) and we got a bit pissed and then, after what felt like hours, Susannah glanced at her watch and sighed.

'I've got to go, Kate.' And she made a little downturned moue mouth.

'Oh no,' I wheedled, cajoled, 'don't go! Not now you're here. This is great! You know you may as well stay . . .'

But she shook her head. 'I can't stay, but it's been brilliant. It's great to see you so happy and it's good to catch up on all the gossip—'

'But you don't understand,' I interjected. 'I'm happy because you're here. I won't be if you go.'

But she carried on shaking her head and smiling a small smile, and I knew I wouldn't be able to persuade her.

'Come here, give me a hug,' she said. And so I did and we clung on to each other for ages and I started to cry. She moved back from me and held my shoulders at arms' length.

'C'mon, it's OK,' she said quietly, gently. 'I'm fine, honestly. And you are too. Take care,' and she hugged me again, 'and goodbye, Kate.' And then she walked out of the room, with one backward glance, and a wink.

And then I woke up and, because of the wink, I laughed. I felt . . . OK (or at least more OK than

I'd felt for weeks). There had been nothing odd or surreal, or even particularly dreamlike about the dream. I told Eric about it straightaway and (no surprises here) he seemed relieved. Perhaps we could start putting this behind us and moving on with our lives without being haunted by Susannah, although if I was going to be haunted by anybody, I figured Susannah would make a better job of it than anyone else I knew.

While I had temporarily transferred my attention from Eric to the desperate business of dealing with grief, I had hoped Eric would support me through it. I couldn't ever quite put my finger on why I felt he had failed me in this respect, but I felt it strongly. Although he had never said or done anything to indicate his discomfort when I raised the subject, for Eric, I think Susannah's death marked the end of our shared romantic fantasy and, ironically, the intrusion of real life. Now that I appeared to be moving forward again, albeit stealthily, into our future, he seemed relieved. But I was also irrevocably changed, and even if I didn't quite know it then, so were we. Because I had lost someone close to me that he had never known, perhaps there was always going to be a limit to his empathy. Susannah, then, had created a gulf in our shared experience.

We left it a few weeks after Susannah's death before we announced our engagement. I told Debra and Caryn over lunch; Daniel over tea at the flat we had formerly shared; my mother over the phone; my father over a bottle of wine (that he happened to be sharing with an old friend, Irina, whose sister Victoria was – in a neat bit of synchronicity – then married to Steve Martin and, more bizarrely still, had starred alongside him in *LA Story*, the film without which . . .); my colleagues after the Monday morning editorial meeting – a control freak in action – and, after I had got the most important people out of the way, the news leaked out the way it always does.

Eric wanted to buy me an engagement ring (who was I to argue?) and took it upon himself to do the research. One evening he came home and said he thought he'd found a suitable contender but that, obviously, I needed to see it.

'Where did you find it?' I said.

'The first place I looked . . .' He paused, smiling. It was unlikely to be Ratners.

There's no escaping the fact that there's something potentially naff about getting engaged in your thirties, particularly if you've been engaged before and your partner is divorced. But despite this, one Saturday morning we drove to Knightsbridge, entered Harrods, bypassed the costume jewellery department and pitched up amongst the hard, shiny, serious stuff without price tags where, to my surprise, my fiancé's relationship to glamorous French jewellery retailers turned out to be roughly analogous to that of Norm's to Cheers – everybody knew his name.

I guess the staff go on courses that teach them how to stage-manage these moments for optimum suspense and glamour because the atmosphere was a bit like the Crucible Theatre during the final of the Embassy Snooker – the occasional whisper and cough, bright lights and white gloves and green baize-lined leather boxes embossed with gold.

'Here's your ring, madam!'

Not only was it beautiful but it fitted. As I stared at the simple gold ellipse with a small (tastefully small that is – rather than, say, amusingly small) diamond solitaire set flush with the shank – I felt both girly and strangely guilty. The assistants melted away, leaving us alone to bicker lovingly.

'This isn't very classy of me, I know, but this ring quite obviously costs a packet and you are therefore bonkers and I really think I ought to know how much it costs and once I know that I think we should go and get a coffee and discuss this further . . .' and while I continued in this graceless vein, Eric just smiled indulgently.

So we had a coffee, talked, went back and he bought it.

Because Eric and I had been together only about four months, it was just after we were engaged that I first met his parents. Eric and Joe were playing football on a Saturday afternoon and his parents came up from their home in Wiltshire for the day to see them and also, presumably, me. I recognized, slightly apprehensively (given that these people would soon be my family, too), that it would always be a struggle for us to find common ground. I am so obviously my parents' offspring, but (apart from their looks) at least on first impressions Eric and Joe were not. Indeed, for all the lack of obvious emotional connections, the boys might have been found by the Finnegans after being dumped beneath a gooseberry bush by some tired stork that had meant to drop them off somewhere else, somewhere urban and creative.

But Eric's parents made me very welcome. Unquestioningly. On my first visit to their little flat we spent hours looking at the traditionally embarrassing old family snaps. There was one small black and white print that immediately caught my attention, of Eric, at about three, standing in a doorway staring away from the camera with those big dark eyes. His body language was acutely uncomfortable (he seemed to be caught on the hop) and he was clutching a large toy rabbit – Bunny. Much later I discovered that this same picture of Eric and Bunny had been used on the invitation to his first wedding, alongside one of his ex-wife at a similar age. I didn't mind too much, though, because both Eric and Bunny and their baggage and, indeed, their family, were mine now. I asked if I could have the picture. What had he been thinking? Where had he just been and where was he going?

When Eric and I had first started seeing each

other I had told him about the astrologer. He read the chart and, impressed, decided to have one done himself. I remember he wrote to the astrologer in big handwriting (much bigger than usual) on a sheet of A4 which he had turned on its side. He may even have used green ink. At the time he was staying in his brother's flat and the reply came back to that address so, for various reasons Eric didn't catch up with it for a couple of months, by which time we were engaged and had come very close to picking a date for the wedding (I favoured September; Eric wasn't bothered).

The delay made the reading even more resonant. Among the expected character analysis (and boy, oh boy was it glowing – when I read it I vacillated between pride and, bizarrely, something approaching envy) was the baldly unequivocal pronouncement that Eric would definitely marry in 1995, sometime close to his thirty-sixth birthday, which was on 21 September. It even turned out that he had an asteroid hurtling around in the deep space outer limits of his chart and that this asteroid was called, of all things, *Kate*. While I didn't think Kate was a very asteroidal sort of a name, there it was in black and white: 'The person in your life with this name will be your teacher', wrote the astrologer. Given that he was the one with the teaching qualifications, Eric thought that was pretty funny.

I was delighted by all this, of course, because I still

believed in 'magic' and 'fate' and the rest of it. But
I was slightly uneasy about the bit of the reading
that compared Eric's planetary set-up to that of a
nineteenth-century saint called John Bosco, who had
been a teacher. Eric was, of course, a very fine human
being and, more particularly, the fine human being to
whom I was prepared to plight my troth for all
eternity – but *a saint*? I wasn't sure it was a good idea
to go around telling Catholics, even lapsed ones, that
they were as good as saintly – they might start getting
ideas. And of course, aside from the trifling and
inconsequential little fact that *I* hadn't been compared
to a saint (although perhaps expecting to have two
saints in one relationship was simply greedy), there
was another, blindingly obvious fact: the astrologer
hadn't ever told me that I would marry in 1995. In
fact, he'd warned me off getting involved for a while,
stating that, although 'marriage was certain' for me,
it wouldn't be until I was 'at least thirty-six'.

I called the astrologer.

'Look, um, Eric and I are getting married. And,
funnily enough, in September, a couple of weeks
before his birthday. Is this the right thing to do?'

The astrologer ignored my brusqueness and
laughed gently.

'Kate, astrology is all about *choices* . . .'

'Right. So you're saying that if I hadn't met Eric I
might have met this mysterious man. You know, the
one whom I would have "married sometime after the

age of thirty-six"?' He had told me several key details about this person a couple of years earlier and I had liked the sound of him a lot. But 'sometime after the age of thirty-six' was the twenty-first century; and patience is not one of my virtues.

'Exactly,' said the astrologer. 'And, anyway, you and Eric are very good for one another. It's a potentially wonderful match.'

So that was that, then. Anyway, if I was honest, wasn't I getting just a bit too hung up on this astrology thing, which was not very Cool and Modern? Perhaps it was because I'd recently given up therapy, having decided that, since I was getting married, I was sorted.

'Enjoy this time. It might be the best part!' joked a (married, allegedly happily) girlfriend about the months between our engagement and our wedding, which we had marked out on a home-made wallchart in the living room. *Order cake*, it said, highlighted in yellow; and things like *Choir? ... Confirm Saturday reception venue ... Flowers for Arts Club? ... First dress fitting...*

But whereas Eric was never less than calm and methodical (the chart was, predictably, his idea), I found myself completely unable to organize anything without getting tense and stressed. And then there was the fact that things didn't necessarily seem to work out the way I wanted them to. For example, having discovered that we couldn't get married in the church of my choice (Eric didn't mind where we got married), only blessed, it made sense to book the register office for the morning of the blessing, but if you want to get married at Chelsea on a Saturday (I wasn't bothered, but it was my local borough register office) it appeared that six months' advance notice wasn't anything like enough; the best slot we could get was 11 a.m. the day before.

Organizing the wedding brought out my very worst control-freaky tendencies, but Eric was rock-like, either ignoring my wiggier outbursts, soothing them or pandering to them, creating numerous computer folders and files that contained our guest list, the (ever-mounting) reception costs and the running order for the church ceremony, leaving me, for the most part, to fill in the creative gaps. He was pretty happy to go with the flow. And, usually, the flow meant *my* flow, while I was constantly torn between wanting him to take over and sort things out and a contrary need to run the show myself. I did let him design the cake, though. He did it on the computer.

I was obsessed with perfection, but we were, like everybody else, on a budget. The average British wedding costs something like £10,000 and in that respect we were absolutely average because that's almost exactly what it cost. Still, I had such grand plans. I would, if I'd been able, have hired Chartres or the Sacré Cœur, the Duomo or Westminster Abbey; I would have worn expensive, dramatic couture and Venetian glass slippers; would have secured Versailles, the Pyramids or a small island for the reception and would have happily fed the five thousand – and then some.

I ransacked old books and magazines for inspiring pictures of weddings and dreamed about how it all might look in pretty much the same way I had when I was a kid. But, for all my centre-stage, limelight-hogging, big-budget bridal fantasies, I did leave a little time to dream, too, of being united in holy matrimony with Eric. After all, we were still very much in love. We were, said my friends unanimously, an obviously perfect match. They had observed that Eric smoothed my hard edges, while I toughened him up.

Organizing the wedding was, of course, squeezed in around the demands of work, now largely defined by my increasingly desperate desire to escape from it. The magazine market had changed and I was under pressure to pick up the gauntlet that had been thrown down by the success of new magazines in our market, like *Loaded* and the revamped *FHM*. I wasn't averse to using sex to sell magazines – my second issue had been devoted to the subject (and – have trumpet, will blow – remains the magazine's best-selling issue, if only because it ended up being racked on newsagents' top shelves), but I thought that sex had to be done with 'intelligence' and, um, 'integrity', which boiled down, in this instance, to an uneasy mix of statistics

and pie charts (long before Eric, incidentally) alongside chicks in their knickers. The upshot of all this
was that I locked horns with the management who
were, increasingly – and not unreasonably – keen just
to sell lots of magazines. As an editor, an unremitting
diet of T&A bored and frustrated me, while as a
woman (who was, of course, increasingly in touch
with her feminine side) it increasingly offended me.
The proper little madam in me resisted the changes,
then, but the editor in me knew they needed to
happen, so I had to get out.

The night the magazine won a prize, International
Magazine of the Year at the Periodical Publishers'
Association Awards, it was a grand feeling to go up
to the podium in the Grosvenor House ballroom,
surrounded by a thousand of my peers and professional elders and betters, but when I got back to
the table my boss's congratulations were disappointingly muted. It didn't take much for me to work out
that, though proud, it was a bit difficult for him to
watch his editor winning awards for making a magazine that he wanted to change quite radically. After
the ceremony I sought consolation and congratulations elsewhere in the room and when I eventually
got back to my table it was empty, the champagne
had been drained and the award was propped up in
the middle.

Fuck it! I thought, bitterly, grabbed the gong and
got a cab home.

Later Eric took a snap of me, grinning, slightly drunk, in the living room, clutching the award – the first thing I'd ever won. I took it in to work the next day and the staff were delighted, but I knew I had to leave as soon as I reasonably could. Fortunately I started being offered jobs, and after several weeks I decided to go to the *Observer*, as associate editor of the magazine. It was exactly the same job and title (albeit on a different incarnation of the magazine and under a different proprietor) as the one Daniel had taken when he had left *Arena*.

I worked out my notice and finally left a week before the wedding. My boss took me, the rest of the staff and some of my favourite contributors out for dinner, where they gave me the traditional leaving present of a framed fake magazine cover. The cover of 'Arena Femme Plus' featured an old *Arena* shot of a bunch of male 'supermodels' with a picture of me, stony-faced, one computer-doctored eyebrow raised, inserted in the middle of them.

Trousers: A Life trumpeted the coverline, then
My life in trousers
Trousers and I
The trousers in my life
The angst in my pants
Trousers – the inside story and, finally:
Girls will be boys, it's a mixed up, muddled-up, shook-up world . . .
Point made. Point taken.

You can't quit, Kate – you're a magazine bloke.
I know – I want to go someplace I can be a woman.

On Friday 1 September, the weekend before the
wedding, nine of the Girls – me, my mother (who
had just arrived from Australia and whose birthday it
was), Debra, George, Caryn, Kelly, Moira, Steph and
Lucy – decamped to a hotel in Devon. That night
in my room there was a pyjama party with pass-the-
parcel (boxes of false eyelashes, bottles of green nail
varnish, bits of highly flammable Anne Summers
underwear and – pièce de résistance, this – a frilly
gingham apron, on which Caryn had scrawled, in
Magic Marker, the word 'Versace'), and then somebody opened champagne and Caryn made a short
speech. Debra got it all on video.

'Just a quick one to say why we're all here, which
is to celebrate our good friend Kate's *forthcoming
wedding!* . . .'

(*much toasting and giggling, then Caryn suddenly
brandishes a red book*)

'. . . and anybody who has got any advice on how
to make a marriage work and how to be A Good
Wife needs to write it down in this book, because let's
face it, she may well need it!'

(*much cheering*)

'And so, Kate Flett . . . *This Is Your Life!*'

Life began at an early age . . . announced the bril-
liantly compiled scrapbook of excruciatingly funny

and tender pictures and captions. I was quite overcome.

On Saturday night we had a formal dinner.

'It's Saturday the second of September, 1995, and this time next week *I'll be married*.' A wide-eyed close-up smile, bathed in flattering candlelight, straight to camera. 'This time next week *we'll be dancing*!' And everybody cheers.

'How's it looking?' somebody asks, meaning the dress.

'I just don't know. Because me and the designers are the only people who've been involved, I try it on and I think *Yes! This is fabulous!* Then I think about what other people will think and I'm like – *Aaaargh!* You know, "She may have been in the fashion business but, *uh-oh!*"' And I do a big thumbs down while everybody laughs.

'It's not you I'm worried about,' says my mother. 'It's the Mother of the Bride!'

I roll my eyes. The Mother and Brother of the Bride shopping trip was scheduled for the following Wednesday.

Caryn took some of the best and funniest pictures of the weekend. There is, though, one snap from that evening about which she had warned me before sending the prints.

'It's really weird, Kate – but I know you're OK with weird, so I thought you should have it anyway.'

In this shot I am sitting on my bed with the

passed-parcel on my lap, wearing a nightdress, the 'Versace' apron and a wide-eyed, rectangular-mouthed Cherie Blair expression. Inexplicably, a bright white streak, like a tinselled bolt of lightning, runs straight down from the middle of my forehead and right into the centre of the parcel, making my already startled features appear even more absurd. And it was on the negative, too – not just the print. But I was OK with weird.

four

for the first
time clearly . . .

Our honeymoon was only ten days, Monday to Thursday week, in France, because Eric had to get back for an OU study weekend. We got very lucky, though – Shirley and Jerrold, the parents of my oldest girlfriend, whom I considered to be almost family, had lent us their house in the Lot-et-Garonne as a wedding present.

Rural south-western France was lovely on the cusp of autumn – fig trees loaded with plump, exploding fruit; aimless legions of languid, honey-freighted bees; vast fields of heavy-headed supermodel sunflowers finally giving up trying to grow; the early morning's fragrant, dew-soaked grass, dried and burnished by a warm, low midday sun and the regular, distant pop and ricochet-*chet-chet* of hunters' gunshot.

On the first day I took a picture of Eric sitting at the big dining table. Wearing Michael Caine glasses and an old jumper of mine, he is captured blurrily inside a dust-mote spattered shaft of autumn light, smiling broadly with his textbooks spread in front of him. We were pretty happy then – though I could have done without the revision.

But the weather turned and so most of our honeymoon was spent dodging dark skies and bitter, spitting rain. The outside world needn't have intruded, of course – we were newly-weds, after all, and had an open fire, an Everest of logs and kindling and a K2 of videos – but it did, at least for me. I have always allowed myself to be far too easily manipulated by the weather and had wanted my honeymoon to be perfect in every way. But we did laugh a lot. On the Friday night we drove to a nearby town where there was an open-air, drizzled-upon free concert given by an ageing blond bouffant-haired leather-trousered rocker of the sub-Johnny Halliday school. Instead of 'Yeah!' and 'Hey!' and 'Phew! Rock 'n' roll' he shouted things like 'Oop-oop!' and 'Icky-icky!'. We clung on to each other and giggled helplessly all the way through his set of mushy ballads and mid-tempo rockular work-outs, while all around us middle-aged *mamans* under umbrellas mouthed the words to the kind of *chansons d'amour* that you just knew had got no further than number twenty-three in 1971. Later we watched a big boules competition, lit by strings of white light bulbs hung amongst the trees of the local park, and became completely obsessed. The next day I bought Eric some boules as an early birthday present, and after that we played constantly, outside on the gravel drive when the weather was clement, inside on the rugs when it wasn't.

The house, though very beautiful, was not really conducive to newly-wed nocturnal romping, with bedrooms functional rather than seductive – although I suppose we needn't have restricted ourselves to bedrooms or, come to that, the night. I was, in any case, on constant spider alert – there were a lot of them, everywhere, and they were very large; and then there was the fact that I had recently become slightly self-conscious about making love, which I figured had something to do with the stress leading up to the wedding and then simply being exhausted after it. I assumed it would pass once we had relaxed a bit but, in the meantime, when there was a clear, rain-free night I would almost rather pile on warm layers and sit on the bench in the garden, waiting and watching for the resident owl to emerge from the rafters of the small tower on the eastern side of the house.

The weather ensured that the pool cover stayed put and in fact it was only on our last day, Eric's birthday, that we again glimpsed a perfect full-blown late summer. Seizing the moment we drove my friends' car to Laressingle, a tiny fairytale medieval walled-and-moated village, and drank beer in the sun. This was far more like it.

As we were leaving Laressingle, Eric, who had been doing most of the driving, accidentally reversed the car into a tree, denting the wing. My instinctive reaction was disturbingly out of proportion – I got out of the car, inspected the damage and ran away to sit on a nearby patch of grass, where I burst into tears and shouted at Eric.

'You've ruined everything!' I screamed, inaccurately and irrationally, quite overwhelmed by both the depth of my anger and the need to blame my husband. We drove back in silence but instead of calming down I became even more angry, while Eric seemed to somehow fold in on himself, his expression opaque, his eyes wearing a look of cold, dispassionate distance which I had occasionally witnessed in the past – although never directed at me – and had dubbed his 'shark eyes'. At the town nearest to where we were staying I got out of the car and asked him to drive back to the house and explain what had happened to Shirley, who was overlapping with us for one night, reclaiming her home. Eric drove off and then drove back past the café where I was drinking hot chocolate and trying to collect my thoughts. Then he disappeared.

It didn't take long for me to regret this stupidity – Jesus, it was just *a car*, just *a dent*; and it was our last day, and Eric's birthday; and because he barely knew Shirley it would be embarrassing for him to have to go back and tell her he'd crashed the car without me there with him; and, anyway, why couldn't I tell Shirley myself?

God, I am so bloody selfish, I must be out of my

mind ... and so, furious with myself, I wandered through the town and bought a large, strange cake for Eric from a depleted patisserie. As I began the mile or so walk back to the house, a familiar figure in a familiar, dented car, pulled over to the kerb.

'Get in! And don't be so silly, Kate. It doesn't matter. Poor Eric is in a complete state but you may as well get your first marital argument out of the way early on,' said Shirley, who had been married for about thirty-five years by this time. 'After all, there will be plenty more!'

Eric was drinking a glass of wine at the dining room table when I walked in. I pulled an embarrassed face and handed him the cake.

'I'm so sorry,' I said. 'I guess I haven't relaxed as much as I thought I had.' And Eric accepted my apology and shrugged it off but, still, I knew I'd hurt him unnecessarily. We ate the cake and, later, we all got a bit drunk. The honeymoon was over.

Back in London I had another week before I started my new job and Eric, who had also left his job just before our wedding, concentrated on studying for his imminent Finals. I spent the week writing thank you letters to everyone who had bought us presents and psyching myself up for work.

There is a picture of me at this time, the last shot on the honeymoon roll of film, in the kitchen of our tiny flat. I am mixing something in a bowl, surrounded by our shiny wedding gifts and look like a caricature of the smug newly-wed – well scrubbed, no make-up, long hair loose, rolled-up sweatshirt sleeves and ancient jeans, doing something creative with food. Subconsciously, that was probably precisely the kind of wifely image I aspired to.

When you're a newly-wed you get treated by others the way little girls treat the twirling ballerina inside the musical jewellery box. They lift the lid on your charmed, secret, mythically blessed new life, sigh, and talk about you in terms which, just a few weeks earlier, would have been considered laughably sentimental. While 'radiant' is reserved for your wedding day (and resurrected for the pregnancy), there are lots of other suitable adjectives.

I was told endlessly by friends how very obviously happy I looked, how relaxed and easy and comfortable I seemed. Even though I was happy, apart from that blink-and-you'd've-missed-it Doris Day photo-opportunity in the kitchen with my new wifely utensils, I don't really think I looked any happier than usual, certainly no more relaxed, easy or comfortable (words that, hitherto, had never been used to describe me, at least not by anyone who really knew me). But apparently it wasn't just me who, reduced to frustrated rage about the (far from magical, antithesis of the fairytale) crashing of the car, hadn't wanted the newly-wed bubble to burst, it was everyone else too.

When, in those first few weeks, people asked

about the honeymoon I would say things like, 'Oh, well, it was such a shame it rained every day,' while Eric, if he was with me, would furrow his brow and shake his head and say, 'No, Kate, it didn't rain every day. It rained quite a lot but not every day . . .' And I would toss my head and say something like, 'Well, it *felt* like it rained every day!' And then anybody who witnessed this was bound to quickly chip in with a hoary old wives' tale about it being good luck if it rains on your honeymoon, or something like that.

I only wish I'd known what I know now, which is that lots of women feel slightly cut adrift after they get married. That having your new wedding certificate prominently displayed on the mantelpiece, next to the swiftly framed wedding portrait, can be as much a poignant public reminder that everything has changed as much as it is a private celebration of the fact. That all the time Eric and I addressed each other, nauseatingly, as 'wifey' and 'husby' in private, we may have been attempting to come to terms with the inescapable fact of our commitment to one another. While friends still billed and cooed about the beauty of our wedding, the perfection of the day, the loveliness of my dress, the blindingly obvious rightness of my and Eric's togetherness . . . it was impossible not to play up and play the game. Nobody wants to hear that your honeymoon period is anything other than what they believe it must be and, of course, neither do you. To a hundred queries along the lines of 'So, how's married life?!' there is only really one acceptable response.

'It's great. It's fantastic!' I'd say. And they would nod and smile and then:

'Well, you look *so* happy. I'm thrilled for you both . . .'

But – and this wasn't about my love for Eric or his love for me or even about us at all: it was about me – there was a small voice that wanted to cry out and say, 'I don't know quite how I feel, but I know I feel different and I want to understand why . . .' which was immediately stifled. Nobody is going to be able to explain to you why, at one of the points in your life when you are meant to be at your most visibly and demonstrably happy, you could feel that in the process of gaining a husband you might have lost a part of yourself; that, say, the ritual of consigning your wedding dress to the mothballs and hanging it at the back of the wardrobe may be attended by tears of regret – partly for the fact that you may never wear anything so extravagantly beautiful again, but also for the fact (and oh! the guilt of admitting this, even now) *that you ever had occasion to wear it in the first place.*

My ham-fisted attempt to come to terms with some of these changes (changes which, for some reason, I found impossible to discuss with Eric) manifested in trying to wrest control of the relationship.

This wasn't hard, because for the first few months of our marriage, while Eric was studying for his Finals and then trying to set up on his own as a management consultant, I was the sole breadwinner, and so, even though Eric and I had a joint bank account (my first joint account), I held the purse strings. Part of this need to control things was, I think, due to an ill-defined and unexpressed discomfort about the fact that we were embarking on married life on unequal terms. Although I was right behind Eric's decision to change careers and held the long-term view that things would inevitably improve, the part of me that still believed in knights in shining armour and all the rest of the monstrous myth hankered after the old-fashioned idea of Eric taking control, at least financially. Eric, though, was not that kind of man and I had known this long before we married.

While far from financially astute myself, I was awash with pension plans and investment advice, while Eric had, for the most part, avoided this kind of dull-but-sensible long-termism. My husband habitually lived for the moment and if he wanted to buy me a Cartier engagement ring on his teacher's salary, then so bloody well be it – he'd just stick it on a credit card and worry about it later. Though more than capable of fiscal impulsiveness and spontaneity, I didn't operate quite like that.

After I had been at the *Observer* for two months and Eric was freelancing as a consultant, having got his MBA, we spent our first married Christmas with Eric's brother, Joe, his American fiancée, Barbi (who had recently moved to London from New York to be with him), and Eric and Joe's parents.

'Let's not bother buying each other presents this Christmas,' I suggested to Eric, partly because we didn't have much money and I thought the money we did have could be used more constructively, like saving the deposit to buy a flat or paying off some wedding debts, but also, I think, because if Eric was going to buy me a present I didn't really want to be the one paying for it. Eric didn't argue but I don't think he liked it very much. I can see why – it was a highly manipulative suggestion, not to mention cold and unromantic, but at the time I didn't care. My parsimony didn't, however, extend as far as the rest of the family. After all, I didn't want them to think we were Mr and Mrs Scrooge.

The proverbial 'they' say the first year of married life can be the hardest and there is no doubt that ours wasn't easy. For a start, both of us began new jobs. For me, having gone from an environment where I was, ostensibly, the boss of a highly creative team, trying to fit in as a member of a team with a boss who was never less than completely in control meant having to adjust. I liked my colleagues but I found the work unchallenging and the inflexibility stifling, so although I had anticipated that newspapers would be very different I also felt, for the first time in my working life, like the needle stuck in the groove. Meanwhile, for Eric, an MBA and a nascent management consultancy meant adapting to no longer being the man to whom people's habitual response, when they discovered he was a caring, sharing, Comme des Garçons-wearing but admirably underpaid teacher of visually impaired children with special needs, was, 'Oh – how *wonderful*!' Admittedly, Eric wasn't making money yet, but he'd already hocked his soul.

Christmas was quiet, spent at Joe and Barbi's flat with Eric and Joe's parents. There were presents (nobody noticed that Eric and I didn't give each other any) and turkey and pudding, of course, and then the six of us watched *Forrest Gump* on video. At some point we found ourselves talking about the millennial New Year. We wondered where we'd all be. Would we hire a house in the country, or go abroad? Better start thinking about it.

On New Year's Eve we went to a dinner party where I found myself having a lengthy conversation with a bloke called Colin. Colin asked me what I did for a living, so I told him.

'I have a secret fantasy about being a journalist!' he said and that was funny because Colin, a musician, had an enviable day job that he was in no danger of having to give up. He told me that his band were working on a new LP, at which point Eric, who had

been involved in another conversation, now introduced himself into ours. After establishing that Colin
was currently in the studio, doing interesting stuff
with computers, he said: 'Oh, I'm a musician, too!'
and so they chatted for a bit and, because I could
guess where the conversation was headed, I felt my
cheeks start to burn with potential embarrassment on
my husband's behalf.

'Well, if you need a hand with anything . . .' said
Eric. Ho-hum – too late.

'Do you know what band he's in?' I muttered into
Eric's ear, but he shrugged, shook his head. The
world was full of musicians who were in the studio.

'Sweet thing, I don't think they need your services!' and I told him who Colin was. But my husband
just shrugged again, unfazed, which said a great deal
more about my potential for embarrassment than it
did about Eric's (or, come to that, Colin's). Eric was
always fantastically unflustered by the kind of stuff
that made me want to crumple myself into a ball and
wait for the ground to open and eat me. It was
actually one of the things about him I really admired.

While Colin and the rest of Radiohead managed
to finish their LP, *OK Computer*, without him, early
in the New Year Eric did find himself a new job
(although perhaps more through necessity than
desire). Working for a small management consultancy
with offices on the other side of London meant a
long, tedious commute which he hated; none the less,

this was at least vaguely the kind of work he hoped to be doing in the future and it paid the rent, so he stuck it out. For a pair of starry-eyed newly-weds, though, it was an unwelcome wake-up call. There was no magic, day to day, it was simply a grind.

In the new year, I changed my name. I did it tentatively, rather in the way I might have tried on an unusual dress just to see what it would look like but not sure if I would be tempted to buy. I didn't abandon my surname completely, though, just tacked Eric's on to the end. I liked the way it sounded – Kathryn Flett Finnegan was, I thought, liltingly alliterative, if far too long. At work, though, it caused all kinds of problems because, as a by-line, it didn't fit easily on the page and sometimes had to be truncated to Kate Flett Finnegan. This looked slightly uneasy to me – even though I am a Kate to my friends, I've always been a Kathryn for work – but I went with it. The first time it came out in print, I showed Eric. He seemed very touched, but a few people didn't approve.

'I can see why you've done it,' said my father. 'It's *romantic*, isn't it, but professionally you're known as a Flett . . .' And he just shrugged. I knew what he meant. If he'd also had a son, he probably wouldn't have minded, but he was the end of this line of Fletts.

Around the same time, Eric and I were invited to a wedding. I had gone down with sinusitis which had spread to my ears and given me tinnitus. Sitting in the church, listening to the choir hit the high notes was, I imagined, a bit like sticking my head inside a speaker stack at Glastonbury. But even though it hurt like mad and I was in a filthy mood (PMT worked its wonders, too), I managed to dig myself into an even filthier one. The couple's choir was professional and immeasurably better than ours had been. I suddenly realized, with a start, that I was *envious of someone else's wedding*. What the hell was this all about?

But even though I was going through an inexplicably irrational phase, Eric was my balm and we were very much an Us, still, even if our tides of loving madness had been, PMT, sinusitis and deadly sins apart, superseded by less tumultuous currents. I had known they would be – must be, if the relationship was to mature. And I knew we could ride them.

I like a challenge. The lease on the flat was due to run out in May and although buying somewhere might, potentially, exacerbate the stress we were already under, at the same time it would give us a new space – both physical and metaphorical – and a home, which I firmly believed would shore up the foundations of our marriage. Initially Eric wasn't anywhere near as keen as I was but it didn't take much to persuade him that it would help us, that we needed it, that our flat was far too small (we could never entertain because more than two people in the living room constituted a crowd) and he saw the sense in that, so we started looking for somewhere to live.

A pattern was emerging in the marriage, even if I didn't, at that point, understand it. I was fast assuming the role of decision maker, troubleshooter (and, even if unnecessary, deflector of potential rock 'n' roll faux pas), while Eric, who had been in most important respects the more decisive half of the partnership before our wedding, was playing a more passive, conciliatory role. I was astute enough to recognize that there was an aspect of my personality that needed to run at least parts of the show, but I didn't need or want to run it all. I believed completely in the idea of a partnership. I would have been happy to compromise if he had expressed strong feelings about a decision but, increasingly, Eric failed to express particularly strong views on anything that affected us as a couple. I didn't want us to drift so I took control and allowed Eric to clamber the curve of his new career.

I think this is a feminine trait. Many men will happily direct themselves almost exclusively towards their work, abdicating responsibility for all the other tedious domestic parts of their lives, including the emotional bits, particularly if a woman allows them to. I went along with it, even while I resented it. Increasingly I had come to recognize that my husband's apparent self-possession might actually mask a gauche unworldliness. Eric appeared to believe that you could get on in life by working reasonably hard and being a nice guy, while I knew that it took a little bit more than that. Even if one didn't like it very much, life occasionally demanded guile and politicking, confrontation and compromise. These words, particularly compromise, were just not in Eric's vocabulary.

I was, in short, becoming a nagging wife.

I knew, for example, that Eric harboured the fantasy of living in a loft space (ideally a fashionable converted warehouse in the middle of town with a couple of thousand square feet of wood floors and white walls), but it was, I thought when he talked about it, precisely that – a fantasy. For a start we couldn't afford it and, anyway, it sounded less like a home (even less a potential family home) and more like a grand version of the bachelor studio pad he had been about to move into before we met. For me, other priorities fuelled the search for our first marital home – dull things, like the fact that we should be able to afford it, that it should be in the kind of area that wasn't about to depreciate, that it should be a practical space that had a good resale potential and that there should be enough room for us to grow into it. In amongst all these desperately sensible 'should's' I had my own dream home fantasies, too, but I knew I'd have to ... compromise.

Winter turned to spring and we started to look. At first we viewed houses – two-up-two-downers in slightly shabby but up-and-coming areas as near as possible to where we already lived. There was simply no chance that we could afford anything decent in the area we were in, although it was the one Eric loved. Every Sunday morning he would go out to buy us takeaway cappuccino and croissants from the nearby deli, the kind of place where you might queue alongside a line of Colin Greenwoods and a couple of supermodels (or even my father, who lived just around the corner). Then Eric would buy me a bunch of flowers – gerberas, usually – from the florist across the road (the one that had done our wedding flowers) and he now had his hair cut at the same hairdresser as me, right opposite the florist. I loved the area too, of course – after all I'd chosen to live there – but I knew we had to move on, at least until we could afford to return to something bigger than a doll's house.

There was, though, something dauntingly grown-up about the idea of a proper house, even if we had found that we could get quite a lot more for our money than we'd thought. It was me who suggested looking in the area where we finally bought, just a mile from where we were already living but a world away in atmosphere. Solidly residential, with street after street of turn-of-the-century red-brick mansion blocks, it was also, I confess, a part of London I knew very well, having spent a chunk of my teens living there with my father, when it was known as 'divorce alley' because of its high density of middle-aged newly singles.

The first place we saw was at the upper limit of our price range but it was immediately obvious why. Mansion blocks can be dark and cavernous, like the spooky hotel in *The Shining*, but this flat was built on a corner and because there was also a light-well in the middle of the block it meant that there were windows on four sides of the building. It was pretty much a flat-pack house, then, in which the sun struck the kitchen first thing in the morning, moved round to the three bedrooms and flooded the living room, which was huge, with both a bay window and double French doors leading to a balcony, in the late afternoon. If there was a proper sunset it saturated one whole wall of the room satsuma.

I loved it and even Eric seemed keen. We looked at a few more flats but I couldn't get this one out of my mind – suddenly, this was something I felt really strongly about. The flat was slightly too expensive but I was sure it was a good investment and I was obsessed with the light and the space and, once we had slapped white paint over walls that were currently a variety of shades from taupe to black cherry yogurt, we could easily live in it until we'd saved enough to do up the bathroom and the kitchen. And there was also enough room for what we euphemistically referred to as a piano – I don't know how or why we started calling children 'pianos', it was just one of our things – but until the arrival of a baby grand, we could have a study each.

'You know I really want to live in a loft, but—' said Eric.

'Dream on, sweet thing!' I said, cutting him short.

'Go on, then!' he said, smiling.

And so I did, although he had to get involved occasionally. Like the time we had to persuade the building society that although we didn't earn enough and we had only been in our jobs for a short while, we were definitely a good long-term proposition (thank god for John, surely the most sympathetic – and creative – building society branch manager in the business). After we had had our offer accepted and the building society had been persuaded that we were the very model of a modern professional married couple on the up-and-up, the flat was ours.

We moved in on a chill May Bank Holiday, the same weekend that Eric's brother, Joe, married Barbi in the Jif-lemon coloured room at Chelsea Register Office. A few days before we made the move, I had an appointment at the flat with an American Feng Shui consultant called William Spear, ostensibly to do an interview for the *Observer*.

'I may have a dragon in the living room,' I wrote, 'but, to my very great relief, I am not disadvantaged by having a lavatory in the area of Wind. Happily, my lavatory is in Water. Not to be confused with the fact that water is, as a rule, also to be found in my lavatory. No, it is my study that is in Wind. Even as I write I am sitting in Wind and contemplating just some of my Fortunate Blessings from the Material World: a jug of coffee, a packet of Fig Rolls and a selection of final demands from various utilities. In a neat bit of synchronicity there is a distractingly stiff breeze currently moving through Wind, a breeze that I could avoid if my study were moved to, say, Mountain, but which would also mean that I'd be writing this wedged in between the kitchen sink and the rubbish bin – correctly perceived to be a fairly extreme form of creative avoidance . . .'

Perhaps, in retrospect, I shouldn't have been quite so glib because, despite my tone, several of the things Bill had said made a strong impression (this was, I suspect, precisely why I didn't put them in the piece). The most confusing, and the one that inevitably stuck in my mind, came after he had asked for both my and Eric's birthdates and made some calculations.

'For you, Kate, this apartment will be like a cave in which you feel safe. It will be your haven and sanctuary and you will be happy here,' said Bill. 'Your husband, however, views it in much the same way as a bird views a telegraph wire.'

One of the things that really bugged me about the flat was the fact that the bathroom window had been mirrored on the inside and then painted shut. No daylight and air was, according to Bill, desperately bad feng shui, so much so that I wouldn't even allow myself to fantasize over unfeasibly expensive Bulthaup kitchen pornography until we'd allowed some air to pass through Water. We ended up unsealing it, noisily and unsociably, at about 2 a.m. a few weeks after we had moved in.

Months later, in the autumn, I returned from a working trip abroad to find a note on the floor inside the front door. *Welcome Home Wifey!* it said, and moments later, in the bathroom, I discovered that the mirrored window had been replaced by sandblasted glass that let in the light whilst also obscuring the view of the block's internal well. It was Eric's sole, although not unimportant, contribution to decorating the flat.

Bill Spear was right – I did treat the flat exactly like a cave and a sanctuary. This was partly because spring and early summer proved to be a difficult time at work. The paper's editor was sacked and replaced, alongside a number of my colleagues. I kept my head down hoping that I might survive the chop simply because I wasn't too closely allied with the outgoing regime and I had a decent track record in magazines. In the event, I did keep my job, but the transition was difficult. I was unused to seeing people summarily dismissed for, apparently, no reason other than that they had been hired by the previous editor. My immediate boss also resigned and although the atmosphere and morale improved, I felt quite cynical about the whole experience, deciding that if I was to stay on

I would like my job description to change. Fortunately, several people in key positions seemed to agree and so I started editing less and writing more. My new boss, Justine, even gave me back my old column, which had been axed by the previous editor when I had written about getting engaged. Too sentimental, he had thought.

I was exhausted by work and the demands of moving house. So was Eric. I knew, and felt guilty about the fact that, I didn't have a lot of myself left over to support my husband, who was still commuting across town and still hating his job and was increasingly reluctant to talk about it. However, in the summer, after having been recommended by Debra's boyfriend, David, it suddenly looked as though he might get taken on by a company that he desperately wanted to work for. All those months ago when we had been drawing up our fantasy life chart, the one that had included my stately home, Eric had written the name of this same company and at that time it had looked only marginally more achievable a goal than moving into my aristocratic pile. Now, though, this same company was talking about creating a special role for him. God, but I was proud.

It was, then, a summer of waiting and hoping. And, for my part, tiling. I spent an unnerving amount of time in Homebase at weekends. It was a pretty quiet life. Domestic, conjugal, safe.

After some procrastination on their part, Eric was

finally offered the perfect job. He started at the beginning of September but, as we hadn't had a holiday that year, we went away almost immediately. He was initially reluctant to go away so soon, but I pointed out that as they had wanted him so badly that they'd invented a job, a couple of weeks' holiday wasn't, surely, going to be held against him.

Anyway, it was our first wedding anniversary. That night I picked a place for dinner out of the *Rough Guide to Portugal*, which was not, perhaps, a very smart idea. We celebrated our anniversary at a tourist restaurant in Sintra and though it might have been funny (laminated menus and Artexed walls, surrounded by a coach party of middle-aged Germans) it wasn't, really. We hadn't quite cracked the holiday thing yet, but there was plenty of time.

five

. . . in the light of
every day

One afternoon, a huge, perfect red admiral butterfly
appeared in the garden of our villa. I became slightly
obsessed with this creature because it never strayed
further than a few feet from us and, as the day
progressed, came closer and closer until, eventually, it
alighted on my dress. As a kid I'd spent a lot of time
capturing caterpillars and keeping them in a vivarium
full of their favourite leaves, watching and waiting.
Rather than the technicolour butterflies I hoped for,
the pupae always seemed to evolve into disappointingly wan moths, but I still loved setting them free
when they'd hatched. This butterfly conjured up half-
forgotten memories and I was more than content just
to waste a day sitting in the sun reading and watching
it resting on me, opening and closing the delicately
illuminated pages of its wings. I didn't really want to
go anywhere until the butterfly had flown away, but
Eric was bored. He was reading A Management
Tome. I was reading *Captain Corelli's Mandolin*.

'What's it about?' he asked.

'Oh, it's wonderful. It's about this man who falls in love with this girl, and he plays the mandolin and it's during the war . . .' and I rambled on for a bit, drawing the plot sketchily, not really wanting to explain, wanting to read instead. I went back to the book. After a while, I started giggling.

'What's happened?' said Eric, looking up.

'Impossible to explain, really, out of context!' I said gently, but dismissively, keen to get back to Cephallonia.

'Well, you could try.'

'Sure, but I would need to tell you so much for it to make any sense that it's not really worth it.'

Silence. A while later I laughed again.

'What is it now?'

'Same deal. You know, it's just a nice line. Um, why don't you read it when I've finished?'

'I don't want to read it. You know I don't read novels.'

'But you want me to tell you every nuance of the plot?' I wondered if I was missing something here.

'Oh, forget it,' said Eric, sighing. I couldn't work out what I'd done wrong.

Moments of pleasantly unravelling relaxation were frequently countermanded by Eric's obvious uneasiness and occasional snappiness. For example, I wanted to get hold of a kitschy poster we had seen pasted up in the local village, advertising a bullfight to be held on his birthday. A few days later I mentioned taking the car and going off on my own.

'Just forget about the bloody poster, Kate!' he said suddenly. He'd guessed, then, and even though it was just a small – and, worse than small, obviously desperately predictable – gesture, I was hurt. I knew that he really wanted a semi-acoustic guitar for his birthday, but because we were in deepest rural Portugal I didn't know how to find one, although I did go as far as suggesting that we drive across the Spanish border and on to Seville – a city, surely, that would have every conceivable kind of guitar. We didn't, though and in the end I panic-bought him a copy of The Manic Street Preachers' *Everything Must Go* at the airport and promised to make it up to him at Christmas. While we hadn't quite cracked the holiday thing yet, it looked as though I hadn't cracked the present-buying thing, either. But there was plenty of time.

The single biggest problem, the seething subtext to all this uneasiness, was that sex had become an Issue and I found myself becoming extremely emotional and inarticulate whenever we tried to talk about it. I was upset by the deterioration in our sex life and I couldn't work out why it had happened. The intimacy of our lovemaking had been one of our strongest connections, and now it was breaking. Eric said he was hurt by the fact that I didn't seem to want to make love any more, and though this was partly true, I couldn't find it in myself to explain why this might be the case.

The thing was that, although were still attracted to each other physically, there was now a subtle, sneaking, impossible-to-ignore emotional distance. I saw Eric's shark eyes more and more these days and I felt sure it was my fault. I was letting him down. I was too bossy. I nagged. I whinged about stupid things, like the fact that he didn't hoover or do the washing up. Obviously, Eric had assumed that we were the kind of couple who were going to rise above bickering over domestic trivia; that I was, somehow, clued in enough to recognize that we couldn't let stuff like this stand in the way of our tides of loving madness. For my part, though, I would catch sight of a new expression – of detachment, disinterest – when he looked at me, and I felt my pedestal begin to crumble. I worried that I wasn't good enough for this extraordinary man with the big heart and the wise old soul, the man I had long before lovingly dubbed 'the alien' (Eric having voluntarily deserted his people and come down to earth to mingle with the human race). But what had once seemed to be a typical lovers' joke was, increasingly, an extraordinarily apposite analogy, and in my panic to bridge the gulf, I seemed to make all the wrong moves, and somehow widen it.

My alien was, then, presumably seeing me for what I really was – just an ordinary wife, after all,

like several million other ordinary wives, the kind
who actually cared that her carpets and her dishes
should be clean; who didn't go out on Wednesday
nights because she would miss *ER*; who read *Hello!*
avidly and not as ironically as she might have; who
said things like, 'Don't you think Princess Diana looks
lovely in powder blue?' and – good god – actually
meant it; who got headaches, of all clichéd things;
who was, yes, often so tired after a hard day at work
that she didn't always – didn't, in fact, often – want
to have a long conversation about the meaning of life
but would rather curl up on the sofa with a blockbuster novel; who could be, if provoked, petty,
cutting, cruel, dismissive and derogatory just as easily
as she could be warm, funny, supportive, insightful
and strong; who sometimes thought it was a good
thing to clear the air with an argument. Eric, though,
would always go out of his way to avoid arguments
or confrontations of any kind, preferring instead to
retreat and, these days, fix me with his shark eyes. An
impasse, then.

I was a disappointment. I could see that. And yet,
in contrast to Eric's new emotional opacity, I didn't
think I'd really changed very much. I hadn't, for
example, ever tried to hide any of those less attractive,
less 'special' or pedestal-worthy aspects of my personality. Apart from the issue of sex, about which I
admittedly felt confused, I was, I hoped, up-front and
honest. I didn't know what I could do to counteract

Eric's inexplicable, unfathomable and steadily increasing distance. It had been a difficult year for both of us and, anyway, I knew that marriages were like this sometimes – ups and downs, lots of compromises and the necessity for boundless patience. But if things were a bit sticky, I certainly didn't for a moment think the marriage was doomed.

Recently, while clearing out a small landslide of papery ephemera from the spare room, I came across a few old sheets of A4, covered with my scrawl, the leftovers of a game we had played one night, just a few months after we'd moved into the flat and which pretty much summed up our world. I had named the game 'At Home with Mr and Mrs Armstrong' and the idea was simple: I was 'Mrs Armstrong' and came up with a selection of boring domestic phrases which Eric, as 'Mr Armstrong' – an astronaut who had never quite recovered from Boldly Going – would then translate into language suitable for an earthbound Apollo mission.

For example, 'please tidy up' became the urgent-sounding 'engage entropy reduction activity', while 'open the front door and let the cat out' (we didn't have a cat but I was trying to be domestically inventive) evolved into 'disengage the extra-environmental disclosure facility to enable feline geo-location shift'. On and on it went.

'Turn down the stereo!' I'd shout.

'No problem, wifey,' said Eric, 'I'll immediately

minimize the co-presence of the configured frequency relayer!'

'Darling, could you get up and go and get the papers?'

'Sure! I'll engage vertical orientation and information acquisition sequence to gather polyexemplarous reconstituted lignin global data-conveyance devices!'

And 'Good night, sweet dreams! Have you set the alarm?' became 'advantageous nocturnal timeframe and maximally sucrosal subconscious semi-random image juxtaposition, darling! and, affirmative! – have activated the pre-configured time-horizon delineation device . . .'

Which not only reduced me to tears but also convinced us (wrongly) that we'd come up with a winning idea for a sitcom. Frankly, it would have been pushing it as a sketch.

Our good times were small, intimate and delicate, and when we laughed it was triggered by precisely the kind of private, untranslatable jokes and observations, like 'Mr and Mrs Armstrong' that characterize any relationship. As a metaphor, however, 'Mr and Mrs Armstrong' sums up a lot about the way the relationship was going, if only in hindsight. At the beginning we had communicated directly; now things were becoming more complicated. This was a quiet struggle. We certainly never rowed, there were no crises and we carried on laughing. Inside our new front door all was apparently calm and equable, although around this time I did decide to have hypnotherapy to give up smoking. I thought Eric might kiss me more often if I didn't taste of Consulate.

Eric was in love with his job, liked his new colleagues and enthused endlessly about the projects he was involved in. To be honest (a bit like Mrs Armstrong) I didn't understand much about the specifics of his work which, as far as I could tell, bridged a mysterious gap between marketing and PR, but I wasn't bothered that I didn't understand, I was simply happy that he was happy. We were, I felt, finally on our way.

I went abroad twice in late autumn and early winter, and prior to the first trip Daniel called to tell me he had just got engaged to his girlfriend. They planned to marry the following June, and although that was several months away, I was so excited by the news that I immediately persuaded Eric to go shopping for a suit. Under my direction he ended up buying a madly expensive midnight blue single-breasted pinstriped Helmut Lang. Silly, I know, but it was very important (if only to me) that Eric should hold his own, suitwise, at Daniel and Samantha's wedding, which was certain to be an express train headed straight for Fashion Central.

My first trip was to Jamaica. Alongside a clutch of other journalists, I flew first class, stayed in glamorous hotels and worked and played hard. Although I was away for a fortnight I didn't miss Eric too much. I'd always thought it was healthy to spend time apart from your partner and, anyway, I was busy. When we spoke on the phone, which wasn't every day because I was moving around so much, I was full of it.

A few weeks later I was away again, for just a few days this time, to do another travel piece about an exclusive private island resort off the coast of Miami. There was only one other journalist on this trip, and I didn't want to spend all my time with her so I filled my days with beauty treatments in the hotel spa, a tennis lesson with the resident pro and my first ever golf lesson – which, to my surprise, I loved. We were put up in little villas adjacent to a man-made beach (the sand had been shipped in from the real Caribbean) and each resident had their own golf cart to get them around the island. Although coddled in luxury in this bizarre island enclave peopled only by the very rich and/or very famous, I took to doing late-night circuits of the island in the golf cart and felt like the Prisoner. The atmosphere was highly conducive to losing one's plot. You could, for example, jog down the beach, and the only person you would see jogging towards you would be – blimey! – Oprah, who might give you a little wave. And then, in the villa next to mine, Bono was having a quiet break with his wife and kids and their nanny. I spent quite a lot of time watching the off-duty Mr and Mrs Hewson and family. Most nights, after the kids had gone to sleep, they would leave the island in a big stretch limo and I wondered what they could be doing. They obviously led a life that was glamorous but at the same time entirely grounded, and I thought about Eric and me, sometime in the future, having a holiday with our not-quite-a-twinkle kids, and wondered if we'd be as relaxed and easy and interested in each other as Bono and his family so obviously were. Bonkers, I know, but I was envious of them, and it had nothing to do with their fortune or their fame and everything to do with them looking so much like a family. I called Eric several times in those few days. He called me once.

I was starting to find a niche. Before Christmas I found myself working on a story about yet another posh hotel, though this one was on home turf, just over a mile from where we lived. I spent two nights there, researching my piece and suggested to Eric that he might want to come and stay too. It could be a laugh, I thought, to have a mini-break in a grand London hotel, with a room-service breakfast in bed before we went to work.

'Too busy, wifey,' he said. And then, 'No point really, is there?' I didn't know what to say to that. I had thought it could be fun.

Shortly after this I landed a surprising piece of freelance work. I'd occasionally road-tested cars and written very lightweight, girly pieces for the magazine ('boot big enough for lots of shopping; goes very fast'). One day at work I got a call from Porsche UK: would I like a few days with the only Porsche Boxster in the country (it had yet to be launched) and write a piece for the Porsche magazine, *The Marque*, available to fans and would-be customers? Well, of course I would.

It was delivered to me at the office and so, well aware I was in the only Boxster this side of Stuttgart, I drove it out of the car park and up the Farringdon Road at about ten miles an hour, but the car didn't seem to like going ten miles an hour. By the time I'd got to Kings Cross and was heading down the Marylebone Road towards home, I knew I was going to be making a lengthy detour because the heads started turning at the very first set of lights. Other (male) drivers rolled down their windows and shouted their approval; pedestrians halted in mid-stride, jaws open, and I realized that not only are there a lot of Porsche fans in the world, but that if a Porsche fan sees a not-yet-available model they've only read about, the reaction may be quite extreme. I have never been whistled at so much in my life. I wasn't even wearing lipstick.

I was very flash, driving round Piccadilly Circus, loving the attention. Somehow I found myself on the A40, and then the M25. Eric was waiting for me at home but I didn't want to go home, I was having too much fun. I felt a bit guilty about that because I should have driven back and collected Eric and then we could have gone away for the weekend. But I loved being in this car, on my own.

'I'm sorry!' I said, when I finally got home, at about ten. 'I got carried away.'

'Can I have a go?' he asked.

'Well, it's only been insured for me,' I said, nervous as hell. I could have let him, I suppose, but I didn't, so all weekend we roamed around London in the car and the only thing Eric was in charge of was the stereo.

I don't remember the context, but we had an argument in the Boxster, driving through Hyde Park. Except it wasn't really an argument because we didn't argue. I just remember, at one point, saying: 'For God's sake, Eric, we can't carry on like this.'

But Eric just kept very quiet and stared out of the window while passers-by smiled and waved and I drove on in silence, jaw set, exasperated. Still, although I don't remember what prompted the outburst, I do remember that it was said on impulse. I didn't think it was important and the moment passed. But Eric obviously did think it was important and, for him, the moment was stored away.

Coincidentally, both of our offices had their Christmas parties on the same night. Eric's workplace, unlike mine, threw legendarily over-the-top affairs, in which all the staff were encouraged to participate. Eric had planned a bit of a musical turn, singing a few Oasis songs, with one of his bosses doing Noel on guitar. I'd never seen Eric sing, although I knew he could (I still treasured the tape of him singing 'My Funny Valentine' that he'd given me on our first Valentine's Day the previous year). I was looking forward to it.

'Well, Kate, the thing is the company doesn't really allow us to have guests,' he told me a few days before the event. 'It's kind of a private thing, so y'know, you're not really invited. Sorry about that, but it's out of my hands . . .' and he shrugged. I was hurt, but if rules were rules then I wasn't going to make a big deal out of it. I would go to my own, legendarily under-the-top, office party instead.

Eric wore the Helmut Lang suit, and his Liam Gallagher impression was a big hit, apparently. After the party (he got back very late, long after me) he was like a kid, excited about having been on stage performing. It had reminded him of his days in the band with his brother. He went on and on about it. *Bloody hell, he thinks he really is Liam Gallagher*, I thought, and although I considered this was a bit uncool in a thirty-seven-year-old man, I was also pleased with the Christmas present I'd bought him, which he was so obviously going to love.

One night I went to meet Eric and his boss after work for a drink. When Eric went off to the lavatory, the boss, whom I liked a lot, asked me what I'd bought him for Christmas.

'A guitar,' I said. 'An Epiphone Casino semi-acoustic – apparently Noel Gallagher plays one. And some plectrums.'

And Eric's boss, slightly the worse for wear, put his arm round me and said, 'Oh Kate, that is *so* perfect. He's going to love that so much! I'll tell you something,' he added, 'my guitar was given to me by a girlfriend and even though we split up, I still think of her every time I pick it up.'

'Sweet!' I replied.

Then he paused and looked me in the eye and said, apropos of nothing, 'Kate, just a word of advice. I – er – think you should cut Eric a bit of slack. You know, let him go out a bit more with his mates, that kind of thing . . .'

My cheeks burned. *Cut him some slack? . . . Let him go out a bit more with his mates? . . .* When had I ever stopped him from going out? He hardly ever went out because, if truth be told, until this new job he hardly had any mates to go out with, but if he did I had never, ever stopped him. I would, in fact, have been perfectly happy for him to go out a lot more, so where was all this coming from? Was Eric saying things about me? I felt confused, and slightly betrayed, but I shrugged it off with a joke when I caught sight of my husband returning to the bar.

We moved on elsewhere for another drink and I

found myself in an alcohol-fuelled debate with Eric's boss about the validity of a new project he was then involved in, which I happened to think was a waste of money. Eric's boss was young (younger than Eric) and the company they worked for was equally young and creative rather than stuffily corporate, so by expressing my opinion I wasn't in any way jeopardizing Eric's relationship with his boss, who gave as good as he got and seemed to enjoy our good-natured argument. I was astonished, though, when Eric weighed in against me, siding with his boss and, clearly, very genuinely, angry. I watched his shark eyes flashing while he argued with me coldly. *Jesus*, I thought, *how did we get to this? Since when did he care about the bloody Millennium Dome?* I really didn't recognize him. Eventually the subject was dropped, and conversation moved on to celebrating their mutual triumph at the Christmas party. Eric's boss turned to me.

'Kate, it was great – you should have been there!'

I paused. Somehow I knew this moment was crucial. I had to judge it right. Not leap to any conclusions.

'Uh, well, I didn't think I was allowed. I thought it was just staff,' I said brightly.

Eric's boss laughed.

'Not at all. Of course you could have come!'

And I glanced at Eric, whose expression (before,

that is, he turned away from me) hinted at a mild panic.

'Oh well,' I said, feigning a breezy cheerfulness while I sensed my world imploding in slow motion, 'perhaps you'll do it again next year?'

Much, much later and because I was the only one still sober, I offered to give Eric's boss a lift home. He invited us in for a coffee and it turned out that he lived alone in a minimalist loft with a stainless-steel kitchen, polished wood floors and black leather sofas. The bed was on a platform, the shower was a kind of free-standing tube in one corner of the room and there was a red semi-acoustic guitar propped against one wall. It was the epitome of the well-heeled 1990s bachelor pad – though, for me, too clinical and veering towards cliché. I looked at Eric, staring at the flat, and then I looked at his boss, playing his guitar, and it suddenly all made sense.

This was everything that Eric wanted.

But I didn't want any of it. I wanted to go home.

One Friday night before Christmas, while I was watching TV at home, alone, the phone rang. A girl's voice asked if Eric was there, and I said no, he was out, to which she said, obviously embarrassed, that she thought she'd rung his mobile number. Eric's mobile, if it wasn't switched on, redirected calls to our home.

The girl was very polite, told me that she was a

colleague of Eric's and that we'd actually once met at a party somewhere, a long time ago. Oh, had we? I said and then, because I am quite polite too, added that I was sorry but I didn't know where my husband was. She quickly apologized for having taken up my time, felt the need to explain that he'd given her his mobile number because a bunch of people were planning to meet up after work and she'd only just left the office, but never mind, etc. etc. . . . and after a bit of this, the awkward little conversation ended, and I put down the phone. I wasn't, perhaps surprisingly, particularly bothered about this girl, but I did feel a sort of intuitive dread about the context of her call.

I was already in bed, though wide awake, ceiling-gazing, when Eric got home, late. I told him straight away about the call, and I must have been obviously upset because he perched on my side of the bed and proceeded to reassure me, gently, that everything was fine, that there was nothing to worry about, that I was being silly. But it didn't really help. Why couldn't I trust him? He had never done anything to lead me to believe that he was anything other than trust-worthy. Then again he never used to stay out late with gangs of colleagues.

That night, I remembered a conversation we had had not so long ago, in which Eric had mentioned, in the abstract, quietly, guiltily, the fleeting thrill of meeting an unknown girl's eye on the tube and the subsequent rush, the 'What if? Maybe, if only . . .'

feeling, and how a life might be full of moments like that. I had nodded, understanding (what a very mature marriage this was, I'd congratulated myself). 'Yes,' I'd said. 'They're great, those moments, aren't they!' and Eric had looked slightly shocked.

It dawned on me, slowly, that this had been tantamount to a full-scale confession; that Eric had been trying to tell me that he had these moments all the time (no surprise. My husband was handsome. Frankly, I'd have been disappointed if women didn't try to catch his eye on the tube – as long as that was all they caught) and that they made him feel guilty, because if you were a married man who met other women's eyes on the tube (and, heaven forfend, even found them attractive) then it followed that something must therefore be wrong with your life outside of the tube.

But when all I'd said, in effect, was that yes, this happens all the time (is, indeed, one of the few things that makes travelling on public transport interesting) he had been shocked, disappointed. Perhaps he'd thought it only happened to him. For Eric, a waft of pheromones across from the Up to the Down escalator apparently constituted something else – something scary, something bigger, something perhaps as bad as adultery. Maybe there was even a little Jiminy Cricket voice that said: *'Eric, if you are attracted to other women, you can't really be in love with your wife.'*

I wondered, over and over, how it had come to

this so soon. And because of the strangely twisted part of the female psyche that habitually assumes total responsibility for tending the emotional landscape of a relationship, I truly believed that if Eric felt he had to lie to me about meeting colleagues for drinks, I must have done something very wrong to make him do so. I was probably an insecure, jealous, nagging wife and he couldn't stand it.

It is one of the Great Domestic Clichés, but everything came to a head that Christmas.

It was my and Eric's turn to do the decent thing and have all the in-laws over, plus a spare aunt. And perhaps because it was such a one-sided family affair – my father was abroad, my mother and brother at home in Australia – and because I felt that I was in some kind of free fall, I became even more desperate than usual to take control.

I don't like turkey much, so – sod everyone else – I ordered an organic goose. Then I chose just about the biggest tree we could fit in the living room and dressed it as though we were recreating Sandringham in Beverly Hills. I persuaded Eric to borrow a long folding table from his office and went mad with table settings and decorations – pyramids of pine cones, scented candles, posh crackers, linen tablecloths and napkins, the wedding-present best crystal wine glasses and all the rest of it. I was planning to purée parsnips and make chestnut stuffing; carrots would be grated and sautéed in butter and sugar, then there would be roast potatoes and mash, bread pudding, cranberry sauce, gravy, beans and peas. The crackers, pudding and mince pies were all from Harrods (regrettably, I couldn't quite build the making of the pies into my tight, perfectionist schedule) and we had bought literally piles of presents for the family.

Eric's parents and aunt arrived on Christmas Eve and were dispatched to Joe and Barbi, who had, conveniently, embarked on their married life in a rented flat just around the corner from ours. Late in the evening Joe called and said that they really couldn't wait, they wanted to open their presents at midnight and so would we come round. I remember thinking, *How pathetic, how immature. We're not children*, but we went round anyway and received Joe and Barbi's gifts, telling them that we were saving ours for tomorrow.

Christmas Day dawned unexpectedly mild and bright – at least in terms of the weather. I, on the other hand, was feeling monstrous. On discovering that the goose was too big for our oven we made an emergency call to my brother and sister-in-law and carried it around the corner. At some point during a basting session, I singed myself on a baking tray and burst into drama-queen tears.

'I want to go home,' I whined like a five-year-old in my husband's arms, and so we did. I smeared butter on my finger and made an impromptu lavatory-roll bandage, then ran a large bubbly bath in which I sat, whimpering. The finger was a distraction, some kind of focus for my pain, because I wasn't really crying about a small burn but about a greater, unspecified wound. Eric perched on the loo seat, watching me while I sobbed in the bath.

'What's *wrong*?' I begged. And he shrugged. Calm, detached, completely in control.

'I don't know,' he said, brow furrowed and pondering rather hard in a bid to give me a straightforward, honest answer.

'But something's wrong, isn't it?' I asked.

'Yes.' He sighed. 'Something's wrong. But I don't know what it is.'

But it was Christmas Day, and although my finger throbbed, even while my heart, the rather more important organ, felt as though it had been pounded with a steak tenderizer, I didn't want to speculate on what that something might be. Suddenly I was an urban thirtysomething Hyacinth Bucket, desperately keeping up appearances.

Eventually our goose came home to roost, and I puréed my damn parsnips and sautéed my bloody carrots and lit the candles and poured the wine and pulled the crackers, and we ate our happy family Christmas lunch in convincingly festive conviviality. Eric sat at the head of the table and I was at the other end, on the side, opposite the aunt. Everybody praised the meal and so, having achieved what I'd set out to achieve, I relaxed slightly, anticipating – despite everything – Eric opening his present.

I had told Eric that I had only bought him one present (but that it was a very nice one) and, to throw him off the scent a bit, I had wrapped a few plectrums in a tiny box and put them under the tree, hiding the guitar elsewhere. On Christmas Eve a similarly small box from Eric appeared under the tree. We handed out our gifts to the family first, saving ours for last. Eric passed me his box with the words, 'I thought this was appropriate . . .'

Appropriate I didn't like the sound of. *Appropriate* was not 'I thought you would love this' or 'I saw this and I couldn't resist it'. *Appropriate* was businesslike. It said, 'It is Christmas and we have to give each other presents so here is a present.'

Inside the box was a pair of plain gold hooped earrings.

'Thank you,' I said. 'They're lovely.' I put them on. Everybody pretended to be interested, but there are limits to how interested you can be in a pair of plain gold earrings. I remembered that several weeks previously Eric had made slightly desperate enquiries about what I might want for Christmas and, at a bit of a loss, I had mentioned earrings. Well, now I had my earrings.

I thought I hid my disappointment rather well, but Eric must have picked up on it.

'I went into our place' – by which he meant Cartier – 'but it was very expensive!'

'Of course!' I said brightly. 'That would've been silly!'

But Cartier hadn't been too expensive when he had loved me. And six hundred pounds hadn't been too expensive for his guitar.

He started to open his small box and while he was scrabbling with the paper and Sellotape, I left the room to get the guitar. By the time I walked back in Eric was holding the plectrums, and as everybody else turned, whooping and cheering at the sight of the black guitar case, he looked right at me, and the look, though outwardly impassive, I had no trouble reading at all. It said, *OK, you win, but I think I almost hate you for giving me the thing you know I really want at a time when I really don't want it from you.*

And after that, while he played his guitar and posed for a picture or two in front of the tree, he avoided my eyes. I wanted to shout, *You cold bastard, I hate you too!* – if only in self-defence. I didn't, but as we all embarked on a bloodthirsty game of Pictionary, I knew it was just a matter of time. All I had done by giving him the guitar was to buy myself a bit more of his guilty time and a stay of execution. This Christmas, nobody mentioned the millennial New Year.

On Boxing Day a 'family' group of us met for

lunch. There was Eric and me, Joe and Barbi, the in-laws, the aunt, Joe's ex-wife, Kelly, and her boyfriend Nick, and also Kelly's parents, to whom Eric's parents were still quite close. At the end of the meal, just as we were all about to leave, Kelly and Nick gave us a present. It was a framed photograph taken outside St John's, just after our blessing and it was perhaps the best of all the many similar pictures we had seen. Eric glanced at it briefly, said something polite and then went to collect the car. I was at a loss as to what to say, but what eventually came out was: 'I look at that dress now and I think it was ridiculous!'

Kelly looked slightly shocked. 'God no, Kate. It was stunning. You looked completely amazing.'

Eric's mother, who had been hovering nearby, appeared equally perplexed. She laid her hand on my arm, gently.

'I will never forget, Kate, how incredibly beautiful you looked walking down that aisle . . .'

And I thought, *You are a kind woman, but you have no idea. No idea at all.* Still, I smiled, wrapped up the picture and put it in my bag. These were the last words my mother-in-law ever spoke to me.

Shortly before New Year we went round to visit a couple of friends, Barry and Tatiana, who had recently got engaged. After dinner we played a game in which each of us took it in turn to pick a page number from the *Concise Oxford Dictionary*, then a column number (one or two) and finally a word number. Then we looked up the resulting word, as if we were consulting an oracle.

Eric's first word was 'anabranch'. Barry read out the definition: 'It's a stream that leaves a river and then re-enters it further downstream.'

Eric started, went quite pale, glanced at me and immediately looked away.

His second word was 'tat'. Tatiana – popularly known as Tat – giggled nervously and Barry looked slightly perturbed. I can't remember Eric's third word.

'I don't like this game very much,' I said.

At New Year we stayed in on our own and watched TV.

The next few weeks became a waiting game. Only I didn't know quite why or for what I was waiting. For the most part, Eric retreated further and further into himself, with occasional lapses. We went shopping in the January sales, for example, where Eric spotted a perfect, much-needed sofa, so we ordered it. He also bought accessories for his guitar, I bought a pair of too-reasonable-not-to-indulge Gucci loafers, and then we went to see *Shine* at the cinema (I cried; Eric didn't). At times like these it was possible to be'ieve that everything was going to be OK, that the comforting banalities of married life were, somehow, a defence against any unwelcome and potentially disruptive intruders. Like emotions, for example, or honesty, or sitting down and admitting that something was wrong.

As the stillborn early days of 1997 unfolded, Eric would sit playing his guitar in silence, shark eyes trained on me, while I wanted to shout and jump up and down – anything to break through his steely carapace. But so great was his control of the situation that shouting seemed childish. Shouting would annoy him, I knew, would make him retreat yet further, because, increasingly, he didn't like it when I was less than calm or logical. But I didn't feel calm and logical. Part of me wanted to say, *Look, do you still love me? Tell me truly*. But the implied neediness made speaking this awful cliché impossible. And anyway, I knew what he'd say. He'd say, *Yes, Kate, I love you*, but his shark eyes would tell me otherwise.

I even tried to convince myself that it was OK when I tried to initiate sex and he didn't want to know. Couldn't, to be blunt, get it up.

One Sunday morning he went out to buy us cappuccinos and came back with gerberas for me. He hadn't bought me flowers for a while but because he had been out for a very long time that morning, I think they were guilty flowers.

by waterloo station i sat down and wept

Stumbling through January. Lots of *Nice day at the office dear?* and *Sorry, but I'm going to be a bit late home tonight; so-and-so's invited us over for dinner on Thursday* and *Do you need that shirt washed?*

I shed a dimension somewhere along the way, seeking sanctuary in the most uncontroversial, doggedly non-confrontational little-womanish behaviour imaginable. Busy thumbing cookery books and comparing swatches of curtain fabrics, I felt Eric's shark eyes on me, sensed him loathing all this, and me, and I knew I didn't have long to wait. I could have lain on the Persian rug clad in a French maid's uniform, had Marco Pierre White's recipe for *blanquette de veau à l'ancienne* on the hob and instigated a stimulating discussion about European Monetary Union, but when Eric walked through the door after work he would still have shrugged off his coat, picked up his guitar and settled in any of the rooms I wasn't in.

A couple of days before we were due to go to

Bruges on a 'romantic weekend', which I had been asked to write about for the travel pages of the *Observer*, George and her boyfriend BJ came round for dinner. I cooked risotto and tried to play the perfect hostess, but Eric had retreated so far by now that his near-total silence during the evening was embarrassing. I cleared the table, and George and I carried the plates to the kitchen.

'Kate, um, what's going on?' said George.

I sat at the kitchen table, head in hands, and, to my own intense surprise and perhaps relief, managed to articulate the thing I had barely dared to admit to myself.

'I think he wants to leave me.'

A few hours later, long after George and BJ had left, I couldn't bear any more of the torturous silence, the mutual denial, so I said it.

'You want to leave me, don't you ... *Don't you? You* want to *go?'* And even as I said it, part of me still believed that he could deny it, would deny it. He sighed. He looked me right in the eye.

'Yes. *Yes*, Kate, I want to leave you.'

And I could hear his relief.

'No!' I shouted. 'No. No. No. NO. NO. *NO* ...'

Thursday 23 January 1997
6.46 a.m.

The night before last I had to remove my engagement ring because the diamond is suddenly a bit loose. As of last night Eric wants to move out. I guess the therapy starts here. He spent what little remained of last night at Joe and Barbi's. I haven't managed to sleep. I wonder if he has? I suppose I've known it might come to this all week, which is probably why I forced it. That doesn't make it any easier, of course. Last night George and BJ came over for dinner, which was a bit awkward. But I didn't think that within two and a half hours of their leaving, Eric would be doing the same.

I'm very frightened. Very lonely.

His leaving isn't meant to be the end. Or The End. It's meant to be an 'anabranch'. He goes off, like a little stream, 'finds himself' and rejoins the river later. En route he probably stays out late, plays a lot of guitar . . . God, I don't know. Anyway he's meant to come back, eventually, stronger, nobler, wiser. Meanwhile I think he thinks I'm supposed to do something similar, which is quite presumptuous on his part. After all, he's the one who wants to go. I don't want to him to go, particularly as I'm not sure he'll come back. I don't think he is, either.

It's not like I haven't been aware that there have been problems. I'm not that thick-skinned. It's just that I hadn't realized they had reached quite such an insuperable level. I feel a dull throb inside, and a kind of speedy heartbeat. I also feel – I'm ashamed to admit it – embarrassed. I know that's pathetic but I can't help it. Already I'm steeling myself for the call to the office later this morning. 'Sorry, but I think I need the day off. My husband is leaving me.'

I feel numb just thinking about the practicalities of it all: Eric finding somewhere to live. Moving out. What will he take? What will he leave? Do I ask for his front door keys back? Do I let him keep them and ask for a spare set of his new keys? Will he offer them? Stupid stuff. Gut-wrenchingly painful stuff.

Fuck. Fuck. Fuck.

I hate the idea that I might drive slowly by the window of his new flat late at night, looking for signs of life. Not getting the reassurance I need whatever I see. It kills me to think of him with someone else. I can't believe this is happening. Perhaps it's even scarier that I'm writing this down.

I tried to let him go on a cheery note. Ha!

'I think we're very brave,' I said, bravely.

We'd pulled ourselves together after some very painful stuff. Breast-beating, primal wailing. Howling, really. I can barely think about it without shuddering and scrunching my eyes tight shut to make it all go away.

7.11 a.m.

The road men have just arrived to start making holes or filling them in or whatever it is they're doing in Elgin Avenue. The sky is deep violet. Apart from the office, I don't know who to call. Probably no one.

I wonder how it feels when your partner dies? Thinking about that should put it all in perspective. But it doesn't. Nobody feels embarrassed when their partner dies. Or jealous. I must have disappointed him very much. I think Eric used to think I was – oh, probably magical, precious, irreplaceable and if not actually perfect then still somebody he couldn't not be with, perhaps despite himself. Although that's more likely to be my romantic spin on things.

7.28 a.m.

A cup of tea – the balm for all Great British Pain – and a rather acidic clementine. The sky is Air Force blue.

When Eric left, at about 3.45, I booked an alarm call for 9. Like I thought I was going to blithely toddle off to bed and sleep like a pet lamb. Of course I couldn't sleep, so I read a bit of *Birdsong*, but it was the particularly harrowing bit where Stephen nearly kills the prostitute, so I chose again.

I'm writing this in the room that William Spear, the Feng Shui man, said represented the Family and all our emotional baggage. He said we should keep it tidy (which we didn't – until very recently. It's a spare bedroom and therefore a potential dump. A kind of ritual burial ground) and put up pictures of ourselves and our families at a time when they were happy. There is just one picture: Eric and me, freshly hitched, grinning fit to burst on the steps of Chelsea Register Office, surrounded by our in-laws. Everyone looks absurdly happy.

I love him. He says he loves me. The love hasn't gone, then, but something has.

7.41 a.m.

I have five Consulate left, which will get me to about 9 a.m., by which time the shop next to the station should be open. Perhaps everything isn't an evil conspiracy after all.

We're still meant to be going to Bruges at the weekend. Perhaps it will be useful in some way.

The sky reminds me of a pad of Basildon Bond I had when I was a kid. They probably called it Dove Grey, but they should have called it January.

I wonder whether Eric is awake. I wonder if he stayed up talking to Joe all night, or if he just slept. Or lay there. I wonder if I'll watch the street at 8.30 to see him go to work. I'm sure I will. It's the kind of thing I do.

I really hope that – and I almost daren't write it, but I'll tempt fate anyway – perhaps he'll change his mind. That perhaps he'll think that trying to work it out, somehow, anyhow, by whatever means necessary is perhaps the bravest thing we can do. The more I think about bravery, the more I think that it is about working with what you have, rather than letting it go. It's a tough one, that.

The car was booked in for a service this morning. I don't expect it will make it to Tufnell Park. Although I might come over all sensible later. It's never too late for sensible.

I just went into the living room and switched on all the lights so if he walks past he'll see I'm awake. Although he'll probably just think I forgot to turn them off. Shipwrecked sailors and lighthouses come to mind. And prostitutes.

I suppose I'm really trying to say, 'I'm here. I'm available. Come and get me.' But I detect a new steely single-mindedness in Eric. He might not come in to shore. He might sail right past and keep on going. I hope not.

8.04 a.m.

Crap sky. There's a man in green wellies and a Barbour outside the window. He's about fifty miles adrift. The whole neighbourhood is walking past on the way to the tube. I go to work so late that I never see it.

8.19 a.m.

The cavalry from St John's Wood Barracks just came by.
They blew their horns. I've never heard them do that
before. It wasn't quite the Last Post, but plaintive
enough. Beautiful horses.

Eric saw me at the window and came in. We talked.
We drank coffee. Well, I talked and he listened and
drank coffee. Joe said lots of things to him that made
perfect sense to me. I thought he might just say to Eric,
'Good luck and good riddance,' which just goes to show
how very wrong I can be. I can learn from that.

I think it was good. I hope it was good. We're going
to try to do everything we can to make it work. If only
so there are no 'if onlys'. I hate 'if onlys'. I don't want to
be on my death bed and have a list of them. I don't think
he does, either. I hope we can be very strong and very
brave. I know we have to try.

11.17 a.m.

I've just come back from dropping off the car. Sensible.
Wandered around Tufnell Park in a sort of hyper-dream
for a while and then got a cab back home.

The sun has come out.

I called the office and I've left a message with my
therapist. I'm too tired to sleep but I'm too tired not to. I
wouldn't say I feel better but I feel optimistic about the
possibility of feeling better, which is a start.

6.45 p.m.

Spoke to my therapist. Just hearing her voice makes me
feel good. She's agreed to see us both but wants to see us

separately first, because she and I have a history and she doesn't want Eric to feel squeezed out. I think Eric will like her. I hope so – it's practically impossible not to.

24 January
12.53 a.m.

Eric got home quite late, about ten. I cooked organic sausages. He looked very tired and, I think, kept his distance a bit – physically and emotionally. We talked about ordinary stuff. Earlier today I felt good about the possibility of making progress. Now, though, the insecurity is back. I'm not sure his heart is in it. I think maybe he feels he has to go through the motions. Please God, I hope that I'm wrong.

He's now deeply asleep. Hasn't stirred. Didn't respond when I tried to make our shape. It's entirely stupid that I should feel hurt, but I do. The fact is, he's exhausted. So am I, but I can't sleep just yet. I wonder what it is that he needs? What it is in himself that he feels will make him happy? Sure as hell I'm not providing it, but then I don't think it's possible for me to do that. He needs to make himself happy. I need to make myself happy. Then we might be able to make each other happy too. Simple. And so bloody complicated.

I keep thinking back to the early days. Long mornings in bed, eating croissants, watching kids' TV, making love and giggling. He's always up before I am these days. I can't think the last time we spent a morning in bed just being together.

My biggest fear is that he's already decided that he doesn't want to be with me, so that any kind of therapy we go through will be used by him to engineer a result he has already planned. We're still going to Bruges tomorrow, though.

In a way, we were already travelling. Eric's quiet stoicism and determination and my predictable tears, anger, recriminations and shock tactics had already laid the tracks, precipitating our own, separate journeys away from each other. Out of either a kind of masochistic madness, perhaps, or denial, we decided to go to Bruges to carry on the negotiations – me trying to persuade him to stay, him building his resolve to go – on neutral territory, because at home even the half-empty packets of pasta, loo rolls and old magazines seemed to throb with a hitherto unnoticed and powerful significance: they said *all this will no longer be as it was.*

Adjusting to the fragile etiquette proved a test. We didn't speak much on the train and I spent a great deal of the three-and-a-quarter-hour journey to Brussels in a different carriage, accompanied by Sebastian Faulks's *Birdsong* and several large bags of crisps. When Eurostar entered the Channel Tunnel, I thought that if something horrible happened, that might be that. Of such mordant fantasies are tragically romantic train journeys made.

As the train hissed into the late afternoon darkness, through *Birdsong*'s First World War killing fields, I thought about my maternal great-grandfather, Cecil Jenkins. A few years previously I had become the first member of the family to make the pilgrimage to Cecil's grave. He'd already spent two bitter winters in the trenches but, during the Spring Offensive of 1918, it was news of the death of his wife, Kitty, from diphtheria, that sent him blindly over the top and straight into the enemy's embrace. Cecil had a tiny son, my mother's father, waiting for him in Australia, but it wasn't enough. He loved Kitty – the proverbial ancestral Great Beauty – too much.

Cecil was buried in a tiny War Graves Commission graveyard with views over the River Somme and his headstone was engraved with the words Wilfred Owen made his own – *Dulce Et Decorum Est, Pro Patria Mori*. I had wept when I'd seen them there.

I didn't cry on the train, though. Even when I thought about Eric, me, Cecil, Kitty . . . *we don't have a love like that.*

On to Brussels, where we made the connection to Bruges on a desolate platform at Brussels Midi station and sat opposite each other on a squeaky, plasticky, cruelly lit train for fifty minutes, not speaking, just making eye contact and, when it all became too much, which was often, sighing and looking away.

The cab journey from Bruges station to the hotel took about ten minutes. Our driver was cheery: 'First time in Bruges? Ah, Die Swaene is one of the very best hotels, possibly the best. Do you want to be recommended a restaurant?' And I thought to myself,

You think we're Mr and Mrs Happy looking forward to our lovely weekend; and I also thought, as we chatted with him, what great actors people can be.

Die Swaene was three old townhouses of four storeys, with a dimity reception and a creaky lift. The welcome was warm. Our suite, number 50, in the eaves, had a shower room, a separate bathroom, a little living room with a squashy leather sofa and a bottle of Moët in a bucket on the coffee table. The bedroom was dominated by a vast bed surmounted by a large gold cupid. The furniture was mostly of the dark, old, eclectic, heavy, oppressively European variety. Two tiny casement windows overlooked a deep-frozen canal. The view was of cobbles, trees, ancient buildings and iced water. Although we were in the middle of town, it was completely silent.

We arrived at 9 p.m., just in time for dinner, and were given the best table in the back of the restaurant, which had been converted into a conservatory. Our package – oh irony! – was called the 'Romeo and Juliet' weekend and included two set meals, one of four courses, one of six, with wine and, according to the brochure, the threat of champagne being opened with a sword, which is the kind of thing I hate. I wondered if we could borrow the sword afterwards.

The food was sublime and talking about it enthusiastically, with a courtly politeness ('No, no, what were you going to say?'; 'No, after you'), nearly got us through the evening. We were given an oyster each, as an *amuse bouche*, followed by a roulade of wild boar with goose liver pâté; tiny bread rolls with walnuts; a 1993 Riesling selected by the female sommelier, who revealed that her favourite wines were old burgundies; stuffed envelope of cod with wakame, accompanied by a sprightly Médoc; wood pigeon in an orange sauce; a cityscape of a chocolate pudding with cinnamon; tiny petits fours and coffee that was brewed on the table in a Frankenstein-type contraption attached to a Bunsen burner. There was enough to keep us occupied. There was also a lot of 'When was the last time you ate anything like this?'; 'When was the last time you stayed in a hotel like this?' We realized that we'd never done anything like this together; we hadn't got around to it yet.

With the coffee came more tears, more stoicism. The carefully cultivated atmosphere of 'romance' was proving difficult because, obviously, we were here to sift and scavenge through the detritus of romance, not feast on it. We were the last to leave the restaurant, and the marriage summit resumed in suite 50 and went on until about 4 a.m. before it faltered and was abandoned.

Inevitably to bed. Turning down the cover revealed two single beds, pushed together, but made up separately. For Eric it was probably a relief, but it seemed strange. After all, it is not unreasonable to assume that most couples staying at Die Swaene would probably want to be close, but to do so in suite

50 you had to negotiate a no man's land of tightly tucked-in sheets. I turned my back to read and left Eric staring at MTV. We agreed that the new U2 single was a disappointment.

The following morning brought a late room service breakfast of scrambled eggs, little pastries, coffee and orange juice – perhaps the very best thing about hotels – then out into a perfect winter day of high blue skies, fogged breath and blood-coagulating cold. We had a map, but the city is made for meandering. Bruges in August is apparently nearly as unbearable as Florence – and even in January no cobble, spire, bridge or canal was left unsnapped by grinning, hand-holding couples. Base emotion or no, I found it in me to be jealous of them all.

There's not much to buy in Bruges except lace and chocolate. I couldn't see a place for lace in either of our futures, but sought short-term consolation in the purchase of several pounds of dark chocolate from Leonidas – shockingly good. Neither of us was in the mood for culture, and my usual passion for churches seemed to have abated – they make me wobbly at the best of times – which meant that I took a picture of, but couldn't quite face entering, the beautiful twelfth-century Basilica of the Holy Blood in the cobbled Burg, one of the many European churches which claim to own a clot of Our Lord's platelets.

We had a cheap, delicious lunch – chips, mussels,

beer, what else? – in an unpretentious, if touristy, restaurant in the Simon Stevinplein, a small square dedicated to the man who introduced the decimal system to Bruges and invented dykes. We barely spoke. Shortly before sunset, we boldly took one of the 'romantic' horse and carriage tours of the city that leave from outside the Basilica. Actually, even if one was feeling romantic, they're not romantic at all – the guides are too good, talk too much and crack too many jokes. For 900BF (plus tip), our guide, Toon Defauw, and his horse, a bay called Wilco, gave us a scatter-gun history of the city at a cracking trot. Toon took a picture of us sitting to attention in the carriage, with horseblanketed knees and big, brave, camera-friendly smiles, with the Lake of Love behind us.

As the sky turned dark, we retreated to the hotel for coffee and downtime. I read, while he watched television, both of us building on our reserves of strength for the evening's six-course dinner, and all the rest of it.

Dinner: bavaroise of crab and turbot with caviar; a glass of Sancerre; roulade of ray with a cherry beer sauce; a glass of Chardonnay; lobster tempura; lamb; a heady Médoc – of which Eric observed, with faux pomposity:

'It smells a bit like dirty, medieval, treacherous velvet. Thick, historical, Inquisitional. It's like Donald Pleasance as Pope.'

After tasting it, he admitted that it was 'actually Vincent Price as Witchfinder General'. Which made me laugh for the only time in Belgium.

Back in suite 50, after a deep-fried Camembert with orange and a pudding called a Zephyr with rose petals, and coffee and petits fours, I felt a dull heavy pain in my solar plexus which I would have liked to have blamed on courses four to six, but couldn't. We talked until late, again; and I couldn't sleep, so at 5 a.m. I finished *Birdsong* on the sofa and when I did, finally, sleep, I dreamed dark, medieval dreams.

The following morning something like a routine emerged among the chaos – a second identical breakfast. I ached from the previous day's walking, all over and inside, and as we went out into a Bruges Sunday the skies were no longer high, but just above our heads, and our feet hit the cobbles hard. From a church belfry came, bizarrely, a discordant carillon of 'Land of Hope and Glory'. It was too cold to walk for long, so we went back to the hotel and drank hot chocolate in the tiny wood-panelled bar until it was time to leave. Upstairs, the bottle of Moët remained untouched on the coffee table.

For such a beautiful city, Bruges station is hellishly ugly. And if you have to wait a couple of hours for a delayed train, Brussels Eurostar terminal is hellish, too. We did it in silence, letting go. On the return leg we travelled first class and were served strange pâté and prawns by an endlessly smiling Belgian girl. The journey was slow – left Bruges at 1.50, got to London at 8.30. As compensation Eurostar offered everyone free single tickets.

At Waterloo, people were being met by their partners. As I watched mine striding ahead to the taxi rank, I felt him let go even more, uncouple, move on.

27 January

I know now that Eric is going to leave me. I have told my parents. I wrote a letter to the astrologer, which I showed to Eric. And then I sat down and wrote my 'Party Girl' column for next Sunday's paper.

Later, a phone call. Eric answered. It was Debra, just back from holiday. I sat on the floor and listened while he made appallingly stilted small talk. She must have known something was up.

'Tell her!' I hissed. I don't know why I wanted him to do it when it should have been me. Maybe I wanted to see how he'd handle it.

'Tell her!' And I watched his scared eyes – marginally better than Shark.

'Um, well, things aren't great actually. Kate and I are splitting up.'

I couldn't imagine Debra's response to this and I felt appalling for not being the one to tell her, but I really wanted him to do the work. I wanted him to squirm. He didn't, though. He talked as if he was rescheduling a couple of conflicting appointments.

29 January

I saw my therapist yesterday morning and Eric saw her
in the evening and he came back and he told me that he
wouldn't be seeing her again. She told me in the morning
that she couldn't see both of us unless Eric wanted to stay
and work it out, so this means that he is definitely,
unequivocally going. She has recommended another
therapist for him who, rather scarily, lives about four
doors away from here.

Last night we started talking about practical solutions
but it is so hard for me. I couldn't sleep with Eric
sleeping on the sofa, so I picked up the duvet and made a
nest for myself on the living room floor near him. I got
some sleep, eventually, but then at about 4.30 a.m., Eric
woke up, saw me on the floor and was shocked. He
suggested we both went to bed.

Today the full import of everything has finally hit
me. I feel so angry and hurt and afraid. I feel like I could
punch him and punch him and punch him. I want him
to suffer and to feel my pain. I don't believe he really
wants us to work. I don't believe he wants us both to
'run and run and run until we stretch the elastic so taut
that we ping back together'. I don't believe him, even
though he says it over and over. I am consumed with fear
and jealousy. I think he is going to go and find a new life
for himself and a new relationship. I don't think he will
suffer, I think he will be fine. That makes me so furious.

I want him to go immediately. And yet I don't. He
called me today at work and asked if I'd done anything
'pragmatic'. No, I haven't done anything 'pragmatic'. I
am hurting. I am in pain – even if he is unable to see
that. I don't want to have to speak to banks and building

societies. I don't see why I should be put through that. I hurt so much that I feel like I just want to lie down and give up.

He is being so cold and controlling about this. I recognize that he needs to do that in order to get away. That he needs to break free of 'the anchors', as he calls them, but I hate him for it. I just want him to – please – hurt the way I'm hurting.

I wish I'd never met him. I wish I'd never married him. I wish he'd never said all that stuff that he said to me at the beginning. He didn't know what he was talking about. I really think I might hate him for that.

And yet, of course . . . oh, I don't know. I love him so much. I love him more than anybody. Madness.

He says he won't wear his wedding ring.

He says he 'may very well sleep with other women'.

He says he will 'probably want a divorce'.

We will never kiss again. We will never make love again. I have lost him and I'm screaming inside. And for what? For what?

There is nothing else but to deal with the truth: he wants another life away from me. I can hardly bear it.

30 January

Last night was the first night I managed to sleep through without Eric beside me.

Had lunch with Debra and Caryn. What they did, which is something Eric seems incapable of doing, was allow me not to feel guilty about my rage. I am, apparently, allowed to be angry and allowed to feel hurt because, however Eric may like to define it, he is leaving me, rejecting me, without giving me any tangible reasons, or even the hope of real goals to aim for. Debra had a lot of interesting things to say about Eric and me, his personality and ability to intellectualize emotions, rather than actually feel them. Caryn didn't like the long piece of elastic idea very much. She said it sounded like being blindfolded and dumped in a field somewhere, in the middle of the night, and told to find a way home.

3 February

So much has happened. I can't think properly. I think maybe Eric is on the edge of a breakdown. This is his poem from yesterday, when he walked for miles, alone, from about 2 p.m. till midnight, and just thought, and felt.

> *This is the closest*
> *I get to crying*
> *reason I don't want*
> *reason anymore*
> *It turns me into nothing*

Oh, god. I now understand that Eric's problem is that he can't feel, he can only think. Eric is The Tin Man.

7 February

Susannah died two years ago today and – God help me – I forgot to light her candle. But I think she would have understood, because tonight was my and Eric's last evening under the same roof and, while he tried to pack, I just sat in front of the stereo and played all 'our' songs back to back in chronological order for about two hours. It was an unspeakable nightmare but I had to do it. I think that music is the only thing that affects Eric emotionally.

8 February

Our seventeen-month wedding anniversary. I bought Eric a tiny tree in a pot for his flat and a card on which I copied out a poem I wrote years ago, before I met him, but which seemed suddenly strangely appropriate. Then George came round and we went to Battersea while Eric moved out.

Battersea Dogs' Home is not for the faint-hearted. Inevitable, then, that on perhaps the most faint-hearted Saturday of my entire life, George and I went there to purchase a lovably dysfunctional four-legged companion as some small compensation for the sudden departure of my adult male hominid life partner.

It wasn't a dog I was looking for, but the Home also has cats. I had visions of the perfect cat: large, fat of face and pendulous of belly, snooty with strangers but devoted to me, one that would find inner peace on the sofa sharing a packet of Kettle Chips during *ER*, a cat that, if it couldn't exactly contribute to a mature philosophical debate, would at least stare at me sympathetically while I indulged in periodic bouts of inner demon-wrestling. In short, a cat with the ability to know a) when I needed it to be co-dependent and sit on my solar plexus and purr and b) when to keep a low profile and give me lots of personal space. It would also need to have a very high maudlin-song threshold. This was asking a lot, but I was optimistic.

We paid fifty pence, and took a deli-counter ticket and a form, which was quite intense: *Why do you want a cat? . . . Is a new baby expected? . . . Who owns your accommodation? . . . Are there any other comments you would like to make to support your application?* Eventually we were ushered into an interview room. I was nervous – was my answer to the question 'What type of cat are you looking for?', 'Adult, female, short-haired, happy living inside, must like risotto but needn't do the washing up' – too specific? Was 'companionship' too desperate an answer to the query 'Why do you want a cat?', or not desperate enough? Should I have owned up and told the truth – 'abruptly re-spinstered thirtysomething needs a distraction'. I needn't have worried, I got the OK with the proviso that, living in a flat with no easy exterior access, I must look for an 'indoor cat'.

The cats are on the second floor, divided into free-range and indoor. Unfortunately they appeared to be fresh out of the indoor variety so I hovered around the free-range section, peering into the cages, seeking a connection. I spotted Arnie – large, black, pendulous, old, used to going out – and felt an umbilical tug. I wanted Arnie, even though he was a bloke, and I wanted him bad. I went back to my interviewer.

'Are you sure I can't have an outdoor cat if he's very old? I mean, he might just want to put his feet up by the fire these days...'

She was polite but firm. 'Indoor' only. OK, I could cope. Arnie was a man and I didn't need a testosterone-fuelled tile-prowler who would love me and leave me, I needed sisterhood.

'Kate! Over here! Look!' George was hovering by the indoor section, where there was a lone cat we had failed to notice. This was a stunning-looking creature, also black and, frankly, obese. The card on the pen announced that it was a four-year-old girl called Sheba who 'doesn't like being picked up, is very affectionate on her own terms but can also be a bit of a madam'. It was like looking in the mirror. Sheba roused herself from her indoor torpor and stared at me, then started to gently, affectionately, head-butt her door. She was patently bonkers. It was love.

But when a 're-homer' called Dawn came to remove her from the cage, Sheba threw a major hissy-fit. After Dawn had donned a scary-looking pair of cat gloves, Sheba lost the plot completely, snarling, scratching and hurling herself around the cage like a woman possessed. Dawn looked pretty upset. Sheba looked like one of Satan's familiars. My empathy knew no bounds.

'I'm afraid I can't re-home this cat. She shouldn't be up for re-homing, actually. If I let you take her, I wouldn't forgive myself.'

'But she's been so affectionate. She just doesn't like being picked up . . .' I nearly whined.

Sheba cowered in the corner, wearing an expression of righteous indignation, coupled with rage.

Dawn shook her head. 'I'm sorry. You can come back, we'll have some more indoors soon.'

I was stoic, recognizing that I needed a creature that wanted to live with me, rather than one that had been forced into a desperate compromise. Although Sheba was a woman after my own heart, right now we were probably better off with separate lives.

9 February

Phone call from my father re my Bruges piece in the *Observer*. All he managed to say about it was that it was 'the oddest travel piece I've ever read'.

The doorbell went at about six. Debra and David . . . who else? I was initially reluctant, but it was good to see them. At one point they were on the verge of turning into Mr and Mrs Bickerson. 'I can't stand it. Stop it, both of you!' I had to shout. Pretty funny, actually. I do love them.

10 February

My first Monday morning without Eric, but a compensatory letter from the astrologer. Although so much has changed since I wrote to him in my 'noble', coping tone, the other week. Anyway . . .

Dear Kate,

I debated whether to give answer to your letter in terms of a full reading, but decided it was best to be as brief as possible. I wish I could have met with you! Yes, the strains and currently separative tendencies in your relationship are shown: Saturn (loss, separation) right on the 'marriage' point. The year will not be easy here, particularly during March/ April. You are also going through some fundamental emotional changes. Stay with the relationship, however, to the extent that you can, for this heavily testing period will come to an end. That is what your relationship is going through, a testing, a purifying. As the Joan Baez song has it 'Carry it on, carry it on'. Give it all you can: it is worth holding on to.

Sincerely,

DB

PS: Yes, let Eric have some distance if he wants but make it clear that you will wait.

I think I have probably come to the end of the road with astrology, but, but . . . I'm interested in the things he didn't say about Saturn.

Wrote a note to Eric and drove it round and shoved it through his door. My old pattern. More predictable than sunrise. Went out to buy books, lots of books. And although I am incredibly wary, I did come back with Liz Greene's book about Saturn, to do some detective work.

According to Liz, Saturn in my seventh house refers explicitly to me in relation to marriage:

'It is unlikely that the individual will find the qualities he seeks happily expressed by a partner. It is more likely he will attract to himself situations which

involve some degree of pain, isolation, rejection and
disappointment until he begins to re-orient himself
toward an inner search . . .'

And on and on . . .

'Venus/Saturn appears to strike at a person's
happiness, and the usual feeling . . . is a nagging
discontent . . . the feeling that one will never be able to be
happy or take pleasure in life . . . loneliness and rejection,
in the case of people with Venus/Saturn contacts, can
ruin the entire life [and] although he stands to lose much
– and usually must spend a good portion of his life
without a companion or without true companionship –
he also holds the key to a relationship which is lasting
and real . . .'

Right. My life is probably ruined and I will probably
spend most of it alone – but hey!

'Regardless of how badly the person with Venus/
Saturn wants to express sexually and emotionally, there is
usually an equally intense unconscious fear which makes
defence necessary at all costs . . . It may be said of people
with this contact that there is often a feeling of being
unloved, and in consequence they find it difficult to
express love themselves – except in that slightly
demanding, sometimes possessive, discontented yet
painfully sensitive and vulnerable manner which is more
often seen in children of about three or four years of
age . . .'

Fuck this.

'There is often much sophistication in people with
Venus/Saturn contacts because their search for happiness
may take them into some strange byways in pursuit of a
love that does not bring pain . . .'

Enough. It's unbearable.

11 February

Get to work and discover that everybody seems to have
read 'Waterloo Station'. Congratulated all day and even
received fan mail: 'the best piece of writing I've read in
the *Observer* for a very long time, if not ever . . .' from
somebody called Alex. I wish this made me feel better,
but it's all too weird. And then, because it's also National
Marriage Week, I was interviewed for tomorrow's
Independent. Great – my husband leaves me and it's my
finest professional hour.

12 February

Skulked by the bedroom window and watched Eric
arrive for his therapy. He came the long way round so
he wouldn't have to walk past the flat and then left in
the same direction. I immediately called him on his
mobile and he sounded fantastically cheerful. Why did I
call?

Did paperwork – there's so much – and went to
work late. Read more 'fan mail'.

'I don't know how you can do it . . . so brave!' people
keep saying.

I don't know how to respond to that. The fact is I
don't know how I can't . . . There's nothing very brave
about a writer writing. In fact in my case it might be a
far braver thing for me not to write, but I'm coping in
the only way I know how, by turning events into words
and sending them out into the world. If I was a double-
glazing salesperson or a merchant banker or a dairy
farmer, nobody would say 'how brave you are to go out
and flog patio doors/get even richer/milk Daisy, what
with everything you're going through . . .' I just write

because writing is what I do and, now, seems to be the only thing I can rely on. I don't mind being praised for my 'honesty' – but this bravery thing is embarrassing. I get up in the morning and spend most of the day in front of a computer screen, so I don't know the meaning of the word.

13 February

Managed a full day at work, so some sort of a breakthrough. Lunch with Lindsay, who was great. There's so much flattering fuss about 'Waterloo' that if it carries on I'll soon be too terrified to write anything. Miss Eric very badly tonight, very badly. Dreading tomorrow . . .

Valentine's Day and I delivered dead roses to Eric's office, which was satisfying for about, ooh, six seconds. Late afternoon I received a phone call from our favourite florist.

'Hi, we've got some flowers here for you. We can get them to your office in about an hour. Will you still be there?'

I didn't dare ask who they were from, which I could have, but instead weighed up the likelihood of them coming from Eric. Well, they were from our florist, so what other evidence could I possibly need? But . . . own up, girl! He'd left me a week ago so, realistically, might not be inclined to send me flowers lest his intentions be misconstrued. But they needn't be roses. They could be something tasteful but non-committal, like arum lilies or just a load of green stuff. A call from reception.

'Flowers down here for you. Well, more of a tree, really . . .'

So, noncommittal flowers it was, then. Fine. I plucked the card from out of the arbour of arum lilies and miles of waving fronds.

Dear Kate – it read – *Thank you so much for that wonderful article you wrote six months ago, and happy Valentine's Day! Yours, a person in public relations.* Or words to that effect.

I wanted to tell anybody who worked in public relations that exercising the corporate credit card at my favourite florist on 14 February to schmooze somebody they'd only ever spoken to on the phone was, well, a really lousy bit of PR.

I left the office, gibbering, with the vast tract of greenery slung over my shoulder, and got home to find another bouquet, from my second favourite florist, leaning against the door.

From all of us said the card. This meant, presumably, the Girls, the sisterhood, my posse, the gang, the network, the soul-sisters, the support group. So that was OK. No corporate Amex paid for these. Feeling profoundly wobbly, I slashed and burned the arums and undergrowth that I could have sworn was still growing, crammed it all into a vase and plonked it on the living room table. No plant food. Delicately trimmed the stems of the second bouquet, added plant food to the water and dropped a two-pence piece in the bottom of the second vase. Put them in my bedroom. Then I had a long, long phone conversation with Debra and felt much better, before dressing for a party that I surprised myself by suddenly wanting to go to.

15 February

Woke feeling . . . OK. Phone rang. George told me that BJ had proposed to her last night. Burst into tears, equal parts desperation and joy.

Phoned Eric. Told him the monumental news. Silence. Mumbling. To fill in the gaps, I apologized for sending him the roses.

'Oh, I wasn't at work yesterday. I haven't got them.'

'Ah. Well. I'm sorry.'

'Don't be, it's very sweet of you to send me flowers.'

'No, it isn't, really. Believe me, it's not sweet at all. They are dead.'

'Ah, I see . . .'

We changed the subject. Foolishly, I told him what the astrologer had said, about waiting for him.

'Don't wait for me,' he said. 'There's nothing to wait for.'

He unequivocally stated that we will not have a relationship and he wants a divorce . . . An hour later we were still changing the subject. An hour after that, we gave up. Oh, except that I told him that I never wanted to see or speak to him again under any circumstances, ever.

22 February

I haven't written the diary this week because so much has happened.

It began badly. On Sunday night I found myself in a very dark place. Debra had to make a late-night emergency visit and brought me a hot-water bottle and a cuddly toy. Woke on Monday feeling much the same, although back from the brink. The therapist was wonderful – I told her everything I had thought and felt and done and she said it was normal and fine and even healthy. But I don't feel normal, fine or healthy (probably because I haven't eaten a proper meal since Bruges), I feel desperate.

I have decided not to see Eric again. He really is an alien – so cold and so distant and unshakeable in the belief that everything he thinks is correct. I can no longer have him in my life because he is too undermining and damaging.

I don't think I can keep up this diary, either.

'is it getting better?'

Who the fuck am I?

Shouting at the bathroom mirror jolted me straight out of the dramas and dreams of the past and the future and hurled me back into the moment, where I caught sight of my reflection as if for the first time. The woman who squinted back from the silvered glass, apparently surprised to find herself there, was not looking her best.

Thirty-two years old, badly in need of a haircut and with a face so pale under the bloodless February skin that, aside from the clearly furrowed forehead and little crease between the messily plucked and thinly arched brows, it appeared almost featureless. Her eyes were Dulux colours on sale only in the Purgatory branch of Do-It-All – 'Brackish Pondlife', perhaps, set off by rings of 'Insomniac Grey' and highlighted by splashes of 'Cry-Baby Pink' – while the tiny, slightly mean-looking mouth (which she disliked only marginally less than she disliked her legs) was almost invisible. She was wearing a pair of plain hooped earrings, her great-grandmother's wedding ring on the fourth finger of her right hand, a three-coloured gold Russian wedding ring on that hand's little finger, a black zip-up fleece top from The Gap and a favourite pair of second-hand Orange Tag Levi's which, as a direct result of having eaten nothing but bowls of soup and slices of pitta bread for the past few weeks, were now hanging (fashionably) low on the hips. A chaotic curl of Consulate smoke added to the vision of existential gloom.

'What a bloody mess.'

So I fished around in the glamorous professional make-up case that Eric had given me as a present on our first Christmas and did something half-hearted with the mascara wand, a bit of blusher and an inappropriately garish red lipstick, transforming myself from killer zombie into a characterful extra, fit for half a dozen frames of a Fellini movie.

I had recently taken to stalking. Eric had reluctantly agreed to carry on paying half the mortgage on our flat for a few months and had moved into a basement studio flat a mile away from me, close to the area where we had first lived and which he loved, but this time very much on the wrong side of the tracks. It was so easy to cruise past his windows late at night and, though the main room curtains were always drawn, I could get out of the car and, hidden from sight in the shadowy side street, peer into his kitchen and even, if the door was open, into the bed-sitting room beyond. A week or so after he'd moved in I watched him for a while through that window, perched ascetically on the edge of his new futon, eating fish and chips from a bag and staring at the wall. He looked small and blurry, like the image on a badly tuned TV.

I rang the bell. The door opened. Startled eyes. A near-comical level of politeness.

'Come in, come in . . .'

Did I want tea? And so, after a quick tour of the premises (the little tree I had given him when he had left was, I was glad to see, flourishing in the kitchen), I sat on one of our chairs with one of his mugs and I tried, really tried to be calm, but it couldn't last. We embarked on a pointless Gordian knot of a conversation – the same old stuff we'd been covering night after night for weeks. He was fine, he said. Happy to have his space. He didn't know what his plans were but he hoped we'd be able to carry on seeing each other. Once a week maybe, on neutral ground, or perhaps once a fortnight if that was easier. And I knew, as I had known for a while, that I wasn't getting anything like the truth, simply because despite his apparent calm and intense degree of self-control I had never seen someone (apart from myself) look less fine and more vulnerable. Even up close the impression was of a man who had somehow shrunk, whose words told one story but his eyes quite another.

They were no longer the eyes of a shark but quite a lot closer to the eyes of the small boy who stood in a doorway clutching his Bunny while his mother — or was it his father? — took the picture thirty-three years ago.

It shocked me to discover that I started to find something of lasting value in the relationship only when I had lost it. I hadn't found security or peace, whatever they were, in the easy reciprocity of an apparently 'happy' marriage, and I was starting to wonder if security and peace were things with which I would be comfortable even if I had them — if only because what I had now was a tangible sense of aliveness that appeared to be linked directly to my pain and which, though almost unbearable, seemed, bizarrely, somehow more real and more important. And, terrifyingly, much more familiar.

I was unable to eat, lost weight swiftly and stopped caring what I looked like, stigmatized by circumstance. But who noticed? Alone in bed, I often rocked to and fro, curled like a sea horse, because in the first days all I could think of, feel and see were the things I had loved and the things I had lost. Senses alerted, I craved Eric like an addict in the early stages of rehab. Longed to touch the soft threads of dark fur that covered my husband's chest and ran down to his stomach, making a delicate whorl around his belly button; conjuring up the tea-stain birthmark on his lower back or the muscled curvature of his bottom.

The thought of never seeing or touching these parts of him again was the source of protracted, desperate bouts of weeping. I missed his gentle, elegant hands, both the look and the touch of them; his eyes, pre-shark; his big, uninhibited laugh. I missed the stupid rituals, like saying 'dark' and having him reply 'dark' before we switched off our respective bedside lights. I yearned for our night-time spoon-shape and for hearing him spontaneously say the word 'love' simply as a calm statement of fact rather than a question or as a pet name.

'Yes,' I'd reply, 'love.' Safe at last, a ship come into harbour.

But as the days and weeks passed and I started to be unable to conjure the memory of his physical presence quite so easily there was something I began to miss even more, something we'd never even had and now never would.

One of the reasons I had married Eric was because at some point I wanted his children and there had even been a vague plan for me to get pregnant this year, which was perhaps one of the reasons he escaped when he did. Like most women I'd fantasized about what kind of person our genetic jigsaw might create – obviously the best bits of both of us and more besides. Increasingly, then, the greatest loss seemed to be what might have been; I could feel the onset of a creeping intuition that children might not now be a part of my life. Strange, then, but though I missed so much about Eric himself, what I soon found myself missing even more was the future. I felt completely betrayed about the direction of the rest of my life.

How could I ever begin to trust anyone again when I had taken my marriage vows so very seriously, and so recently? The easiest, safest way, I knew, was to avoid having to trust, but I also knew that easiness is not satisfying, the struggle is all. If not, why else was I feeling so highly charged, so insightful, so attuned to being alive? Even so, shiveringly lonely, more than anything I wanted to escape the pain that apparently came as part of the deal. The early weeks were extraordinarily difficult because, though focused only on pain, I also started to see things with a clarity that constantly surprised me.

In the previous few weeks we had been through so much that I had started to learn a great deal about the man I had married. I had learned, for example, that so intense was his fear of expressing emotion that the only way I could get him to do it was by screaming at him until, bludgeoned, he had no option but to reveal at least some of what he actually felt. I threw something (a Birkenstock sandal) only once. I didn't even aim at him but he made a great show of ducking and looking scared. The shoe bounced off a white wall in the living room and left a scar.

But aside from this demonstration and some occasional shouting, our split had mostly been con-ducted like a management think-tank sorting out a personnel crisis and I felt, on occasion, less like a rejected wife than a redundant employee. He even encouraged me to read one of the few books of his that had haunted our shelves – it was called *Uncoupling* (such a cool, detached Eric sort of a title) and he said it had helped him a lot when he had split with his first wife. New wife, old tricks, then. The book was full of the typically dispassionate language he loved so much and that I had come to loathe but which I had also learned, after having to almost bully him into saying how he felt, was really the only way I could communicate with Eric effectively.

One of the worst nights before he moved out was spent having a bit of impromptu quasi-group therapy with Debra and David at their house. My best friend was in her third year of training as a psychotherapist at this point and she used every skill she possessed in trying to find out why Eric was leaving me. (I'd failed. All I ever got was, 'No, there is no one else,' 'Yes, I still love you,' and the old favourite, 'If, for example, we were joined by a long piece of elastic and we ran and ran until we got incredibly far apart, then we would ping back together . . .' which sounded to me more like a first-year physics experiment than a practical solution to our problems.) Debra was, however, much more successful than me when it came to communicating with Eric on his own terms, using calm, specific language to tease out the things all of us wanted or needed to hear. Because it wasn't just me – all my closest friends were struggling to understand.

I sat at their dining table, then, next to David, who was playing the role of best friend's ideal boyfriend above and beyond the call of duty, and we both listened while Debra tried another tack, asking Eric yet again what it was he hoped to gain.

This time there was a pause and Eric peered at the ceiling, gathering his thoughts. Then, very, very calmly, he said:

'Look, it's like this. If you're playing football and your boots are hurting, what do you do? You get off the pitch.'

At which point I couldn't control myself.

'How fucking *dare* you compare me to a pair of football boots. You *bastard*.'

And Eric's expression never changed.

'But you know what, Eric?' said David (an Arsenal season-ticket holder) calmly, squeezing my hand in sympathy underneath the table. 'After a while you get back on the pitch.'

'Yeah. Maybe. If you've changed your boots...' said my husband quietly, stealing a glance at me. But it was only much later that I picked up on the possible meaning of those last few words because at the time I was too busy crying in David's arms while Debra tried to hold it all together. I found out much later on that she spent the following day in bed, nursing a migraine.

So, after I'd stalked Eric and he had perched on the side of his futon and I had sat on our chair with my tea and we tried to talk, I vacillated so furiously between bouts of manipulative calm (it was the best way to get him to talk) and white-hot rage (my feelings would keep getting the better of me), I knew we wouldn't get anywhere. After several fruitless hours, then, I left and went back to my bed and another sleepless night.

We had one of our 'dates' (endorsed by our respective therapists) the following Wednesday. He told me he was going on holiday for a week ('Oh yeah, on my own. Definitely. I'll probably just sit on a mountain and think about things . . .'), and I ended up running out of the restaurant in tears.

'I just thought I'd phone and, um . . . if you want to talk, then please give me a call. But obviously I quite understand if you don't . . .' It was an unsolicited message on the answering machine from Eric's first wife, right at the start of the week he was away. This turned out to be the very worst week since he had moved out, during which three events, of which this was the first, revealed that almost everything I had ever believed about my relationship with Eric was wrong.

It took me days to find the nerve to call her back and, when I did, it took even more nerve to stay on the line. I didn't want to hear what she had to say but I knew I needed to and so I listened while she described her marriage to Eric in terms that made me feel as though she had been a fly on the living-room wall during ours. One of the most important things I had believed was that my and Eric's relationship was unique, but here, suddenly, was concrete evidence that it had been far from that, that it was, in fact, virtually a replica of hers. We talked for well over an hour, maybe two, and we haven't ever spoken since but we haven't needed to. It was she who said, as had I, that at the beginning Eric had shown her 'what love could be . . .'

The following day I had an appointment with the therapist, who lent me a book.

'I know it looks trashy, Kate, but I think you'll find it useful.'

That night I lay in bed and inspected the American paperback's cover. The title wasn't actually embossed, but it was gold. **MEN WHO CAN'T LOVE**, it screamed, and then there was a subtitle: **How to recognize a commitment-phobic man before he breaks your heart. The Ground-Breaking *New York Times* Bestseller.** And then, **As Seen In *Cosmopolitan*.** On the back the hype was raised to new, increasingly feverish levels: **As seen by millions on *Donahue/Oprah Winfrey/Sally Jessy Raphael/Hour* magazine.**

Right. Great. My husband has just left me and I'm trying to find out why by reading self-help manuals that have been serialized in US *Cosmo*. Was this the saddest-of-sad thirtysomething clichés, or what? But I started reading...

> When a commitment-phobic meets a woman he's attracted to, the intensity of his interest often seduces her into thinking she has the upper hand in the relationship. At the beginning he often makes her feel so secure that she tends to ignore the clues that give away his problem ... the typical commitment-phobic is confused and confusing. On the one hand, he has a tremendous desire to get involved in a relationship. On the other, whenever this happens, he is overwhelmed by his need to get away. That is his problem – until you become involved with him, and it becomes yours—

... and of course I didn't stop. By the time I'd finished I'd chain-smoked virtually an entire packet of Consulate, crying almost constantly.

According to my unlikely new bible, the least damaging kind of commitment-phobe was the man who asks you out and then, after one great evening, inexplicably vaporizes, leaving you confused and hurt in the short term, but capable of a full recovery. The most potentially dangerous kind of commitment-phobe – mercifully quite rare, apparently – was the type that won't settle for less than marriage and once he succeeds, sooner or later he runs.

I didn't sleep, I cried. (Where did all this liquid come from? I had visions of legions of little eye workers – a bit like Woody Allen's cast of sperm in

Everything You Ever Wanted To Know About Sex –
tipping great vats of salty water down highly polished
stainless-steel tubes – 'C'mon, guys! Big trauma here!
All hands on ducts!') I cried hard and long because
there had not been a paragraph in the entire book
which had not described some aspect of my relationship with Eric. I hadn't ever imagined that my
marriage could be defined so sharply and accurately
in a pulpy best-seller, and the revelation that it had
been far from either unique or profound, coupled
with the crushing realization that I had married an
emotional conman (albeit an emotional conman who
didn't know he was one), made me feel firstly weak,
then nauseous, then angry and finally, after the water-
table of tears had been depleted, just tired.

Something very peculiar happened. My *Welt-
schmerz*, weakness, sickness and anger passed, to
be replaced by complete numbness, physical and
emotional. The next day I met David and Debra for
breakfast and I was close to monosyllabic. Toying
with my food, pale and unmade-up, eyes ringed with
exhaustion, I glanced up at one point to be confronted
by the sight of my old love, the musician, entering the
café with a pregnant woman, obviously his wife. He
caught sight of me and came straight over.

'Hello, darling! How are you? How's married
life?'

I smiled, sort of. 'Over,' I said.

He made the right noises before introducing us to

his wife – 'The baby's due in June!' – then he scribbled down a mobile phone number.

'Call me sometime. Any time. I'll buy you lunch.' And I smiled – ish. I knew I wouldn't call and I think he did too, but I appreciated the gesture.

Afterwards Debra, David and I walked by the Regent's Park Canal and I told them that it was very odd but I couldn't actually feel my feet.

'What can you feel?' said Debra.

'Nothing,' I said. 'I can't feel anything.'

'And does that bother you?'

'No. It doesn't bother me at all. I feel as though nothing can touch me.' Debra went quiet at this and we carried on walking. After a bit we stopped for coffee.

'I think it might be shock,' she said.

'Maybe,' I replied, 'or perhaps this is how Eric feels all the time.'

And so I banged my deceased feet on the floor and pinched my faraway skin a few times just to check if I was still there. I felt incredibly cut off from everything but I didn't care. The pain had dissolved but so, apparently, had I.

At home later that day I got a call from my friend Neil-the-Philosopher, inviting me to come and stay overnight with him and his wife, Liz, at their home in Oxford. I was still numb, but I went anyway, warning them that I wouldn't be much use. On the Sunday morning Neil persuaded me onto a runcible spoon of a bicycle and we wobbled across the Banbury Road and down Aristotle Lane towards Port Meadow, flooded and lovely, along the canal and then to Corpus Christi, where Neil did his philosophizing. We drank tea inside the college's mellow walls and I felt pleasantly distracted.

We discussed the philosophy of mind. My mind, mostly.

'Perhaps you think too much,' observed Neil (fabulously flattering coming from him) as I made randomly illogical connections between the fact that when I had got in the car to drive to Oxford the first thing I had heard on Virgin FM had been Terry Hall's 'Sense' – Our Tune. And debated what, if any, bearing that event might have on the fact that Saturn was currently in both my seventh house and Venus, and that my husband had left me three weeks ago. Despite having a good day with Neil and Liz, when I was on my own, driving home, I was anxious. By the time I'd hit the west London 'burbs, I had all the symptoms commensurate with an imminent outbreak of masochistic stalking.

I drove past Eric's bachelor basement and happened to spot (actually I had to park, skulk and peer) a girl doing the washing-up in his kitchen. She was slim and androgynous-looking, so much so that at first I took her for a boy (which gave me a nanosecond's pause for thought – Jesus, he's gay!) but, no, it was definitely a slip of a twentysomething girl wearing a tight T-shirt and jeans – Mia Farrow, *circa* Frank Sinatra. Timing is everything and so I drove home in an unsuccessful combination of first and fourth gears and immediately phoned Debra.

'I have to go back. Now.'

'You're not driving. I'll take you,' she volunteered.

I grabbed cigarettes, money, my keys, some strength of will and the two boxes of boules that I had bought Eric on our honeymoon. Armed, then, with both actual and metaphorical balls of steel, we returned to the scene. Debra parked and lurked. I rang the doorbell. He answered.

'Right,' I said calmly. 'You have five minutes to get her out, and then we're going to talk.' He looked nervous. Debra and I sat in the car and watched as the girl left. She was wearing a fake fur coat and made eye contact, briefly, as she walked past. I picked up the boules and went in.

'For your next honeymoon,' I said. He rolled his eyes.

Oddly, my anger was not so much about there being another woman, but about the fact that he had lied by telling me that there most assuredly was not one. Had, in fact, been adamant about needing this important time alone. That getting into another relationship was the last thing he could bring himself to do.

He sat on his futon and said that she was a colleague (no surprises there), they had got it together in mid-February (Valentine's Day?) and had just been snowboarding together in the French Alps (so much for the holiday alone, then). He also volunteered the information, somewhat cruelly and unnecessarily, I thought, that he had told her he loved her.

'But it's different this time. I've told her I love her but I've also said that I don't really know what love is.' He said this calmly, earnestly, big brown eyes wide, beseeching me to understand. I looked around his room and noticed the feminine touches, things he hadn't had a couple of weeks earlier, like a TV ('Yes, she gave it to me. I think it's her granny's or something.'), an empty bottle of champagne ('a house-warming present'), the essential oils, the well-burned candles ... girl stuff, the signs of a fledgeling and, I had to assume, inevitably doomed relationship. I finally recognized that the man I had married was an emotional liability.

I told him (perhaps foolishly) about extreme commitment-phobics, but of course it fell on deaf ears. And I even found it in me – pass the halo – to feel sorry for the girl, swept off her feet by my husband, who was turning out to be a real pro at this. Even now she was probably thinking that he could be the One, as girls are wont to do. As indeed had I.

'We can stay in touch. We can always talk ...' he said, with awesome nerve as I put on my coat. I smiled tightly. 'You're dead to me now, Eric.'

All this had taken so long that Debra, who had been parked nearby, had left an hour or so earlier. When I finally got in the cab, my biggest regret was that I hadn't chucked the bloody boules through the TV while I had had the opportunity. Still, he had them now – and balls of steel were something he probably needed a whole lot more than I did. I felt a lot of things at this point, but at least I wasn't numb any more.

The next time I passed the flat, months later, in non-stalking circumstances, I noticed there was a blind over the kitchen window.

So we didn't meet again, but we did continue to speak occasionally. And three days after I wrote about that weekend in my column (no longer 'Party Girl', which had been ironic anyway, but rechristened 'Girl Overboard') I received a letter. *Strictly Private and Confidential* it said on the envelope.

12 March 1997
Dear Madam,
    We have been consulted by your husband, who has sadly come to the conclusion that the marriage has broken down irretrievably.
    In these circumstances, he feels that there should be a divorce and financial settlement at this stage, rather than waiting for a two year period of separation. His suggestion is that you divorce him on the basis of his adultery.
    Bearing in mind the fact that our client

wishes to reach a speedy and amicable settlement
with you, he would appreciate your desisting
from writing about the breakdown of the
marriage in your column of the *Observer* from
now on.

We enclose a copy of this letter for you to give
to your solicitors and look forward to hearing
from you or your solicitors as soon as possible.

Yours faithfully,

Indeterminate Scribble

'His suggestion is that you divorce him on the
basis of his adultery.' A legally sanctioned lie was
what was required, then? While I didn't admire Eric's
adultery it was, to me, barely grounds for a divorce.
Why should I have to do the divorcing, anyway?
Why should all the paperwork have to read Kathryn
Alexandra Flett (petitioner) v. Eric Frank Finnegan
(respondent), when it was so obviously Eric Frank
Finnegan v. Kathryn Alexandra Flett, and the only
basis for a divorce was on the grounds that Eric *had
stopped loving me and had found someone else*. That
made me mad. Bloody, bloody, bloody lawyers.

The name on the letterhead looked familiar. It
took me a while to make the connection but, when I
did, I had to laugh. Eric might be living in a basement
bed-sit in the wrong part of Notting Hill but it hadn't
stopped him hiring Farrers, the firm which represented Charles when he divorced Diana.

I wrote back promptly. I'd be the one to decide

when he could get his bloody divorce and in the meantime nothing was going to stop me writing my column. It was the thing that was keeping me going. Anyway, I didn't have a solicitor and I wasn't about to hot-foot it over to Mishcon de Reya.

'She's a fan of your column,' said Eric, of his lawyer, when I phoned him later that day. *What did he want me to say to that?* – 'Ooh! Thanks, Eric! That makes everything OK, then!'? The conversation was predictably tortured (Eric even cried, asked me to be his 'friend') and afterwards I sat in the loo at work and cried, too. At lunchtime I left the office and went across the road to Hatton Garden, my wedding and engagement rings in my bag.

The first two shops weren't interested, didn't even want to see them. At the third, a bored-looking man umm-ed and aah-ed and pawed them.

'How much are you looking for?'

'How much are you offering?'

'It's difficult . . .'

'They're Cartier!'

'Well, the wedding ring I'm not too sure about, to be honest. Do you know which branch?'

'Harrods, actually.' He looked sceptical. I wanted to punch him. 'Look, *I was there when they were bought.*'

He slipped into a back room, consulted somebody, returned with brow furrowed.

'You see it doesn't really matter that they're by

Cartier. Well, not much anyway. We make rings absolutely identical to this ourselves. All you was paying for was the name.'

I was having a hard time holding it together.

'Funnily enough, I didn't actually pay for them myself.'

He ignored me.

'Well, I can give you £300 for the engagement ring and just the weight in gold for the wedding ring.'

I remembered my rings glittering on the green baize at Cartier. In that environment they had been worth £2,000 and £900 respectively.

'Which is how much?'

'Ten pounds a gram.' He ambled over to a weighing machine. 'A hundred quid.'

I just managed to withhold a sneer.

'Forget it.' And I looked at my beautiful, apparently barely saleable rings and I felt strangely sorry for them. It should have been till death for us, too.

'What sort of price were you expecting, love?' He made eye contact, was suddenly trying to be nice. I supposed he saw a lot of bitter, betrayed and overdrawn wives looking for a fast buck.

'Oh, maybe a business-class return flight to somewhere very far away.'

'Well, I'm sorry I can't even offer you a single economy fare.'

I put the rings back in their box and left. Halfway

down the street I got them out again and put them on the third finger of my right hand. They felt horribly wrong so I took them off.

That night I dipped my nib into a convenient jar of vitriol and wrote a letter.

14.3.97

Eric – I feel so confused and unhappy after our conversation. Since our confrontation I had been very certain that I did not want any contact with you at all, under any circumstances.

But communication with you is fraught with contradictions and our conversation today both moved me (it was your tears, I think – the first real tears I've witnessed you shed over our marriage) and depressed me. Your need to be understood somehow turns me into a martyr. I listen, I hear, I advise, I confess too many things about my feelings. Things which you should no longer be privy to because you are no longer a part of my life.

You left me not for the reasons you talked me into believing (and believe them I did, like a fool, because I trusted you. The same way I trusted you when I said the marriage vows), but to sleep with some girl with whom you have convinced yourself you are in love. It is inconceivable that this can be the case so soon.

I doubt that she is very emotionally healthy either. There is so much hubris involved when a woman finds herself in the situation she is in. She'll believe that she is 'better', in some way, than me. A woman always thinks she is better than her predecessor, when the fact is she is merely different.

I have thought back over the last few months we were under the same roof – your aloofness; keeping me away from your office Christmas party so you could pursue your, er, future; your nastiness that night we went out with your boss; your obvious frustration and anger that it was me who had given you the Christmas present you wanted so much; the fact that you would just stare at me silently, day after day, with your 'shark eyes', playing guitar after having got out of bed very early to avoid me. Whatever . . . you had already left me then, caught up in the escapism of your potential new life, despising everything I was and stood for, my 'wifelyness'. I remember you going out that Sunday to buy us coffee . . . for two hours. Coming back to me with a bunch of gerberas. It is obvious to me now what you were doing, even if you were only doing it on the phone. Guilty flowers . . . it makes my flesh crawl. Then there was that night I got the phonecall that had been re-directed from your mobile . . .

And of course it started the very day you went to work at that place. God, I was so excited for you then. I really wanted to see you fly in an environment where you seemed to be so happy. If I'd only known how fast and how high you were planning to fly. God, Eric, I was so blind.

So you lied. And though I may still love you in some ways, how can I like and respect someone who is so weak, who simply bails out as soon as

the going gets a bit bumpy and the first bright-
eyed little girly comes along? It is, I think, no
coincidence that she is ten years younger than
you. You know that I would have liked to have
got pregnant this year and I suppose that was a
terrifying prospect. You've bought yourself more
time now ... you are free, you can still avoid that
level of commitment even while you appear to
commit to her.

I am impatient, emotional, volatile,
demanding, perhaps impossible to live with – but
I am not a fool, despite being made to look like
one. I am also willing to trust and love (or rather
I was. God knows what the future holds) and I
am prepared to suffer the lows in order to reach
the highs. I know I can live on my own. I do not
need you to make me feel better about myself
(particularly as you have now made me feel so
bad), so why do you want to keep tabs on me?

Why do you want to create some kind of
strange 'friendship', whilst also being so desperate
to divorce me? I cannot be your new 'friend',
Eric, because I am your estranged bloody wife.
Unfortunately, you keep hooking me in, again
and again, and each time I find myself trying to
believe what you say and I respond to you
instinctively. But I should stop trusting my
instincts quite so much because my instincts led
me to you in the first place.

You cannot have the proverbial cake and eat
it. You betrayed me, lied to me, cheated on me
and, finally, left me under false pretences. You
will, of course, get your divorce and I will throw

away the stupid wedding pictures and the dresses
and the cake and all the rest of the meaningless
junk that surrounded our pointless marriage and
I will carry on. And I will do it alone because
you, of all people, are in no position to help me,
just as I am in no position to help you.

I refuse, then, to be drawn in by you and your
strange, perverse charisma. You must get on with
your life and deal with your past because you are
an emotional vampire and I must not allow
myself to be bled dry. Your motivation to remain
in contact with me is entirely selfish, although you
wouldn't see it like that. Indeed I genuinely
believe that you think I can benefit, in some
absurd way, from your 'help' and your
'friendship'. What, though, can you possibly give
me, now that you have taken everything away?

You can send as many lawyers' letters as you
like, but I will only deal with the divorce when I
am ready and not before. You have called all the
shots so far and I won't play the game any more.

Stop trying to manipulate, insinuate and
pretend to understand emotions of which you
have no conception. I do not know you and I do
not trust you and I am not here for you, Eric,
now or ever, so please go away and get on with
whatever adolescent fantasy it is that passes for
your life . . .

Not only was this not funny, not clever and not
grown-up, but it was also not sent. Not this or any of
the dozens of others in a similar vein. But writing it

felt so good. That week I also took delivery of the
sofa Eric and I had ordered in the sales, selling the
shares given to us as a wedding present by my father
to pay for it (after all, it *was* the perfect sofa), and I
received a letter from my friend, Richard, an American professor of critical theory. He had never met Eric.

Dear Kate,
    Your news came as a real shock to me ...
    It's terrible that this man has betrayed you. It
sounds as if this has been a complete withdrawal
of his promises and responsibilities to you, and I
can hardly suppose there is even a question of
reconciliation. I don't know about you, but I'm
not too good about forgiveness. The point is,
when a rupture happens, everything changes, and
even though everybody still lives and breathes, it's
necessary to build a wholly new framework in
which to deal with whatever is left over. The very
idea of forgiveness implies a stable context, and
the possibility of remaining oneself. I find it easier
to assume the opposite: because of what has
happened, one will have to be someone else, and
the task of making that (new, improved) self can
be useful ...
    Is this useless? I suppose I am proposing that
you take seriously the possibility that you're now
starting a whole new life. And in that process,
everything is up for grabs, even things that had
nothing to do with him ... I guess I'm suggesting
that you cut bait and run. I don't even know
what your status is – whether you have to deal

with this guy, how much practical shit has to
be done to extricate his traces from your
surroundings – but I just hope it happens quickly.
Will you move house? Will you restore your old
name? Is your trip in April a vacation somewhere
nice? Maybe you're already shaking it all off? . . .

Well, I was trying.

A fortnight later, on 1 April, my thirty-third
birthday, I boarded a plane bound for Bali. I was
theoretically going to write a travel piece for the
magazine, but personally I was hoping to get much
more out of it than that.

On arrival my first impressions, powerful ones,
were olfactory. This was surely the most beautiful-
smelling country in the world? Heady incense was
burned everywhere and the fumes, mingled with the
scent of frangipani and magnolia, hung heavy in
the humidity. Drunk with exhaustion, infused with
romantic scents, I checked into a large hotel at Nusa
Dua on the island's southernmost peninsula, and was
allocated one of their newly built stone cottages.

My gorgeous temporary home had a thatched roof,
a garden featuring a couple of pergolas, a pond (with
carp and frogs posing cutely on lilypads) and a
swimming pool heated to blood temperature. Behind
a tree I discovered my very own household temple.
The interior, though described as 'traditional Balinese
design', was definitely of the Conran Shop school of
'traditional design'. For instance, a little parchment

scroll invited the guest to select precisely what density of pillow and texture of sheet one would require for the following day. I chose duck density and linen texture.

This was a bittersweet venue for misery because everything conspired to remind me how alone I was. The cottages on either side of mine were occupied by Australian honeymooners whom I never saw, but heard. And every time I called room service a polite voice would ask if my order was for one or two. When I filled in another parchment scroll asking if I would like my temple blessed a) every day, b) on request or c) never, and I ticked a), the Mangku who came to perform the ceremony sat in the garden beside me in silence for several minutes. I assumed he was meditating, but after a while he said:

'We are waiting for your husband?'

'No, I haven't got a husband. Or rather, I have got a husband but he's not here.'

Which just made it worse.

'It is sad he is not here with you?' he asked, lighting incense.

'He's in London. With another woman. We're getting a divorce. That's why I'm here. Um, partly. But also to work.' The priest looked askance. They don't really go in for divorce in Bali. Once we'd cleared that up, however, the ceremony began. I had grains of rice stuck to my temples, forehead and throat and was sprinkled with holy water and petals while the priest prayed for me. It felt good, even if it didn't last. Two hours later the eye workforce was on overtime again as I lay in tears on my duck-stuffed pillows in one of the pergolas, accompanied only by the casual croaking of insouciant lily-pad dwellers and the sound of Mansun's LP, *Attack of the Grey Lantern*, which had become my soundtrack of late.

For a week I travelled through Bali accompanied everywhere by my guide, Darnata (Dar for short), and a driver. Temple after temple, rice paddy after rice paddy, mountain after mountain, lake after lake . . . Dar told me everything I could ever need to know about Bali for the purposes of my piece and so I took only desultory notes and drank in the landscape. In the evenings, staying in different hotels all over the island, Dar was off duty and so I was left to my own solitary devices. I had brought a lot of books. I kept a journal. I had long baths and long meals but, even so, there was still a lot of night left over.

In a temple at Pengosekan preparations were under way for the Balinese New Year. Statues were swathed in black and white chequered fabric, like grands prix flags, while village women brought offerings of fluorescent-coloured rice cakes, flowers and fruit. I had a pidgin conversation with a local man, which turned out to be small talk about Big Stuff – the spiritual significance of the hypnotically beautiful Balinese temple dances.

'The eyes,' he explained, 'are of God, the body

and hands are of Man and the feet represent the discipline of the Soul.' He executed a little impromptu dance, complete with darting eyes, elaborate hand movements and neatly precise heel-and-toe footsteps. After we had shaken hands and left the temple, Dar said, contemplatively:

'You and I are the same. I have to be good to you and you have to be good to me.'

And I felt the tears come hot and fast but I didn't want to embarrass Dar, so I simply nodded and looked away.

We drove through a village where men the colour of polished dry-roasted peanuts took breaks from the rice fields, sheltering from the noon sun on roadside bamboo thrones with canopies. Here we stopped at another temple where there was a cock-fight in progress, the spectators chanting in unison. Dar steered me away, though I wanted very much to see it. In the temple I was smiled and nodded at so much that my face settled into a semi-permanent rictus. Dar eventually leaned over to me and whispered.

'Everyone keeps saying how beautiful you are.' And then, slightly bashfully, 'You are very beautiful, I think?' as if the only sensible response would be, 'Yes, of course!' I rarely feel beautiful, mostly because I'm not, and I was certainly feeling very unbeautiful in Bali among this matchlessly beautiful race of people. In fact I had felt large and white and lumbering ever since I had stepped off the plane.

'That's just silly, Dar!' I blurted gracelessly. 'Balinese women are incredibly beautiful.' He shrugged.

'It is what is different that is always most beautiful, I think.' And I immediately thought of my husband and his new girlfriend – physically the antithesis of me. Apparently there is a country somewhere in the world where everyone gets to feel beautiful and so, even if she was probably considered beautiful everywhere else in the world, obviously she wouldn't get a second glance here in Bali. I had to smile. Thank God I hadn't gone to California.

That night I went to a temple to see a Kechak Monkey Dance and a Trance Fire Dance. Women in elaborate sarongs and highly stylized make-up fought demons while a circle of men chanted 'chuk-a-chuk-a-chuk-a-chuk'. A pair of prepubescent girl dancers synchronized their movements with their eyes closed, while another man walked over hot coals. I felt slightly bludgeoned by strange new sensations and was very quiet on the drive back to the latest hotel, in Ubud. Dar tried to engage me in conversation.

'This hotel is popular with honeymooners, I think.' (Oh dear, I thought, here we go.) 'You might come back for your honeymoon!' He smiled.

'I'm already married.'

'Second honeymoon!' suggested Dar, helpfully. I thought I'd better explain. He was really quite upset.

'I apologize for being personal,' he said after a pause, 'but marriages in Bali are considered to be a meeting of souls from previous lives.' And (c'mon, guys! Big trauma here!) I couldn't hold back the tears.

'I guess that some souls are apparently meant to stay together and ... some are not.'

Spotting the gleam on my cheeks, Dar (himself married and a new father) waited awhile and then delicately, touchingly, changed the subject.

'So tell me, Kate, what is the British national dish?'

Which threw me a bit.

I had had violent nightmares every night since I'd arrived in Bali, waking foggy and depressed. My last day turned out to be Balinese New Year and I decided to make it my own, too. Far from being a riotous night of drunken celebration, Balinese New Year is spent fasting and meditating at home in silence and darkness. No electricity is allowed and special dispensation is needed to travel anywhere. The night-time drive to the airport was memorable. Lights out, with only hazard-warning lamps flashing, we drove through the deserted, silent streets of the capital, Denpasur. It was so dark that you could see the stars and even Bali's legions of sad stray dogs appeared to have sought a quiet place in which to contemplate their canine lot.

Unlike the Kechak dancers I had failed to wrestle my demons into submission, but by the time I arrived at the airport I'd started to come to terms with them.

I had a lot to thank Bali for, not least discovering that the Balinese have life's big picture enviably in perspective. As the plane took off and I watched the darkened island recede from view I thought of Dar spending New Year in his home village compound near Ubud, perhaps contemplating the British national dishes of roast beef with Yorkshire pudding, and fish and chips (which, under the circumstances, was all I'd managed to come up with). I hoped he wouldn't waste too much time on it.

I wasn't going home though, not just yet. Instead I flew to Darwin and then on to Sydney where I was met by an old friend of mine, Graham, who drove me a couple of hundred miles in the direction of Canberra. By the time we arrived at Toad Hall, Long Swamp Lane – a dirt road somewhere in New South Wales – I was exhausted but excited, having planned a surprise visit to a couple of people I hadn't seen since my wedding. I particularly wanted to see if my sixteen-year-old brother really was 5' 11" and growing, and then there was the simple fact that even big girls sometimes need their mother.

I'd worked things out with Graham in advance. He was going to make sure that my mother was at home by telling her he needed to drop by on some spurious pretext (my mother doesn't live in area where dropping by is an easy option) and while he kept her occupied in the kitchen I would sneak round the side of the house and open the back door. From where my mother would be sitting I'd be in her line of sight, although I only had Graham's word for this because I'd never been to the house before.

It worked perfectly. I got out of the car at the beginning of the short drive and hid under some gum trees. When Graham was inside the house I crept like a thief around the side of the building, and, bizarrely, those of my mother's many pets that were roaming free-range around the scrubby front garden – a trio of fat merino sheep, grumpy ram Trousers, Wylie and Bo; four dogs, Murdoch, Pugsley, Nellie and Benny; the vociferous, foul-mouthed galah, Foster; and Eric, the aptly named goat – all played along. Perhaps they remembered me, even though it was six years since I'd last been in Australia. On the back steps I paused, took a deep breath and then swung open the screen door. My mother turned and stared for what seemed like minutes. From inside the gloom of the house, I probably looked like some sort of backlit Old Testament vision. I didn't move a muscle. Eventually my mother got to her feet, in tears, and started running, and so did I. They don't even make movies like that any more.

Later that afternoon we went to collect my brother, Jonny, from school. Being both sixteen and a boy, when he spotted me sitting in the front seat of the car he was initially a great deal cooler than my mother had been, but it was all front, didn't last long.

I stayed for nine days and let my mother do as

with this guy, how much practical shit has to
be done to extricate his traces from your
surroundings – but I just hope it happens quickly.
Will you move house? Will you restore your old
name? Is your trip in April a vacation somewhere
nice? Maybe you're already shaking it all off? . . .

Well, I was trying.

A fortnight later, on 1 April, my thirty-third
birthday, I boarded a plane bound for Bali. I was
theoretically going to write a travel piece for the
magazine, but personally I was hoping to get much
more out of it than that.

On arrival my first impressions, powerful ones,
were olfactory. This was surely the most beautiful-
smelling country in the world? Heady incense was
burned everywhere and the fumes, mingled with the
scent of frangipani and magnolia, hung heavy in
the humidity. Drunk with exhaustion, infused with
romantic scents, I checked into a large hotel at Nusa
Dua on the island's southernmost peninsula, and was
allocated one of their newly built stone cottages.

My gorgeous temporary home had a thatched roof,
a garden featuring a couple of pergolas, a pond (with
carp and frogs posing cutely on lilypads) and a
swimming pool heated to blood temperature. Behind
a tree I discovered my very own household temple.
The interior, though described as 'traditional Balinese
design', was definitely of the Conran Shop school of
'traditional design'. For instance, a little parchment

scroll invited the guest to select precisely what density of pillow and texture of sheet one would require for the following day. I chose duck density and linen texture.

This was a bittersweet venue for misery because everything conspired to remind me how alone I was. The cottages on either side of mine were occupied by Australian honeymooners whom I never saw, but heard. And every time I called room service a polite voice would ask if my order was for one or two. When I filled in another parchment scroll asking if I would like my temple blessed a) every day, b) on request or c) never, and I ticked a), the Mangku who came to perform the ceremony sat in the garden beside me in silence for several minutes. I assumed he was meditating, but after a while he said:

'We are waiting for your husband?'

'No, I haven't got a husband. Or rather, I have got a husband but he's not here.'

Which just made it worse.

'It is sad he is not here with you?' he asked, lighting incense.

'He's in London. With another woman. We're getting a divorce. That's why I'm here. Um, partly. But also to work.' The priest looked askance. They don't really go in for divorce in Bali. Once we'd cleared that up, however, the ceremony began. I had grains of rice stuck to my temples, forehead and throat and was sprinkled with holy water and petals much mothering as she felt able to do, while I bonded with the brother who had still been a kid when I had last seen him, just after my wedding, and was now on the antsy, querulous cusp of adulthood.

One night I helped Jonny with his homework (urban and traditional Aboriginal art: compare and contrast; my use of the word 'contextualization' a bit of a giveaway), then, armed with a torch and a camera, we went wombat hunting in the bush. The stars were so bright it was like walking underneath a floodlit colander and though we disturbed kangaroos and cattle, wombats remained elusive. After about an hour of my brother helping me over fences and saying butch things like, 'If you see a snake, keep perfectly still,' we sat on a boulder for a rest. There was rustling just a few feet away.

'There's one!' hissed Jonny as the creature snuffled and scuffled back into its hole. '*Wait. Very. Quietly.*'

The scuffling resumed and so I aimed the lens vaguely in the right direction and shot.

'Ah! Bedja goddit!' said Jonny. While I betted that I hadn't, we ambled back to the house via the dam, where there were tiny wombat prints in the mud.

'Find any?' asked my mother.

'No, but we did get abducted by cows,' I said, and Jonny and I giggled collusively before slumping in front of *The X-Files* while my mother cooked us dinner, which I love because it hardly ever happens.

My brother and I fought over control of the remote, demanded things from our mother and, because we were both brought up as only children, competing for her undivided attention took getting used to, but we enjoyed the struggle.

Sibling bonding aside, most of the time I was in Australia I was in a mood like an unwelcome, premature outbreak of winter in the antipodean autumn. I had thought that maybe my mother and I might do some serious talking, but in the event I didn't want to discuss any of the stuff I was going through. I just wanted my dinner cooked and my washing done and to stay up late watching dumb TV.

Waiting for the 8.15 from Goulburn station to take me to Sydney to catch a plane to Denpasur, to catch a plane to Jakarta, to catch a plane to Kuala Lumpur, to catch a plane to London, Graham took a picture of Mummy, Jonny and me beneath the station clock. We were all equally useless at saying goodbye. On the train I made friends with Phyllis, who was eighty, had been widowed at thirty and never remarried. By the time we got to Sydney, she had invited me to stay any time I liked.

I had hours to kill so I got the film processed. The group shot under the clock was delightful and I wondered when we might have another one done and how tall Jonny would be by then. There was no wombat.

A week later – ironically, given my fears in Bali –

I was sent to Los Angeles to spend a self-esteem-boosting day with several hundred former Playboy Playmates at the Playmate of the Year lunch and to interview Hugh Hefner. In the event, I didn't feel quite as displaced and, given the statistics on display, desperately inadequate as I would have done a few weeks earlier, even if I did find myself in the unlikely position of telling the happily married Hef, ex-Playboy of the Western World, my own story and asking for his advice on love and marriage.

'My generation seems to have a lousy track record making committed relationships. It's as if marriage is, particularly for men, pretty much the death of hope. I think it's partly your fault.'

Sitting on the edge of the leather sofa in his study, wearing his trademark black silk pyjamas, Hef laughed.

'Well, I will say this. I'm responsible for bringing the question to the fore. Before the women's movement, as we perceive it, there was a men's movement and there is an intimate interconnection. But we are not the enemy. We both want similar things but we express them in very different ways. You're still in pain, aren't you?' he asked gently.

'Yes, of course I'm still in pain. I fell for all the old romantic myths and they turned out to be just that. Romantic love and marriage are nothing to do with reality. And you know something else? I can't believe I'm discussing this with Hugh Hefner!'

'But who better?!' said Hef, draining yet another bottle of Pepsi. 'Who better? Yes, it's dreams and myths, but who'd want to live without them? Even with what you've just gone through, what you still do not want to accept is that it was all a myth. What you want is for the myth to be true. And, Kate, *so do I*. In many ways these September years are the happiest time of my life. I truly mean that. It's the combination of a tremendous sense of satisfaction at a life well lived, looking back at the childhood, loving the boy who dreamed the dreams, recognizing that the dreams came true beyond *anything* I could have imagined, and sharing in a wonderful way with Kimberley and the children.'

I sighed. Lucky Hef – rabbit at rest. He'd already had it all, and now he had even more besides.

After our conversation I showed Hef an old issue of *Arena* that I had edited, a *Playboy* tribute issue which had been instrumental in winning us the award two years previously.

'Ah yes, I remember this,' said Hef, appraising the magazine like the consummate editor it is so easy to forget he still is, while I summoned the courage to ask him to sign it.

'I gotta say, Kate, that this is a damn good magazine.'

And while I blushed with pleasure, the man who had invented the magazine without which *Arena* would probably never have existed took a pen and scrawled the words *To Kate, with love and admiration, Hugh Hefner* and I thought I would explode with pride. Professional vindication from Hef was, perhaps, almost better than meeting Bowie. Almost.

I got back to London on 1 May to discover that Britain had voted in a Labour government. 'A landslide!' announced the captain, and our micro-cross-section of British society cheered as the plane circled over Heathrow. I'd missed not only the election but also most of the campaign, and once home, trying to capture the moment, I immediately fell asleep in front of the TV while the nation celebrated.

Things. Can. Only. Get. Better?

eight

the heart-shaped bullet

I had found myself a divorce lawyer – scarily expensive and desperately chic – shortly before I went to Bali, so I called her when I returned, piling on the shoulder pads for our first (and, as it turned out, last) meeting.

'So,' she said cheerfully, after I had done my spiel, 'why did you get married in the first place?'

'Um. Because we were madly in love and wanted to be together for the rest of our lives . . .?' I turned it into a question because even I could tell that it sounded faintly ridiculous.

She smiled. 'Well, I haven't heard *that* for years!'

I tried not to look too surprised. 'What do people usually say, then?'

'Oh, that they had "so much in common", or that "one thing led to another and before we knew it . . .", something like that. Hardly anybody says what you've just said!'

Obviously, getting married because you're madly

in love and want to spend the rest of your life with someone was not where things were currently at, trothwise. It seemed as if most of her clients did it to facilitate a dynastic merger or secure the stately for future generations, while all I'd wanted to do was skip around holding hands and being happy, which was clearly unrealistic, if not downright childish and pathetic. I emerged into the watery sunlight of a perfect spring day feeling foolish, disillusioned.

In May, I contacted the lawyer and asked her to get things in motion. She passed my case, which was, at least in the lawyerly scheme of things, pretty straightforward, on to one of her assistants, Lucia, and I never spoke to her again.

'Do you still love Eric?' asked a girlfriend, gently, one late spring evening. It was a surprisingly tough one, and so I struggled with various definitions of love because I didn't seem to understand what it was any more.

Love Is . . .? Love is . . . *what?* Both of you fighting for the singular honour of taking out the rubbish without being asked? *Love Is* . . . giving him a neck massage after a hard day at the office? (*Love Is*, presumably, doubled if you can bring yourself to give him a neck massage after a hard day at your office. And quadrupled if you can accept never getting one in return.) *Love Is* . . . celebrating her gastric wind problems, violent PMT and habit of talking over the top of you at dinner parties? *Love Is* . . . laughing dutifully at the dinner party anecdote you've heard ten times before? *Love Is* ... not minding when he talks wistfully about the rare beauty of his ex's thighs? *Love Is* ... knowing the right thing to say when he can't get it up, even though you take it completely personally? *Love Is* ... putting up with her meddlesome and sanctimonious gang of girlfriends or his personality bypassed relations? *Love Is* ... trying to hold it together if he ever gives you that line about having caught crabs from a hotel towel? But, mostly, *Love Is* ... an ad man's irony-free slogan wrapped around an inexplicably naked infantile 1970s cartoon couple.

Love was, presumably, the prime motivation behind the current spate of weddings amongst my closest friends. And also those cheery, supportive 'Haven't spoken for a while, how are you? Hope you're OK?' messages on my answering machine. That kind of normal, healthy love I could understand, but then there was the Dark Underbelly of Love, invoked by people who confused love with lots of things that, I felt sure, love was not. This was the kind of Love that came with subtexts, footnotes, appendices and hidden agendas; Love, for example, of the kind demonstrated by a friend who one evening leant forward over our respective glasses of house white, wrinkled her brow and whispered, 'I'm only saying this because I *love* you ...' and then proceeded to tick me off for some perceived infraction of the unwritten Code of Friendship. And then there was the ex-boyfriend who had recently stood me up for dinner but left a message on my machine saying 'love you loads and loads...'. And the letter from the unknown PR, who knew me so well that she addressed me by my married surname and then signed off, presumptuously, *with love*... How dare she offer me her 'love'? And draw a smiley face in the 'O'? And then there was the Love contained in some of the letters I received at work, in response to my column. The majority of letters in my sizeable postbag were wonderful, uplifting missives, but a few were spooky, *Cracker*esque: *I love you. I can make you happy. Only I can feel your pain...*

So when this friend, who really did love me, asked me if I still loved Eric, I didn't quite know how to respond. Did I still love him as a husband, for example? Well, he was only technically a husband and we hadn't even spoken for two months, so how could I? Did I perhaps love him like a lapsed friend? Obviously not. He was an *estranged husband*. Did I maybe love him in that way that you do when you've loved someone, but it's over? Well, that would presumably depend on how and why it was over. And though there were people I did love in that way, none of them had let me down in anything like the way Eric had let me down. Did I, then, love him because I hadn't got out of the habit of loving him, whether he loved me or not? Possibly, maybe – but it seemed pointless loving someone who couldn't love you back. Could you even call that love? Maybe it was just laziness.

The more permutations I came up with, the more confused I got. I didn't hate Eric, but I didn't like him much, either. Still, did not liking him actually preclude loving him? Although, if I admitted I still loved him, who was it that I was loving exactly? Certainly not the man he was now, because I didn't know that person. Was I, perhaps, capable of still loving the man I had married just because he was *the version of himself who had loved me*? And if that was the case then I might as well confine myself to a dusty attic room wearing 'Pride and Prejudice' and clutching a wedding portrait for the rest of my days. But if I admitted that I didn't love him, wouldn't that also somehow negate all the love we did have?

One Friday at work, while pondering some of these definitions, a colleague offered me an Italian foil-wrapped chocolate which contained a motto.

Mai nessuno e tradito dall'amore puro, it said. *L'amour pur jamais ne trahit*, it added helpfully. And *El amor puro jamas ne traiciona a nadie*. Not to mention *Ninguem jamais e traido pelo amor puro*. Finally: *No one is ever betrayed by true love*.

And I stared at the words and I thought, for the first time: *He didn't ever really love me, then. Not really. And he certainly doesn't love me now*.

And at that point, slowly, reluctantly, I started to

recognize that any pain I was in was now less about the loss of Eric himself and much more about his emotional legacy, which, in turn, reminded me of other, older losses. This, then, was about the things that his rejection revealed about me, particularly the desperate neediness and childish romanticism – *'We were madly in love and we wanted to be together for the rest of our lives . . .'* Pah! – Foolish child!

No, I didn't love Eric any more. *And maybe, just maybe, I never had.* Maybe I had just wanted to feel safe, secure. Maybe I had wanted not to have to worry about loneliness any more. Maybe I had just wanted to be looked after, like a child – even though I'd been useless at letting him look after me, probably because I wasn't a child.

That night I watched my favourite wedding video – originally a startlingly beautiful five-minute Super-8 film in which Eric and I were captured in silent, grainy black and white, like an old newsreel. We had dubbed this film *Mr and Mrs President*, partly because we looked very John and Jackie, dignified and glamorous, but also, we'd joked, because it had a Zapruderesque quality. I watched it over and over, to remind myself not to rewrite the script too much, to try and remember how obviously happy we had been then. And we *were* happy. You could see it.

Chain-smoking, rewinding, freeze-framing the moment where we leave the church and head through a storm of blurry rice towards David's car, the old

Mustang ... and after a while I found I could watch the film and half-believe it was a documentary about other people, each time it became slightly easier to look at that extraordinarily radiant woman and pretend she was someone else, someone to whom I was distantly related, which in many ways she was. This trick was harder to pull off, though, when I looked at Eric.

I finally fell asleep with Eric and me still going through the motions on the TV. Somewhere behind, us, just out of shot, there was probably an unidentifiable man shielding himself from the sun under a black umbrella, waiting to fire a gun loaded with heart-shaped bullets. The clues are always there if you look hard enough.

The following day I dug out the birth chart the astrologer had done for me several years earlier, concentrating on the things I'd usually chosen to avoid in the past. Once I'd shored myself up with all the stuff I agreed with – the nice, flattering bits, funnily enough – I paid closer attention to the rest, reading as if for the first time, bracing myself.

'Your basic motivation is dynamic and goal-orientated and seems to be expressed, more often than not, against a background of questing for emotional security ...' it began.

For you, the Pandora myth is central to your life. On the negative side it can bring a sense of fragmentation, particularly in relation to men. Looking closely at the Sun in House Seven, we find that it is here that you shine and where your strengths are released and tried. Marriage itself, or an intimate relationship with another person, assumes special importance. It is the quality of that relationship which sets the measure for almost everything else in your life . . .

It is as though you are questing for someone who is bigger than yourself and who is able to defeat you in combat. There are several factors at work here, negative influences that arise again and again in the context of relationships. Although the origin of this pattern lies far off, there is something in your early familial relationships which seems to have set it into being again.

Life certainly asks you to earn your keep and the journey has not been especially enjoyable. Here, however, we come to the Saturn principle – that of learning through limitation; learning to cope with sickness and loneliness, with the graveness that lies within you, even within a relationship. The picture is of one who strives for harmony at the end of conflict, an emotional extremist whose life has pursued a zig-zag course.

'Negative influences that arise again and again in the context of relationships . . . something in your early familial relationships which seems to have set it into being again . . .'

How does one learn about love?

In childhood.

In the beginning, then, the condom broke and I was the result. My mother was very sick, couldn't keep anything down in the early weeks of her pregnancy and was admitted to hospital.

'You'll lose this baby if you don't eat, Mrs Flett,' said a doctor, so she forced herself to eat, eventually developing an obsession with curry and charcoal. She suffered from agoraphobia throughout the pregnancy.

I was born, a forceps delivery, at Bushey Maternity Hospital, Hertfordshire, after a long and difficult labour, at 6.40 p.m. on 1 April 1964, weighing 8lbs 6oz. And I wasn't an April Fool because I was born after 12 p.m. A few days later, I was taken home. I was a very 'good' baby, apparently.

How does one learn about love?

My parents had miserable childhoods. My mother was the eighth generation of a wealthy old Australian landowning family. My mother's mother, Alex, a beauty and an alcoholic, doted on my mother's older brother but wasn't interested in my mother, who was cared for by nannies and sent away to boarding school at the age of three. Sometimes she didn't get picked up at the end of term because her mother would be abroad or had just forgotten the date. After her parents' divorce and several subsequent remarriages, my mother watched any semblance of family disintegrate, but as she hadn't ever known emotional stability, she simply adjusted, as children always do, unquestioningly.

My father was the only child of the marriage between a Scotsman and an Englishwoman who had emigrated to Australia. Before the war, Captain Alec Flett had been the skipper of a Commonwealth Fisheries Research steamer, *Warreen*, and established the Antipodean tuna-fishing industry. When he died of a heart attack, in 1945, my father, aged nine, was the one who found his body. My father didn't get to go to the funeral, although nobody told him why. Nobody told him anything. After her husband's death, his mother, Marion, slipped into depression and so my small father, now the man of the house, coped. He was very self-sufficient, shouldering particular responsibility for the housekeeping and simply adjusting, as children always do, unquestioningly.

In many respects, my parents were made for each other. They fell in love, married and emigrated to England four years before I was born.

How does one learn about love?

All through my childhood, I knew about my parents' childhoods. I knew what unhappiness was because they told me about it. My mother, in particular, was a coper and she made light of her pain, often turning it into a series of blackly amusing anecdotes, but the fact was that both my parents had been wholly and completely unhappy, confused and emotionally abandoned at early ages, so they grew up and passed all the love they hadn't had on to me. They did the best they could, of course, given the limited resources. They led by example and showed me how to be resourceful and smart and independent and they did all this because, right from the start, they flattered me into thinking I was a small adult.

But children are not small adults. Children, I think, need to feel safe long before they need to feel smart; children need to be carpet-bombed with affection long before being told they are big and strong enough to stand on their own two feet; children need parental boundaries firmly in place long before those boundaries are removed; children need to be cleverly shielded from learning the harsher adult lessons, at least until such time as they can make sense of them. Children ultimately, ideally, need to be able to grow up and become adults who choose to do the leaving, rather than have their parents leave them, either physically or psychologically, while they are still children. Because if that happens, they often keep searching desperately for 'love', when all they are really looking for is some place they can feel safe.

Snapshot memories.

My parents first split came when I was three and my mother decided to take me back to Australia. We stopped off in all sorts of exotic places en route. One day, in Jamaica, my mother decided to go diving for coral (this was 1967, when a hunk of living coral was still considered a suitable souvenir rather than an environmental rape) and so we hired a man who had a little boat and puttered out into the blue. After an eternity the boatman cut the engine and I sat, clutching my brand-new raffia handbag, waiting for I knew not what. My mother put on a snorkel, said goodbye, slipped over the side of the boat and disappeared. I sat for a while, politely staring at the boatman, who was big and black and smiley, but I couldn't hold it together for long. My mother had gone and I had no idea if she was ever coming back. By the time she did, after what felt like an age, I was distraught, sobbing, and though the boatman had tried to comfort me, it wasn't enough. While I sniffled, my mother tried to cheer me up by giving me a hunk of stinky, crinkly coral, which I put in my bag. The second time she dived, I was sort of used to it. I just sat and waited.

In Australia, for months, I slept with a picture of my father under my pillow but, eventually, we came home. I was a member of the BOAC Junior Jet Club and after my mother and I had circumnavigated the globe and I had become blasé about cockpits and my log book had been stamped and signed by numerous handsome captains whose knees I had enjoyed sitting on at 30,000 feet, I was given my BOAC Wings. I also had an Australian accent. I said 'steerio' instead of 'stereo'.

My father was angry. He was trying to teach me pre-decimal currency and so I sat quietly at the end of the dining table while he explained the theory. But although I could read and write, I couldn't make sense of numbers at all. He got increasingly angry while my mother kept a low profile. I was there for hours, number-blind, trying very hard to do what he wanted because it seemed terribly important. He shouted and shouted and shouted. I couldn't think straight. I knew I was clever at some things, but I was obviously stupid at this. And being stupid at this somehow appeared to negate all the things I was clever at. Stupid, stupid, stupid me. But I did not cry. Crying might have made him angrier.

Idyllic Christmases, invariably spent in big houses in the country with my godparents and their extended family. One Christmas Eve, unable to sleep, I got out of bed and sneaked downstairs. In the dining room there was a dinner in progress. At one end of the table sat my father; at the other, my godfather.

'I fucking hate Brussels sprouts!' someone shouted, and either my father or my godfather picked up a handful and hurled them down the length of the table, at which point someone picked up more sprouts and hurled them back. They *seemed* to be angry but, confusingly, everybody was also laughing very loudly. I watched, riveted, for ages. I had never seen people drunk before and it was very funny.

At five, I started making serious plans to escape to Narnia through my (fitted) wardrobe, and, at night, I 'flew' all over the place, down the stairs, round the house and best of all, outside and up, up and away. Until the age of about nine I flew nearly every night. It was my extra-special secret. One day, though, I told someone at school that I could fly and word soon got around. At the next breaktime my classmates forced me to stand on the milk table in the playground and prove it.

'I think I can only do it at night,' I said.

'Liar, liar, liar!'

So I jumped off the table and took my milk bottle and sat in a corner of the playground on my own. Best not to tell people secrets, I decided.

There were good things, too, of course – lots of them. But the good things always seemed to be overshadowed by clouds of tension and anger. There was often the possibility of shouting, and then my mother getting hit and I would half-wait for it all in my room, where I would read and, if the noise became too much, stick my fingers in my ears and hum very loudly. I wished I had a big brother.

Seven or eight years old. It is night-time and I am sitting in the back of the car near the end of a long journey. My mother is reading the map and she misses a turning we need to take. There is no shouting but the car suddenly stops in a lay-by and my father starts hitting her in the face until she is silent and pale and her head slumps forward and drool comes out of her mouth and I shout: 'You've killed her, *you've killed her* . . .' and I can tell by his shocked expression that he thinks he has, too. Pain and regret are etched on his face. I don't remember anything after that.

At home, when things got this bad, it was usually best to hide, but sometimes I had to go and look. Somehow I couldn't stop myself. Then, whatever I saw, I would run.

One day, when I was nine, I came home from school and put my satchel in its usual spot next to the rocking chair in the living room.

'Um, Daddy has gone to live somewhere else,' she said.

'Oh,' I said and went upstairs to read. I was the first girl in my class whose parents divorced, but frankly it was a relief.

My mother, who I now understand must have been depressed (because, despite everything, my father was the love of her life), started to fend for herself. She had three serious boyfriends in the years after Daddy went – Andy, Philip and Arthur. By the time I was twelve or thirteen, I was left to my own devices a lot. Sometimes I would come home from school on a Friday night and find a note saying she had gone away for the weekend. There would always be money, though, and food in the fridge, so I would play music very loud, eat a lot of toast and Marmite and go shopping.

I became a habitual truant and was sent to see an educational psychologist. I knew exactly what she needed to hear so that I wouldn't have to go back. Easy-peasy.

How does one learn about love?

Philip and my mother bought a house together and I became very close to Philip's extended family. When my mother went off with Arthur while she and Philip were still living together, Philip's father, whom I had looked upon as a surrogate grandfather, turned up at our door to remove his son's belongings. He was very, very angry.

'And you're a little slut, too. Just like her,' he shouted. I never saw him again.

After he'd left his wife, Arthur came to live with us. He was an alcoholic and my mother and I spent a lot of time policing his whisky benders. We would find bottles hidden all over the house – in the lavatory cistern, in the back of cupboards, in the garden – and we'd pour them all down the drain. Not that it made any difference, he just bought more. When he was on the wagon, though, Arthur was great fun.

One day, when I was fifteen, my mother came into my bedroom and sat on the end of the bed and told me that she and Arthur were going to go and live in Australia. I could come if I wanted, of course, but I probably didn't want to, did I? After all, they'd be living in the bush, breeding horses, and there wouldn't be any shops and I'd be a long way from my friends, and stuff, but I could go and live with Daddy. And then she called Daddy and told him, so my Sunday afternoon father had to buy a new flat to make room for me. He said I could choose any kind of decoration I liked, so I asked for a white carpet and egg-yolk coloured walls. He wrote a poem for me too, which he gave me the day I moved in. He tried really, really hard.

My mother and Arthur moved to Australia a month later, just after my sixteenth birthday. Within a fortnight of their departure, I met Paul. He became my first serious boyfriend. We were together for two years.

A few months later my father put me on a plane to visit my mother and Arthur in Australia. They met me at Canberra airport. I was very jet-lagged.

'What's that?' I said, pointing at my mother's vast midriff.

'That's your brother,' she said, smiling. 'I didn't want to tell you on the phone.'

'Oh,' I said.

He was born three weeks later. I held him in my arms shortly afterwards, and felt something approaching unconditional love. I thought I would willingly, happily walk over broken glass to the ends of the earth if he ever needed me to. I'd always wanted a brother. My father met me at the other end a few days later.

'I think you'd better sit down,' I said.

I went back the following Christmas, for my brother's first birthday. We shared a room and I would wake every morning and see his small, smiling face peering at me through the cot railings. As soon as I woke he would giggle. Love, love, love. God, I loved him so much.

That Christmas, Arthur was on a whisky bender. One day, while I was sunbathing in the garden, he came over to me.

'She doesn't want you now, you know,' he hissed. 'We've got a new life here.'

I didn't see my mother or my brother for another six years. They moved around a lot and sometimes I didn't have an address for them. And I never saw Arthur again. In fact it was only after he'd died of cancer, in 1991, that I discovered he and my mother had been married for several years. That I had had a stepfather.

I didn't do very well at school. Instead, I went clubbing and took a lot of drugs. Speed, mostly, but I tried smack and acid and anything else that was going. I was also wildly promiscuous.

'I think it's probably time you went,' said my father, not unkindly, when I was eighteen and I'd just flunked out of secretarial college.

'Yeah, I think so too,' I said, because I wanted to get on with my life. So I went and signed on and found somewhere to live. I was an adult now, anyway.

How does one learn about love?

We pick it up as we go along, I suppose. As I went along, I think I learned a bit about love and a lot about what love was not. My parents loved me utterly in theory, they just didn't necessarily know how to do it in practice, but why would they? I don't blame them. When I was a child my father had violent outbursts (which made him extraordinarily depressed) but they did not continue. He is no longer that man, then, although part of me is still that child.

Love. As an adult I was determined to find the Real Thing for myself by any means necessary – and if that meant a combination of intuition and fate and chance and coincidence and luck and even astrology, well so be it. Perhaps it was no surprise that Eric and I shared confusing childhoods characterized by conflicting messages about what love was and what love was not. When we found each other we both desperately wanted to love and be loved, we just didn't know how.

Right at the end of the astrologer's chart there was an all too brief paragraph about an alleged Mr Right. The astrologer had never promised me a Happy Ever After but he had once described this man as 'the main life partner', which suggested at least some degree of staying power. Have straw, will clutch.

There was, though, no getting away from the fact that, whoever he was, he wasn't Eric. And although the reason for Eric's sudden irruption into my life – and subsequent sudden disruption of it – was, I was forced to admit, becoming much clearer, I just wished the damn astrologer, for all his insight, hadn't once described Eric and me as soulmates (presumably Eric had a wanton soul). But I also knew that even if he had said I should avoid Eric at all costs, knowing my stubbornness I would have ignored the advice. Hadn't I, in fact, been told not to get involved in a relationship in the autumn of 1994? And hadn't I gone and done exactly that? Yeah, well, astrology is about choices, right?

In early June, Daniel got married. The morning before the wedding I was woken by a loud crash, filmic in its intensity. There wasn't much time to assume anything except, obviously, the worst: 747 in the living room, ceiling relocated to the floor, hundreds wounded, raft of emergency services mobilized, that sort of thing. Terrified of what I might find, I nonetheless bolted out of bed.

The bathroom mirror, a large oval in a kitschy gilt frame, was face-down on the marble floor. I started to shake. Glass glittered everywhere, like tears; lodged disturbingly in places where it seemed the most sinister. There were tiny stalagmites in sponges and lavatory rolls, between floor tiles, awaiting bare feet. There is something terrifyingly chaotic about broken glass but this was not just broken glass, this was a mirror.

I eventually calmed down enough to inspect the scene. There was no obvious reason why the mirror should have detached itself from the wall. The big hook remained screwed tightly into the tiles, while the hook in the back of the mirror was also intact. Even stranger was the fact that the mess surrounding my basin – make-up, brushes, aerosols, perfumes, nail varnishes, assorted gloopy unguents – was still in place. I attempted to calculate the trajectory of a three-foot mirror falling onto the floor without making contact with a large basin covered in stuff. It didn't seem to make sense and the more I thought about this, the less I knew I wanted to.

The wedding was very beautiful. Everything about it was choreographed perfectly, from the weather to the church, the food to the music, the bride's dress to the speeches to the burgeoning summer beauty of the surrounding countryside. It was a very different kind of wedding to the wedding Daniel and I might have had (which would have been urban, edgier, messier and less like a photographic shoot for a magazine called, say, *Modern Couples*) or indeed the wedding I did have. Because it was all so very lovely, I put myself under pressure to be on equally perfect behaviour. When I cried in the church, people might have noticed, but there was nothing I could do about that. Fortunately I was tucked away in a corner.

At the reception it transpired that I had been seated between my father and a gay male friend of mine. I was exceptionally conscious that this was a placement afforded that most awkward of wedding guests, the single ex-girlfriend with a marshmallow heart and a face like flint. But who would see this ritual the way I saw it, noticing the nuances and subtle ironies of the situation? I hated myself for feeling that somehow I was at the epicentre of things, when the fact of the matter was that I was merely a hoofer in the chorus line of a production in which the bride and groom were the stars. Which was as it should be.

And yet it was so hard.

At one point, trying to ensure I wouldn't be noticed, I crept away from the reception and wandered down a country lane to commune with nature and order my thoughts. I didn't get very far, however, before I heard running footsteps behind me and turned to see a girlfriend wearing an expression of such deep concern that I felt a kind of boiling rage. *Don't feel sorry for me*, I wanted to scream.

'Are you OK? Shall I walk with you?'

'No.' I said. And turned away. 'Leave me *alone*.'

And my tone was bitterly cold. She left me, though, and I carried on and let the tears come. I wasn't a good and generous person. There was no nobility in my soul and – yes – I was suddenly angry at other people's good fortune and blessings. Self-pity is an ugly little emotion but knowing that didn't stop me feeling cast out, completely excluded from the possibility of the kind of happiness that surrounded me. I wanted to run, but eventually all I did was walk back towards the marquee, my ridiculous stiletto heels scrabbling on the gravel, wiping mascara-smudged eyes on the sleeve of my borrowed white designer jacket, before remembering that it was both borrowed and white. As I neared the tent I saw another friend coming towards me. He too wore an expression of concern, but this was different because – and I hated to admit it – he was a man. Right now, I needed a man.

He held out his arms.

'Kate. Don't cry. I know how you must be feeling, but you will be OK. ' On and on, saying all the right things while I blubbed messily, a weak, self-pitying lummox underneath the constricting armour. I felt like Duckface from *Four Weddings and A Funeral*.

'I should be better than this, *bigger* than this . . .' I muttered incoherently. 'I'm happy for them. I really am. But – oh, God!'

Later, I had the obligatory dance with Daniel.

'*Nice* to see you two dancing together. So civilized!' said a friend, *en passant*.

Oh, good, I was thinking, *I managed it* . . . when another, male, friend lurched drunkenly my way.

'Kate. Little word of advice, all right? Don't be such a fucking victim.'

Oh, I thought, recoiling from the blow, *so I didn't do a good enough job. Right. Must try harder* . . .

'You seem all right these days. Got over that husband, then!' said an acquaintance, when our paths crossed at the bar of my office local a few weeks later.

'Yeah! I'm fine, well, er . . .' but that was obviously all he needed, or wanted, to hear because before I'd finished (although I hadn't planned on saying much more) he turned away and talked to someone else. And I did that thing you do to rescue yourself from a snub, when you've been cut off and you weren't exactly talking about the weather. I glanced about self-consciously, grinning, focusing on the middle distance, both embarrassed and wounded, perhaps more than I could bear to acknowledge.

Back at the table with another, closer friend, I explained why I was slightly pink and bothered.

'You know, I think I'm only able to make small talk about it now.'

'Maybe you only ever reduced it to small talk with some people?'

And I knew what she meant but she was wrong. I'd never made small talk about my marriage breakup. I'd either talked about it properly or not at all. Recently, though, I'd noticed the subtle enforcement of an invisible external deadline. After five months there seemed to be the vague and unspoken assumption that I should be, if not exactly over it, then certainly beyond having to talk about it for any length of time, unless I was paying for the privilege.

This was difficult because, in many respects, by June I *was* all right. I slept through the night and ate solids and talked in properly formed sentences, some of them even quite complicated. I had even survived my former fiancé's wedding. And yet, despite all of this, however much I might have wished I was, I was not 'all right'. In fact I had decided that even when I did get to be 'all right' I would only be as 'all right' as it is possible to be after you have been profoundly hurt. That is, 'all right' but irrevocably different.

So why did I feel guilty?

'Frankly, after just five months I'd be worried if you told me that you were fine. Try not to let other people's preconceptions about your situation dictate your own state of mind,' said the therapist, wisely, when I saw her a few days later.

And I nodded and agreed because this made perfect sense, and I paid and I left and, funnily enough, carried right on feeling guilty about not being all right and the possibility of boring people or being accused of being unnecessarily self-absorbed. The irony lay in the fact that, at precisely the time when people were, for the most part, expecting me to be all right, I was actually starting to come to terms with some of the reasons why I wasn't. And then there was the fact that my weekly column in the *Observer*, which, apart from the ministrations of close friends, was the one thing I had come to rely on to get me through the worst of the earliest weeks and months, was now suffering a backlash.

I had had nothing but support from the readers when I started writing about Eric leaving, and while I felt at my most completely unloved and unlovable by the person who mattered the most I came to rely on this invisible fan club more than I should have. Evenings spent alone and adrift would be eased by reading words of encouragement and support from people I didn't know and never would, and then I would write replies. One evening, though, on the way home from work, I accidentally left a big envelope, full of readers' letters, on the tube and felt both embarrassed by the idea of anyone else seeing them and immensely guilty that I wouldn't be able to acknowledge them. But I didn't want to go to the London Transport Lost Property office, either.

'Yeah, hi! My name is Kathryn Flett and I wonder if you've found a large Jiffy bag full of letters on a Bakerloo line train. What sort of letters? Well, they all tell me how brave and wonderful and talented I am ...'

In the summer, however, although my postbag was still large and overwhelmingly positive, I sensed I should stop relying on it to bolster my self-esteem. After the *Guardian* commissioned from me a perfectly post-modern piece for their media pages, writing about what it had been like for me to write about the things I'd been writing about (accompanied by the most unflattering photograph of me that has ever been taken, so unflattering that the day after the article came out I received, anonymously, a photocopy with a witch's hat drawn on my head, accompanied by the words 'Who the hell would ever marry *that*?'),

I found myself the butt of a satirical column in the same paper, the first of several. And at the same time as I got invited on to Radio 4's *Today* programme to talk about confessional columnists, an article in *Vogue* described me as 'formerly heart-breaking. Now ... embarrassing'. And then, when other, even more emotive first-person columnists started getting a high profile, I braced myself for the hate mail. It was just as well I had anticipated it because when it came, it came on strong. There were a few letters, in particular, which were so desperately vitriolic and critical that reading them was actually physically painful. I still keep them in the top drawer of my desk to remind me that their brand of hate is, presumably, the flipside of an equally perverse kind of love. And all of it from people I didn't even know, and who knew only as much about me as I chose to reveal within the limited parameters of 850 words, every Sunday.

After Diana's death, the work of the so-called confessional columnists, or indeed anyone else who used the 'I' word or touched on any subject that had to do with yucky emotions, was scrutinized, written and talked about by the media as yet further evidence of the increasingly worrying flaccidity of the British upper lip. I was, then, keen both to distance myself from all of this and to stop writing the column, which I felt had run its course. And then, far sooner than

I'd expected, something happened which provided another very good reason not to carry on untwisting my corkscrew life in public for too much longer.

I didn't go looking to get involved with someone. Far from it. I was too terrified, for a start, and the wounds were too raw.

July. A passionate one-night stand. Except it became a two-night stand and then three. Three consecutive nights — now here was commitment. But before terminal panic could set in for either of us, he got on a plane and went back to South Africa where he lived and worked. He knew about me — he was also a journalist, and we had once been colleagues, albeit long-distance.

'Ah well, everybody always goes!' I said, sighing with mock-pathos as we sat in my living room waiting for the cab to take him to the airport. I stood on my balcony and waved him off. I doubted if I'd ever see him again.

The following day I received an e-mail from Africa.

Kate,

. . . London is now a drugged night's sleep away. I think of sitting with you on the grass, watching cricket in that city unable to deal with its summer. And then good-bye and you standing on the balcony looking down, looking resolute.

*What was your resolution? I left wanting to
believe that you were saying to yourself 'go away,
Boy, I don't care', which would mean that you did, a
little.*

*You are extraordinary Kate ... I had a
wonderful time and, for now, I remember.*

Bugger – not only was he not going to go quietly,
he wasn't going to go at all. And what was more, I
felt the swift onset of that familiar, dangerous old
hurtling-down-the-roller-coaster-towards-who-knows-
what sensation. We e-mailed each other every day,
several times a day, for the next two months. Our
hearts were in our fingertips, but our heads didn't
enter into it. I should, of course, have known better,
but I was being wooed with the written word and it
had never happened before (it was also the one way
that was guaranteed to get me). The Boy and I
trawled our respective bookshelves for poetry and
prose; gossiped and giggled; flirted and argued and,
in two months, became urgent, passionate e-mail
junkies. Sometimes I wasn't even sure which I
enjoyed more – the medium or the message. *Hold
tight. Come over here ...* he wrote one day. I'd never
been to Africa. I was due some holiday. I booked a
ticket. And I packed my wedding and engagement
rings because the day after I arrived would be my
second wedding anniversary and I had plans.

That same week the divorce petition arrived in

the post from my lawyer. Apparently I had to go and find somebody legal to witness me swearing on it. Or possibly at it.

I rang the bell of a solicitor conveniently situated next door to my therapist and the door swung open to reveal a large man with a funeral director's sympathetic countenance.

'Hello!' I said, far too cheerily. 'I need to swear an affidavit on my divorce petition. Could you do that?'

'Come in, come in . . .' Into an empty office where no phones rang and we remained standing, rather awkwardly, though not obviously on ceremony, next to a photocopier, on which the solicitor placed the petition before adopting an expression of deep gravitas.

'Do you solemnly swear that the details contained in this document are the, er, truth?'

'Er. Yes,' I said, shifting from foot to foot.

'Fine.' Then he paused, wrinkled his brow, touched his chin with his finger, raised his eyes. You could almost see the invisible lightbulb. 'Oh dear me. You should have sworn on the Bible. Do you want to do it again?'

'Oh, it's OK. We may as well keep the Bible out of it now we've got this far.'

'Well, then, I'll just pop upstairs and get my rubber stamp!' He was easily six foot five and not really the popping type. Indeed, he disappeared for several minutes, while I sat on a low, cheap chair, distracted only by the intensity of the silence. There should have been a dusty, sonorously ticking clock, but there wasn't. Eventually, he reappeared.

'We're all done!' and he settled his huge features into an expression that called to mind Reverend Casaubon. 'Ah, but I'm afraid that there is an oath fee.'

Oath fee! I liked that. It sounded like a swearbox.

'Well, I didn't think it was a free service! How much?'

'Seven pounds.'

Which, for some reason, made me giggle. I gave the solicitor, whose name I didn't even know, a ten-pound note and he fished three warm coins from a trouser pocket.

'Thanks, then,' I said, moving towards the door. But his kindly eyes made me think that he expected something more from me after this insubstantial brush with one of the more complex bits of a life about which he knew nothing, except the obvious. Perhaps he wanted reassurance. 'I'm fine!' I said, pointlessly.

'Good!' But then he smiled the quick, big smile of the professional – all mouth suddenly, and no eyes – and held open the door. I had been mistaken. It was, after all, business as usual.

I flew to Johannesburg on the evening of Diana's

funeral, landed the following morning and, within hours, the Boy and I were lost and just about to run out of petrol in the Kalahari. Though nervous and exhausted, I didn't know the Boy well enough to be anything other than a) quiet, b) polite and c) hopeful. After several hours we were rescued by a local Bushman chief who had suddenly, absurdly, metamorphosed out of the dust and the darkness in a very smart new 7-series BMW.

'Ah! . . .' said the Boy one morning a few days later, unzipping the tent, lighting a Marlboro and staring blearily at an incandescent 6 a.m. sunrise over the Okavanga Delta, '. . . it's a jungle out there.' And I lay in bed giggling, while a baboon relieved itself on the canvas roof.

We hiked through the bush and watched the lilac-breasted rollers doing their mid-flight stall turns with multiple wing dips. We were charged by an angry elephant. We dined under sausage trees by firelight. We rounded up wildebeest and danced on horseback alongside zebra and swam with red lechwe. On one extraordinary evening we punted out into the Delta in a makoro canoe amongst head-high sedge grass and delicately fragrant giant water lilies, while elephants strolled past us and we drank a bottle of rosé at sunset. I wove the Boy a necklace of plucked water lilies which, being a bloke, he preferred to wear as a crown.

During one al fresco evening meal under the sausage tree, half the camp was still discussing Princess Diana while the other half, our half, was getting quietly drunk. I told our guide, John, a Devon pig-farmer turned African bush ranger, that I'd brought my wedding and engagement rings with me and that I wanted to get rid of them. I wanted to do something ritualistic with them, return them to the African earth from whence they may well have originated. The only problem was that my wedding anniversary had passed four days previously and the moment hadn't been quite right. There was some discussion and then John suddenly shouted: 'I know! I've got it!' And as it turned out he had.

The following morning the Boy and I went for our final ride in the Delta. We had a plane to catch at 2 p.m., but when we rode back into camp at 11.30 there was still unfinished business.

Five of us – me, the Boy, John, a French trainee guide called Charlotte and Jonathan, the camp manager's son – made an assignation by John's truck. I sat in the front, the ring box sat on the dashboard. I opened it and showed it to John. He winced. For a moment I had second thoughts.

'Maybe I should keep the engagement ring...' I said feebly.

'Chicken!' everybody shouted. But, peer pressure aside, I knew I didn't really want it.

John had a suitably scenic spot in mind, near the

water, so the truck bounced over scrubby sand for fifteen minutes and then we searched for a tree. A lone, robust tree. A tree with gravitas. We found it — a solitary raintree, strong and tall and old. We pulled up. The Boy and I took a few pictures of the rings in the box, of the tree and of John, who had knotted a ritualistic black band on his arm (it turned out to be an old rugby club tie) and slipped a round into his .458 Winchester elephant rifle.

'Full metal jacket!' he said, and smiled at me.

We stepped back and stuck our fingers in our ears while he fired. The raintree was wounded and so I placed my rings into its skin-deep scar. John leaned on the bonnet of the truck and took aim a second time. There was silence, and then:

BAM.

Raintree bark arced high above us as the shot rang out, scattering a nearby herd of nervy impala. We all screamed and jumped up and down and went to inspect the tree. At first glance the rings seemed to have disappeared completely, but then, peering closely, I spotted a tiny shard of gold, the remains of the sheared shank from my engagement ring. I knew it was the engagement ring because you could see the edge of the diamond's setting, if not the diamond. On the inside I could clearly read one word.

'Cartier!' I said, and John winced again.

'Oh, God. Now you'd better tell me how much they cost.'

So I did. And then I told him what they were worth. And we laughed, near-hysterically, and took photographs, while Jonathan uncorked champagne which we all slugged straight from the bottle.

At High Noon, I removed what remained of the corpse of my marriage from the raintree, put it back into the ring box and presented it to John, while John unloaded the big bullet casings from the rifle and gave them to me. There is a fairly profound kind of bonding to be had with the person who blasts your wedding ring to kingdom come and so, back at camp, there was only one thing I could think of to write in the visitors' book.

'What can I say? You blew me away.'

With heart-shaped bullets.

We were driven to the airstrip to wait for our little plane and there we found a sleepy heap of lions. I found myself unexpectedly in tears when a lioness turned her huge amber eyes on me. She was calm, haughty, seemingly immovable, utterly beautiful and while making that inscrutable feline eye contact she seemed to dare me to outstare her until the hair rose on the back of my neck and I had to turn away. On the twenty-minute flight out of the Delta, I couldn't speak. I thought about my rings and then fantasized about being in amongst the sandy lion fur, dozing underneath a big breathing rug of cats, being licked by a huge sandpapery tongue.

The Boy and I moved on to Zimbabwe and went

white-water rafting down the Zambezi. I only lasted a morning, terrified after being turfed out of the raft on a particularly tricky rapid, but the Boy carried on down the river for the rest of the day. Back at the hotel, drinking rainbow cocktails on the terrace, I was worried about how much I missed him, wondering if he'd drowned. I went back to our room.

The Boy stumbled through the door: 'Christ, I thought I was going to die walking back up that bloody cliff at the end. I'm *knackered*. Fancy a cocktail?'

We carried on travelling, down through Bulawayo to Great Zimbabwe, where we stayed at a wonderful lodge constructed from vast boulders, and on into South Africa, where we drank ridiculously fine wines in the Drakensberg mountains and ate stringy biltong on the high veld. When we got to the edge of the continent we wanted to learn to scuba dive but couldn't get on a course. Instead we found something better – a five-mile-long deserted beach, so we made intoxicating, salty, wave-pounded love in the Indian Ocean. And, yes, by the end of it all we had a song – The Verve's 'Bittersweet Symphony', which has never sounded better to me than it did while cruising an empty blacktop during an African sunset.

Just after I returned from the most extraordinary holiday of my life, I received a bouquet from my favourite florist. *A rose for every day* said the card, accompanying seven white roses – one, indeed, for every day of the week until I was due to collect the Boy from Heathrow. He was coming back. That same day I also received a letter from my friend Richard.

Dear Kate,

You're freshly returned from Southern Africa – surely there will be stories to tell. Perhaps a great deal has changed in your world since we last spoke. Or maybe not. You sounded great, happy, last time, so I hope that some of that mood is still within arm's reach whenever you want it.

I won't conjecture. The Africa trip was a big leap into the unknown, and while I'm curious to hear how you dealt with the world-traveller aspects of it, ultimately it's the romance-adventurer part that matters. And – if you'll excuse the rather distant tone of voice – I'd say the whole experiment is especially important for what it may have shown you about your capacity to deal with 'romance' in general, rather than for what may have happened with this particular guy. Given that your life seems to unfold in large symphonic movements, I don't expect that any single affair can call the tune – a relationship is a symptom of a larger tendency, isn't it?

I don't know what your therapist has been telling you, but it seems clear to me that you are 'recovering' quite strongly. I say 'recovering' because you're not really returning to what you once were, but you are reclaiming bits of yourself that had been wound up in the marriage, and that you can now pick out of the wreckage, having realized that you had not in fact ceded them over to him. You keep telling stories that sound cynical or utterly disenchanted – but I think there's a more subtle point here. You may have invested a great deal of hope in that husband of yours, but his failure has not robbed you of your capacity to hope for great things out of others – it has (perhaps?) shown you that you can never hand over your hopes, even in the best of cases. To leave our hopes to others is always to abandon our own responsibility – like love, hope can be shared but never signed over.

So you'll have to excuse me if I read your sequence of columns as a story with a more-or-less happy ending. It begins with a kind of minimal inventory, which sounds like somebody doing a basic body check after a crash to make sure all the limbs are still there. (Although it's funny, it's also sad-true: you touch on all these little pieces of what seemed to be most 'yourself', and find them somehow unconvincing. I have this impression all the time . . .). Then, as you tell each new episode, the story becomes more and more generic: you recognize patterns, you note the wrenching, irreversible turns with a fatalism that is alternately shocked and anxious to get over it (it's not just late twentieth century people who have read lots of novels and seen lots of films who get this feeling of repetition). What's touching about these columns (if you'll forgive the expression!) is your willingness to keep your responses open, to see what turns up next . . . you sound like someone who finds herself in the situation of having to interpret the whole world over again: all the old significance, centered on a certain life, stable, ordered, is dissolving before your very eyes, and now you see absurdities, fantastic constellations, and even unexpected joy.

It's not your new life that's bonkers – it's your old life, the one that seemed to have been settled once and for all, the one you can write about now . . .

I read it over and over. *Large symphonic movements* . . . bitter-sweet symphonies. Richard, only recently relegated to second-favourite correspondent, had crawled right inside my life.

I met the Boy at Heathrow. His African tour of duty over, he rented a flat a quarter of a mile from mine and suddenly we had a real relationship to deal with. To our surprise the potency of our romance was enough for us to make the leap together back to a winter in west London and a pair of office jobs. And if it ever looked like flagging a little, we ran away and found it again.

Although I'd been to Paris often, it had always been for work and so whilst there I had never been kissed on anything other than the cheek, which didn't seem the correct state of affairs for a sophisticated thirty-three-year-old woman. Paris was reinvented for me, though, when the Boy kissed the bits of my face

that weren't cheeks at midnight on a deserted Pont
Neuf under a full moon, and we held the pose,
laughing, in the floodlights of a passing bateau-
mouche. Hopeless romance junkies. Pathetic.

'I can absolutely promise that I won't leave you
for another woman,' he said one day when I was
feeling rabidly, premenstrually jealous because the
world seemed to be full of beautiful young things
who always stared at him in the street, and then
glanced, quickly, slightly quizzically, at me.

One night, we were with a group of his friends in
a pub when somebody's young, thin, beautiful, ditzy
girlfriend turned to me and said, 'So, um, like, who
are you again? Are you and the Boy related, or
something?'

'Jesus! I hope not!' I said breezily, but underneath
I was simply embarrassed. She'd been sitting with us
all evening – wasn't it, um, like, obvious? But clearly
it wasn't obvious at all. Unless we were actually
kissing and holding hands, the idea that the Boy and
I might be a couple who, like, were in love and, um,
had sex, and stuff, wouldn't have crossed her mind.
She must have been twelve years younger than me.

'Kate's *my girl!*' said the Boy, proudly, putting his
arm around me. And while she went slightly pink, I
peered mistily into my vodka and tonic because,
though he was gallantry itself, at times like this I
knew the Boy was just too young, too handsome and
too bloody lots of things, really, to be with me. Even

though he was with me. And although he'd promised he wouldn't leave for me another woman, I had a pretty good idea what he might leave me for.

'You'll leave me for the rest of the world,' I'd said. And he'd laughed.

Bonfire Night is my favourite pointless annual social activity. Every year Debra and David, whose flat backs onto a chic communal garden, have a Bonfire party and all the residents club together to hire pyrotechnologists. Three years previously, having just fallen in love, Eric and I went to the party and stood apart from the other guests, holding hands, gazing into each other's eyes and, occasionally, watching the fire in the sky. We both agreed these were the best fireworks we'd ever seen. The following year we were newly-weds and did a lot of 'Remember this time last year!', still apart from the other guests, still holding hands, but there was not quite so much of the gazing into each other's eyes. Last year, Eric had said that, actually, this time he really wanted to stand and watch the display with everyone else. Little eye contact, no hand-holding. This year, I went on my own. The Boy was at a friend's birthday dinner and, even if he hadn't been, I didn't want him here, where so many memories jostled for my reluctant attention. While standing under a tree to escape the drizzle, I realized it hadn't rained on any of the recent Bonfire Nights.

A lot of close friends were there, as well as my soon-to-be-ex-brother- and sister-in-law, and just a few members of the *schadenfreude* family, whose company I tended to avoid but who were none the less scrutinizing me intently.

'You look great!' said a girl I know, who used to be a model, as she air-kissed my aura. That night I noticed that all my closest friends said, 'How *are* you?' with feeling, while the shinier set said things like, 'Wow, you're looking so well!' with barely disguised relief. Sometimes, when I spend a bit too much time among the exquisitely beautiful and/or fashionable, I think that their strong identification with the surface of things is just a way of avoiding having to deal with anything too real, too *ugly*. That night it started to grate and so, after an hour or so, I left ('Got a better offer, then?!') and drove across town to where the Boy was. The next day I spoke to Debra.

'Thanks,' I said. 'It was nice evening, but I wanted to leave.'

'Yeah, I know,' she said. 'And did you have a good time?'

'I had a brilliant time. It was . . . totally different.'

'You're moving on. It's good.'

On? Yes, I thought – but does *on* also mean *away?* Then she told me that Eric had phoned her and David the previous afternoon, after months of silence. He'd known about the party and was – she thought

– waiting for an invitation, even though he wasn't going to get one.

'But,' she said gently, 'maybe it's time to build bridges?'

A couple of days later David, rather sweetly, called me to say that he'd been invited out for a drink by Eric, and was that OK? I told him that of course it was OK, but I didn't really want to hear about cosy foursomes at dinner.

'No chance!' said David. 'Not yet!'

And it surprised me how much the 'not yet' hurt.

On 21 December, George, given away by 'Elvis', married BJ at the Little Chapel of Love in Las Vegas. The Boy had recommended a hotel in Tobago for their honeymoon, so they went. Meanwhile, my Christmas was spent with the Boy's family in Scotland, which reminded me of my own childhood Christmases, and New Year on our own in London. I cooked sausages and mash and we overdressed for dinner, drank champagne and undressed, swiftly, giggling, on the sofa, while Big Ben chimed through Radio 4.

'Our first New Year!' said the Boy. Any time we did something new, it was always Our First whatever.

A couple of days later we bought *Tomb Raider II* for the PlayStation, and so winter nights were squandered, rather obsessively, closeted in the Boy's flat in front of the TV. I was merely the bossy back-seat driver while the Boy did all Lara Croft's hard work for her. I loved it.

A few days later I got a call from Neil-the-Philosopher telling me that his wife, Liz, had given birth to a daughter, Imogen Daisy, on 1 January. It seemed like a fine omen.

A mid-January afternoon. My phone rang at work.

'Guess what?' said Daniel breathlessly, so I tried to guess some of the whats it could be. Only a couple of weeks previously he'd called and said exactly the same thing and it turned out that he'd handed in his resignation at work, so I assumed he'd either just accepted the Chair of ICI or he and Samantha were jacking it all in to go and grow organic sprouts on a smallholding in Shropshire.

'I can't guess. What?' I sighed.

'I'm going to be a father!'

So I made the leap.

'Congratulations!' I said.

Sunday, a few days later. I returned home after spending the night at the Boy's flat to find a message on my answering machine.

'Hi, Kate! It's David! It's nine forty-five on Sunday morning and Debra and I wondered if you wanted to come and have breakfast with us? Give us a call – and, Kate, *we love you*!'

I pondered this interesting, multi-faceted little message for quite a while. Debra, David and I often have brunch on Sundays but although David is distressingly bouncy in the mornings, Debra and I are, to say the very least, not, so we usually eat about twelve. A 9.45 a.m. call was, then, unprecedented. And then there was the sweet little suffix – *we love you*! They are a pretty touchy-feely twosome but what was all this about precisely? It was 11 a.m. and I called them at home but they had gone out. I left a message on Debra's mobile before going back to bed with the papers and a bowl of Crunchy Nut Cornflakes.

Late afternoon and the doorbell rang. Debra and David hadn't been to my flat for a while, so they wandered around inspecting *objets* and leafing through magazines while I made tea. Then they got a bit giggly and started hugging each other. I watched them, fascinated. They'd been together for five years, so it was quite distracting to see them being this soppy.

'Guess what?' said David, suddenly, gurning like a twit.

'What?'

'We're getting married!'

And so we had a bit of a group hug and I offered my congratulations. And then I kept staring at Debra, who was definitely doing the radiant thing, and I kept thinking, over and over, like a mantra:

Neil's a father. My former fiancé is going to be a

father. My best friend is getting married. And it's still only January.

My decree absolute – apparently the 4,519th of its type to be issued by the High Court of Justice, Principal Registry of the Family Division, in 1997 – arrived in the post in the second week of January, twenty-eight months to the day after the wedding and the same week I read that Hugh Hefner and his wife, Kimberley, had separated. The divorce certificate was stamped smudgily red with the High Court coat of arms – lion, unicorn, *Dieu et mon droit* – the only attractive thing on a piece of paper of otherwise chilling charmlessness. I stared at it for quite a while, even read the small print (perhaps it was useful to know that the Principal Registry of the Family Division in Somerset House is open from 10 a.m. to 4.30 p.m., Mondays to Fridays) and then I put away the sad and scruffy little document lacking either gravitas or grace, marking the end of a sad and scruffy little marriage which had lacked them too.

As the petitioner, I knew I would have been sent our marriage's death certificate before Eric, so I called him. We hadn't spoken for months.

'Hello. Second wife. Apparently we're divorced,' I said.

'Ah . . .' he replied. 'And how does that feel?'

'Well, you should know, you've been there before.'

'Mmm. Well, I think the funny thing about it is

that when it finally happens you feel kind of . . . *nothing*, really.'

No, I thought, *you* feel kind of *nothing*, but I feel very *something*. It was a short conversation, after which I phoned my parents.

'I'm divorced,' I said, getting used to the sound of the phrase. 'I am a mature and sophisticated divorcée.'

'Ah! . . .' they both said, from their opposite ends of the earth.

I phoned the Boy.

'Ah!' he said. 'Let's have a celebratory dinner!'

Then I went to work where, in the tea-trolley queue, a colleague asked me how I was.

'Divorced, actually!'

'Ah!' she said.

I made a mental note that it might be worth contacting the product development division of Hall-mark Cards and alerting them to the obvious potential for the 'Ah!' card.

In February, I took a three-month sabbatical from the office to write this book. Shortly afterwards the Boy and I went away for the Valentine's Day week-end . . . a breakfast of Beluga caviar smeared on sixty pence' worth of cratered crumpets, eaten in bed in a folly tower in the Hampshire countryside . . . sun burning away heavy mists to reveal a day of astonishing, unseasonable beauty and warmth . . . an extraordinarily perfect day . . . a day which laid last year's ghosts, well and truly.

Six weeks later, I met up with Eric for the first time in a year. For quite a while I'd wanted to tell him about the book and it didn't feel right to do it on the phone. The first time we arranged to meet he called me back almost immediately and cancelled, but a few weeks later he called again and asked if he could have a lamp that he'd left behind when he'd moved out. I couldn't think of a good reason why he shouldn't have it and so we arranged to meet at a café near my flat that same evening. If I'd had any longer to think about it I suppose I might have panicked, but as it was, only about three hours elapsed between his call and our meeting.

Eric looked exactly the same as when I'd last seen him, slightly fuzzy round the edges, hair in need of a trim. He was even wearing an old top of mine and a pair of trousers and shoes from the incarnation before me. The jacket, a Brit-poppy kind of windcheater, was new, though.

'Not lost any more of your hair, then?' I said and I couldn't resist running my fingers through it. He didn't flinch. 'Well, *a bit*. And there's some more grey.'

I told him I was writing a book about our marriage and he widened his eyes and pulled an exaggerated scaredy face.

'Um,' I said. 'Er, I think it's going to turn out quite fair. I *hope* it is. It's not meant to be a hatchet job. I mean, um, it probably takes two people to fuck up a marriage.'

He smiled, raised his eyes to the heavens. I struggled on.

'I think you'll just have to trust me. Or perhaps I'll see you in court?'

He laughed. Shrugged.

'I suppose I will. Have to trust you, I mean.'

We talked for far longer than I'd expected, but then we both knew that if we got it right here and now we'd never have to do it again. We'd done what he'd suggested, had run and run as fast and far as we could and this was going to be our only pinging back together before we finally cut the elastic.

Eric tried to explain, quite candidly, about how being written about every week in a national newspaper had made him feel. But he didn't tell it all (well, he wouldn't, would he?). And anyway, listening to him, full of the same old predictably unemotional jargon that worked so well when we'd played 'At Home With Mr and Mrs Armstrong' but which, I thought, he might now have seen fit to junk, I suspected that he hadn't really dealt with any of it yet. He probably never would. He'd just file it all away and move on. Again.

I tried, though. At one point, exasperated, I said, 'Eric, if we're talking about feelings, perhaps you could try using the kind of language that might reveal that you actually have some.'

He asked me about my relationship. 'I hear you're seeing someone. Anybody I know?'

'If you *knew* them then you'd *know*, wouldn't you?' But I told him a little about the Boy.

Then Eric mentioned that he was trying to read, of all things, a novel.

'*Love In the Time of Cholera*. Read it?' I nodded. He sighed. 'I don't know why I'm bothering, really.'

And I laughed. As it happens, we laughed quite a lot. Before he told me he was getting married in the summer, at Chelsea Register Office.

After tussling with the unwelcome image of Eric and his girl standing in the Jif-lemon coloured marriage room and saying those words that had once been our words, I tried to let it go. If, as this seemed to indicate, our marriage no longer meant anything to him, then I would have to learn, somehow, to make it mean nothing to me. I didn't really know how to do that, but because I was happy, because I was *in love*, I could afford to be generous – I could change the subject.

I was due to have dinner with the Boy ('Oh God,' he'd said when I had called to tell him about meeting Eric, 'I suppose you'll stare into each other's eyes and he'll realize he made a huge mistake and you'll run off into the sunset together.' I told him I doubted it, but even if he did I wouldn't have him back, particularly as the Boy and I were just about to go to Spain for a fortnight) and so, after a couple of hours in the café, I said I had to go and asked Eric if he'd like a lift to the nearest tube.

'It's OK.'

'It's no trouble . . .'

'No, no. I've got a, er, scooter.'

So we left and walked across the road to where he had parked his black Piaggio, and I couldn't help smiling because one of us was wearing a snowboarding jacket, would soon be celebrating their third wedding and their thirty-ninth birthday and was riding a scooter, while the other one of us hadn't had the slightest desire to ride one since about the time the Jam had released *All Mod Cons*. Apart from a failed marriage, I didn't have anything in common with this person any more, so while my chameleon ex-husband put on his helmet and prepared to ride back to his flat in too-cool-to-live, too-young-to-diet Notting Hill, I prepared to walk away from his world – whichever world it was he currently inhabited – for the very last time.

'Have a nice life!' I said cheerily, and as I got into my beat-up Fiat I suddenly realized that I'd just managed not to do something I'd never managed not to do before. I hadn't looked back.

So I went on holiday. One hot afternoon, on sun-loungers by the pool, the Boy was reading a heavyweight history of Europe, while I was racing guiltily through some romantic trash.

'What's it about?' he asked.

'Oh, it's wonderful rubbish. It's about these four debutantes at the turn of the century . . .' and I banged on for a bit, drawing the plot in great detail, wanting to explain. After a while, I started giggling.

'What's happened?' said the Boy, looking up.

'Ah well, you see the bitter and twisted over-the-hill society beauty is angry because her dull debutante charge is far too plain to get painted by Singer Sargent.'

'Oh no! She's not going to like that at all, is she?'

A while later, I laughed again.

'What is it now? Tell me everything.'

'But it's your turn. I want to know what's happening in Europe.'

'Cheese. I can tell you all you will ever need to know about significant developments in European cheesemaking in the last thousand years.'

The holiday coincided with my thirty-fourth birthday, and because he knew I liked to be in another country on my birthday, the Boy took me on a day trip to Africa, from Tarifa to Tangiers. When he told me he loved me, later, over dinner, his tone revealed a level of intensity and intimacy I had never heard when he'd used those words before. We talked about coming back to the same hotel soon, maybe in September.

This relationship was, then, turning out to be exactly what Richard had indicated it might be – I had embarked on an emotional adventure and I learned about my capacity for 'romance', and what

I learned, above all, was that I still had a capacity for 'romance', with or without apostrophes (but I guess that's critical theory for you).

We had another rather dark little running joke, the Boy and I.

'I promise I won't dump you while you're writing the book,' he'd say.

'And I won't write about you when you do,' I'd reply.

But we both broke our promises. I hadn't imagined the relationship would be over before we'd finished *Tomb Raider*. We had only just got to the last level.

I struggled through the first week of it, attempting to kick-start the coping machine – old dog, old tricks – and I did OK for a few days but, you know, this time I couldn't get my head to do the stuff I wanted, needed, it to do. I couldn't, in point of fact, actually believe it was already over because it just didn't make sense. In contrast to Eric, there had been no break-down in communication, the Boy had been so *very* with me so *very* recently, in Spain, a fortnight ago, for God's sake, and now...? And the more I thought about the sudden illogical brutality of it all, the more I felt close to a kind of madness. Eric had simply stopped loving me, had met someone else and had lied about how he felt, and although this had been excruciatingly painful, it had at least made sense. It was just one of the predictably disappointing things that people did. This, however, didn't make sense. There had been no beginning, middle and end to my relationship with the Boy, just a long beginning and a very short end. I tried to understand, though, sought out clues. Much later, in one of our old roller coaster era e-mails, I found one.

> *K,*
>
> *Trust. I think I once saw a movie about that. The usual metaphors: girl throws herself off wall, boy catches girl, girl laughs at boy's foolishness and wanders off to find man. Hmm, trust is a bad one. I don't trust myself in the grander scheme of things and, given your recent experiences, I think perhaps your trust is something I should earn with more than a few words. So if you need a dragon slain, give me a call.*
>
> *I can only promise you that I will be honest. I can tell you about my commitment problems, about jumping continents and wandering the world full of self-hate because of a poisonous fear of the word 'forever' but I will spare you. All I know is that I have now met somebody who is different to anybody I have met before.*
>
> *But that is no reason to trust me. I have destroyed good things just to feel the pain, so god knows where all this will go. I am walking on glass here, fully aware of the damage I could do if I tread too heavily. I can only tell you the truth and that I will continue to do . . .*

He'd kept his word in one respect. He'd always told the truth.

'I hurt so much. I can't believe how bad I feel,' he said, vehemently, on the phone a couple of days later. 'You know, I'm not leaving you because I don't love you any more.'

'Yes, I know. You're leaving me in order to avoid the possibility of not loving me in the future. And for the rest of the world?' I said, understanding, coping. And he agreed, relieved. I'd given him *The Times Atlas* as a Christmas present. Now it was apparently time to use it.

He told me he was going away for a few days, that he'd call me when he got back. I discussed it with friends, with the therapist, with anyone who would listen, and they all said this sounded like a hitch, not a real ending. But I thought about the Boy, who prided himself on never going back on a decision once he'd made it, and I wasn't so sure – *I have destroyed good things just to feel the pain*. But none the less, a few days later I turned up unannounced on his doorstep, seeking masochistic clarification.

I rang the bell. The door opened. Tired eyes. A warm, but wary, politeness, so I knew the score.

'Come in, come in.' And then: 'Oh yes – it's *over*,' said the Boy. 'But I can tell you I have never felt as bad about the end of a relationship as I have about this one. It really hurt.'

Maybe he thought that telling me this would help,

so I half-listened, crying, while he carried on talking in the past tense, not just about the relationship but also about any pain he might have felt over its unravelling. Could this be love? Could this ever have been love? Why did I keep on confusing romance with something more enduring? Maybe because romance is at least a doorway to something more enduring, and you've got to start somewhere.

And I really believed that. Right up until the point when I couldn't believe it any more.

When I felt myself suddenly spiral out of control, the first impression was of watching myself do it. There was the 'me' that was clearly collapsing and disintegrating right there on the Boy's living-room floor, and then there was the me who was looking on and thinking: Now *this* is interesting. I hadn't known that this kind of thing could happen so fast or be so terribly physical, but it did and it was. And while I waited, watching myself, I felt a tiny, still moment of triggered tension, felt the heart-shaped bullet make contact with its target and held my breath while something very, very tired inside of me half-sighed and then simply died. I think it was hope.

Immediately after that, I stopped watching myself.

nine

here come the
karma police

I am in Debra and David's house, rocking back and forward. *Who am I?* back and forward and back and forward and back and forward. *Who am I?* I don't know any more. Debra tells me she wants to take me to hospital, but David has made some calls and the hospital won't take me.

five days

one

A doctor arrives. I won't look at her. Silent tears. Shaking. Now I am on medication but the pain doesn't go. It arrives like a tsunami and knocks me down, drags me under. I try to fight it, rocking, holding myself tight and feeling everything.

Fight it. Fight it. *Fight it.*

Every time I shut my eyes I am so scared. Fear floods me and loneliness amputates me from the rest of the world. *Drowning.*

Who am I?

Caryn is here too. I don't look at her, but I can tell she is crying. Debra and Caryn and I sit all in a row on the sofa and I look at the floor. I try to explain how I feel: I have run out of love because I gave what I had left over after Eric to the Boy. Now he doesn't want it and I haven't got any left. And a life without any love is no life at all.

two

I am very small. I sit on a chair and even though my feet touch the ground it feels wrong, it feels as though they should swing. I am so small and so young that I can't speak. It's as if I haven't learned yet. Debra seems to understand this and cuts up my food and I eat it with a spoon. Sometimes I cry.

three

George arrives. I understand now that my friends are keeping me under surveillance in Debra's house while they decide what to do with me. I spend the day lying in bed, thinking of ways to escape. I am very tired. Very, very, *very* tired and I still can't speak. This can't go on much longer.

four

Phone calls all day. People talking about me while I sit passive, waiting. Debra tells me that I must see another doctor and that I will have to get in a cab and go across London, but that she will be with me. Inside the cab and out in the street there is terrible noise everywhere. People. I hold Debra's hand tight.

'*Why are we here?*' I shout at the doctor. He says I need to go to hospital. He has a very loud voice. We get in another cab and go back to Debra's house. More phone calls. People talking about me.

five

The doctor who saw me on Day One arrives with a psychiatrist. I don't look at them. They are NHS and prepared to section me but I have got very lucky – I am being sent somewhere private. I am conscious that some people are paying for this, but I can't think about that now.

'*Get me out. Go away. Why are we here? What's going on?*' I shout. I can tell that they are nice people, but I really want them to go because the only person I really trust is Debra. Still, they look at me and talk about me for a while before they leave, and then Debra and I get in the cab. I can tell she is very tired. I feel bad for making her so tired.

'It's a shame you didn't get a look at that psychiatrist, Kate. He was so handsome I could hardly speak.' And she squeezes my hand.

*

The room has peach yogurt coloured walls, motel chintz, a school-of-Bayswater-railings watercolour and a bedside table covered with an overgrown doily and a lamp that doesn't work. There is a fleur-de-lis motif on the single-duvet cover and the window overlooks a light well that is masquerading, courtesy of some dusty urban greenery and a couple of park benches, as a courtyard retreat.

'Title you wish to be known by?' asks a man with a clipboard.

'Dame,' I mutter lamely. 'And now I suppose you'll have to write down "delusions of grandeur".'

But he ignores that and carries on. Different people keep coming in and out of the room and all the while I make absolutely sure I'm on my best behaviour, perfectly polite and accommodating. Someone gives me a multiple-choice form with questions like 'Do you feel everyone else is to blame for your problems?', 'Can you hear voices inside your head?' and 'Are you feeling blue?' (No/A little/Quite a bit/Very/Extremely). I do not feel that everyone else is to blame for my problems, nor (slightly disappointingly) am I hearing the internal voices of the paranoid schizo – but 'Feeling blue?'. I snort derisively. I have the blues badder than a blind, bald, one-legged man sitting alone on a Mississippi veranda nursing a three-string guitar, an empty bottle of Jack Daniel's and a grudge.

A softly spoken pretty Irish nurse arrives. She

empties my bag, tells me she is taking my purse, keys and a bottle of anti-PMT starflower oil capsules packed out of habit. This week I'm kind of beyond PMT flower remedies and on to high doses of temazepam.

'Oh, I wouldn't do it like that!' I say breezily as she confiscates my packet of Gillette Blue IIs. 'Way too messy.'

'How would you do it?'

Uh-oh – a Good Cop. I shake my head. I'm not going to play the game.

'You can have them back in a few days, but if anyone asks if they can borrow them – and they will – don't let them.'

So far I have been trying to kid myself that I am taking a brief holiday in a three-star London hotel conveniently close to a selection of main line stations, but this comment (along with the red panic buttons by the bed and in the bathroom and the fact that there is no shower attachment and the window opens only five inches) effectively dispels the illusion.

Some food arrives. A meat dish, fluorescent gateau and a bread roll. Afterwards I light a Consulate. The rooms are non-smoking. I exhale via the five-inch gap.

For the past five desperate and difficult days Debra has helped me salvage just enough of my life to get me to this place. We have been through all of this extraordinary stuff together and now we are here, simultaneously hyper-talkative and blearily exhausted. I am relieved to be feeling technically 'safe' and contained but am already conscious of how much Debra has done for me and of how inadequately I will ever be able to thank her, even though the time when this might be a practical rather than an abstract dilemma seems inconceivably far off.

My psychiatrist arrives. I have only spoken to her once, on the phone, three hours previously. I didn't talk then, really, I howled. Now she is here I do not howl but I cannot look at her, either. Somehow, though, I am aware that she is small and gentle and instinctively I like and trust her. This is important because even though I am trying very hard to be a model patient, I do not trust many people. I, myself, am a godforsaken place, but now, here, presumably I must be safe. Within these walls, surely, the fragmented me can lie down and let other people piece me back together again? These are professionals, they must have the technology.

I want to be helpful so I engineer an attack of articulacy. It upsets me that even though I understand very clearly exactly why I am here and can recite my *taedium vitae* at length, this doesn't seem to make any difference. The unadulterated rawness of my pain, the complete sense of loss and rejection, the terrifyingly unprecedented loneliness and isolation and a near-total evaporation of any sense of myself cannot, this time, be talked away.

For the first couple of days I sleep, take my medication and wander the corridors, enervated, dissolving. I can't read anything more challenging than a *Hello!* picture caption and neither can I write. Without either of these distractions to act as a crutch I am thrown back into my fractured self and it is not a pleasant place to visit, even briefly. I structure my day to avoid too many inner confrontations. Seeing my psychiatrist helps, but is invariably preceded by excited anticipation and followed by bouts of introspection which start off grey and spiral into choleric blackness.

Nurses come on and off duty and stick their heads around my door. I make a lot of cups of tea and Marmite soldiers in the communal kitchen and warily check out the other patients congregating around *Jerry Springer* and *Oprah* in the lounge. But I'm not ready to make friends yet. After all, these people are probably mad.

My 'ward' (though we have separate rooms) caters for Depressives – Manic (for which the hip description is bi-polar), Clinical (which is me, apparently) or plain old-fashioned depressed Depressives – and is on the ground floor, presumably because we are the most likely to jump. Above us is the Eating Disorders Unit. Some of the EDU girls are occasionally to be found in our kitchen, scavenging for scraps like runty strays. Their kitchen is locked. One evening I spot a girl scarfing some of my cold leftover chips. She eats with her head right down to the plate and uses both hands but as soon as she sees me she runs, taking my Hermesetas with her. These girls unnerve me. When I come across them scuttling and cringing in the corridors I just want to shout 'Shoo!' because of their darting eyes and sneaky, feral demeanour. As a fellow inmate I know I should be more compassionate but each category of fuck-ups tends to gang together and the Depressives' running joke about the EDU girls is that they are lucky because they're the only ones who could potentially escape through the windows. The EDUs are, say the nurses, also the ones that used to get the spur-of-the-moment late-night visits from the sainted Diana. There are pictures of her in all the nurses' stations.

Elsewhere in the hospital there are wards containing alcoholics, other assorted addicts, the sectioned (which sounds like a Stephen King novella title), self-harmers and schizos. There is also the fourth floor, notable as the place where Michael Jackson (plus entourage) once stayed for a few days, weaning himself off prescription drugs. The nurses all have Wacko anecdotes. Despite this rich tapestry, I am certain that the Depressives ward has the most entertaining patients and staff. One night I am told by my favourite nurse, an Irishman called Malachy, that usage of the words Nervous and Breakdown in close conjunction is pretty much banned.

'You could have had a Personality Fragmentation,

though, Kathryn,' he suggests drily, while the two of us watch Dana International cavorting in a Jean-Paul Gaultier designed rooster on *The Eurovision Song Contest*. Saturday Night In The Bin – It's a Top Night In.

'Either way it sounds like bollocks . . .' I mutter. Malachy tut-tuts, shakes his head and ticks me off for my attitude. He is always ticking me off. He is the only one who can get away with it because he is the only nurse who manifests at my bedside just when I seem to need it the most and then makes a nuisance of himself until he's dragged it all out of me.

'Would you ever press the red button, Kathryn?' he asks me one evening as I lie on my bed, arms crossed, refusing to make eye contact and staring at the ceiling.

'No. Never, ever. Absolutely not. Under no cir-cumstances. Well . . . maybe if I thought I was having a heart attack.'

'And why is that?'

'Can't ask for help. Won't.' A fat tear squeezes itself out of the corner of an eye but Malachy is not prepared to indulge me. He sighs, rolls his eyes.

'So, have you heard from him recently?'

He doesn't mean Eric, who doesn't even know I am here and wouldn't call if he did, or even my father, who does and has. He means the Boy.

'Um. Yes.' More sighs. I sigh on an heroic scale at

present. 'I miss him. But then I'm always missing someone.'

Psychiatric illness cuts out the crap. Some days I am so naked and stripped of any sophistication and personality that I feel like I could quite easily communicate with dogs or dolphins or aliens. This isn't to be confused with hearing voices, it just means that as many of the bits I recognize as me have systematically disappeared I am now so emotionally attuned that I pick up on other people's moods like a satellite dish receiving distant signals. This is both a good thing and a bad thing. Good in that it means the only way might be up; bad in that I am the proverbial walking wounded. The thirty-four-year-old veneer has cracked and so, as vulnerable as a small child, it is easy for me to be hurt.

I am hurt by virtually anything that smacks of neglect or desertion, which currently encompasses not getting sent flowers by people I would like to be sent flowers by and coping with visitors having to leave me. Intellectually I know they have to go and I have to stay, but emotionally I identify much more strongly with dogs, who apparently believe that every time their owner walks out of the front door they are gone for good.

I hate asking the nurses for help but then I am also sulky, introverted and, eventually, angry if they don't somehow guess that I need it. I diagnose myself as Passive-Aggressive, thanks to one of the Cognitive Behavioural Therapy classes we are all persuaded to attend during the day. It works for lots of people but I hate the classes in CBT, perhaps because of the lists and flip charts, which remind me of Eric. I very much do not want to be 'taught' how to get better by shiny-haired twentysomething girls with Oxbridge psychology degrees. A fellow Depressive, Giles, is particularly scathing about these girls.

'What the hell am I going to learn from someone who hasn't been through it themselves?' he mutters one day during a group in which we have been asked to break up into sub-groups and, um, analyse each other's problems. 'Have you ever been sick?' he enquires of today's sparky, clean-limbed young positivist. She shakes her head, smiles wryly.

'See!' he says. 'What would she know?!'

I nod vigorously. I was a rebel at school and I am starting to rebel here. I have decided that CBT will not, under any circumstances, make me better, but for how long can I sit alone in my room without ending up even more bonkers than I already am? So I go to groups, if only to pass the time. One day in a group we are given a photocopied sheet – the only bit of the CBT notes (and there are a lot of notes) that I actually read:

> *To laugh is to risk appearing foolish*
> *To weep is to risk appearing sentimental*
> *To reach out for another is to risk involvement*
> *To expose feelings is to risk exposing your true self*

To hope is to risk despair
To try is to risk failure
To live is to risk dying
But risks must be taken
Because the greatest hazard in life is to risk nothing
The person who risks nothing
Does nothing, has nothing and is nothing
He may avoid suffering and sorrow
But he simply cannot learn, feel, change, grow, love
    or be
Chained by his opinions, he is a slave
He has forfeited freedom
Only a person who risks is free

I am much better one-on-one with my psychiatrist, with my clinical psychologist, with Malachy and with some of the other patients (we always refer to ourselves as the Nutters). There is, though, one nurse whom I loathe because, in my freshly peeled-and-salted emotional state, I can tell she doesn't really give a shit, that she's just here earning a living. This nurse has that old-fashioned patronizing 'Now-now! Tch-tch-tch! Naughty girl, Nursey knows best!' bedside manner. She talks slowly, as if to an idiot child, and cocks her head to one side when she asks the question that is to nursing what 'Going anywhere nice this summer?' is to hairdressers: *'And how are we feeling today?'* This approach might conceivably work with the wrinklies, who probably expect nurses to be like that, but everyone on my ward under about ninety can't stand her because, as old lag Carol (seven weeks in the Bin and counting) observes, 'She's got the rule book shoved right up her arse.'

On my ninth day in hospital, my second Sunday and my fourth day on Prozac, Nursey-Nursey is on duty and I am having a Black Dog of a day. While the hospital has worked very well as a kind of containment facility to save me from myself, now I am simply feeling mutinous, cabin-feverish and angry because I am not getting better fast enough, dammit. It turns out that there is no magical cure and no technology. Apparently I have to do most of the work myself.

It is oppressively hot outside and the thin streak of blue sky I can see from my window further depresses the Depressive me. I don't want summer, I was happy in winter. There is no breeze and no air-conditioning and only the five inches of open window to admit the lead-heavy air of the Marylebone Road directly into my room. Nonetheless I stay there all day, alone, lying on the bed, adrift on currents of rage, purgatorial loneliness and all-purpose hopeless-ness. Weekends in the Bin are deadly. Lots of people check out, go home for visits or out with friends and family, but I am terrified of home and horribly agoraphobic, so these are not options. The phone doesn't ring. I can't (won't?) call anyone because the weather is so hot I know that all I will speak to is a series of answering machines and that that will feel like rejection. I have no visitors.

Lost.

I've come on a bit in the past few days, though. I can now read newspaper picture captions and some poetry, if not novels. This afternoon I choose to read Rilke, over and over . . .

How I have felt that thing that's called 'to part',
and feel it still: a dark, invincible
cruel something by which what was joined so well
is once more shown, held out, and torn apart.
In what defenceless gaze at that I've stood,
which, as it, calling to me, let me go,
stayed there, as though it were all womanhood,
yet small and white and nothing more than, oh,
a waving, now already unrelated
to me, a slight, continuing wave, – scarce now
explainable: perhaps a plum-tree bough
some perching cuckoo's hastily vacated

For the first time in weeks, I scribble some stream of consciousness gibberish into a pad given to me by one of the nice nurses ('You're a writer, you're bound to want to write, aren't you?!' she'd said kindly. I didn't want to tell her that real writing, in proper sentences, containing thoughts and observations, was next to impossible. And that not being able to do it was just as scary as the thought that I would, eventually, have to if I am to carry on earning a living). After a while, though, I get spooked by my handwriting. It is edgy and nervous-looking, leaning perilously close to the edge of the page. Never mind what I've actually written, this is plainly the hand-writing of a Nutter.

The nurses are meant to look in on us often, for obvious reasons. Indeed a torch is shone on us every hour on the hour throughout the night but, because I am always sedated, I only find this out from a Nutter after about thirty-six nocturnal inspections. (First reaction? Panic. I sleep in the nude. The nights are hot and muggy and it is a very small duvet. Floodlit views of my naked arse – even if it is diminishing at a rate of about a pound a day – may well constitute an experience above and beyond the call of a nurse's duty.) Today, though, Nursey-Nursey ignores me. Needy as hell, I am torn between resentment that she is ignoring me and resentment that she might decide not to. No win.

After a day of prolix pointlessness coupled with loneliness, Debra and David suddenly arrive. Outside in the light well David nods off in what's left of the sun while Debra and I sit on a bench and I listen to myself talk. This is, increasingly, an out-of-body experience. I don't think I make much sense, mutter-ing about Rilke, slowly and fuggily, dressed like an extra from *Deliverance*.

When I arrived in hospital it was cold, so I bought fleeces and tracksuit bottoms, fuzzy, out-of-focus clothes that co-ordinated nicely with my inner state.

Then it got hot and so I bolted across the road to M&S and bought new underwear, T-shirts and a flouncy dressing gown that makes me look like Tammy Winceyette. In M&S I convinced myself that everybody was looking at me because I was so obviously not one of them. 'Them' being normal people, presumably fully functioning in the outside world that terrifies me so much. I felt highly conspicuous in the shop but immediately completely invisible when I was out in the street again. I scuttled back to the Bin, clinging to the walls of buildings like a cockroach. After this I ventured no further than the chip shop on the corner and the newsagent directly opposite, which is right next to the dole office where I used to sign on when I was eighteen.

Every time you want to go out you have to ask permission, then, if granted, the nurses buzz through to reception who, in turn, buzz you out when they've identified you. There is obviously a problem with bolters, though, because after a few days a new manned and coded security system is in place at the front door. I think they should issue swipe cards to the Chosen Ones, balls and chains to the Nutters. Still, a Chosen One can easily slide the slippery slope to Nutterdom and, this being a hospital with the prime objective of getting you better and getting you out, presumably vice versa.

I am, despite my initial wariness, making friends. There is Cindy, twenty-nine, mother of two, stepmother to two more. Cindy defines herself by motherhood, despite – or perhaps because of – the fact that she didn't get any decent mothering herself. In her room Cindy has big studio portraits of the kids and an endless supply of copies of *Bella* and *More* and lots and lots of comfort food. Cindy is generous with her Ovaltine and herself. Sometimes, because she is so busy making sure everyone else is OK, it is easy to forget that one of the reasons she is here is because she is married to a violent man.

Carol is twenty-seven and has been a money dealer in the City for ten years but has recently, spectacularly, burned out. Carol is six feet tall and five feet of her is, easily, legs. One of my visitors, a fashion industry veteran, assumes she is a model but Carol has the self-esteem of a gnat, so when I tell her this she blushes and does a 'Who, me?!' face. Twenty-seven may well be too late to start modelling but she should give it a try.

Giles is also twenty-seven and works in the city. Analysing futures, or something. He is the one who gives Ms Vorderman serious competition during our daily *Countdown*-watching sessions in Cindy's room (I am embarrassingly bad, even at the bits with words. Carol and Giles do *The Times* Quick Crossword while I read *More*). Giles has had to give up work, however, because he has severe panic attacks. He was admitted a week before me and both Cindy and Carol were extremely impressed because he had a nurse on guard outside his door all through his first night. We are also very jealous because Giles has the biggest and most exotic cocktail of prescribed drugs out of any of us – every morning and night he ingests an entire Damien Hirst spot painting.

This unlikely quartet is a gang, then. After a few days Cindy, Carol and Giles confess that when I first told them I was a journalist they decided I was undercover, pretending to be bonkers, and that I was probably going to write about them. I tell them I'm not that bloody good an actress. Then I admit that I've been writing a book, but it's on hold.

'Oh!' exclaims Carol. 'I wanna be in it!' It turns out they all do. Despite the fact that even thinking about finishing the book seems impossible right now, I ask them to choose their own pseudonyms.

'No, no!' says Cindy. 'We want you to use our real names!'

'You don't, not really . . .' I say. 'They're all pretty identifiable!'

'Exactly!' says Giles. 'We want to be in it.'

'OK,' I say, but I change them anyway.

Conversation turns to the disappointing lack of celebrities in the hospital, which is a well-known haven for addicted soap stars and anorexic models. We wonder what it might have been like to have had Michael Jackson sharing at a Cognitive Restructuring class – 'I'm bad, I'm mad . . .' – when Malachy in-forms us that our sibling hospital, which is out in the green belt and has a proper garden and chandeliers in the restaurant, is currently heaving with celebs.

'Who?'

'Who?'

'Who?'

'Who? Oh, *go on!*'

But he won't. We all beg to be transferred.

'You don't need to be, you've got Kathryn!' he says mischievously. I gaze heavenwards. Carol looks suspicious.

'Are you famous, then?'

'No,' I sigh, 'not even slightly.'

'She is too!' says Malachy.

'Oh *God*, Kathryn's famous!'

'Look, I am *not* famous, all right? You haven't heard of me, have you?'

'No, but do you get your picture alongside the things you write?'

'Well, yes, sometimes, but . . .'

'Ha! Kathryn's our celebrity and we didn't even know it!' exclaims Carol triumphantly.

I shrug, put on a mock self-deprecatory 'OK, you've sussed me' expression, while Malachy grins.

'Look, I'm really sorry I'm such a crap one.'

'Your turn to make the Ovaltine,' says Cindy.

Prozac doesn't, I think, agree with me. I feel like the Peter Finch character in *Network* – I Am Mad As Hell And I'm Not Going To Take It Any More. And then there is this dislocation of self, during which

I feel as if I am observing my every action and word. Sometimes this is a good thing but on the whole I'd prefer to be able to control it. Even given the situation in which I find myself, my mood swings surprise me. After a week I come off Prozac, before it even kicks in.

The Boy visits me twice, bringing flowers, Jaffa Cakes, grapes and unsuitable paperbacks. I reject *Regeneration*, partly on the grounds that I can't read books at the moment but even if I could this one is set in a hospital full of victims of First World War shell-shock and a romp through even a prize-winning fictional account of post-traumatic stress disorder doesn't currently appeal.

He tells me that he has handed in his notice at work and rented a house hundreds of miles away and will be leaving London permanently in a matter of weeks. Do I think he's done the right thing, he wonders, and I can hardly contain my emotion at the fact that he has already managed to push our relationship so far away from him. *Do I think he's done the right thing? Um – that's a tricky one.* I don't know why he comes to see me other than to assuage some presumed guilt, seek absolution. I daren't even think that, maybe, he just cares about me.

'Finished *Tomb Raider* yet?' I wonder.

'Haven't touched it. Can't. Look, do you blame me?'

'No,' I reply. 'You were the catalyst, not the cause.'

And this is true. Still, because I love him it hurts to see him and because I love him it hurts not to see him and so after two visits I attempt to decipher which hurt is the greater hurt and decide that seeing him is worse, so I tell him, and he leaves. I feel a desperate sense of déjà vu.

Malachy is on duty tonight and he knew the Boy was coming to see me. He watches me as the metaphorical storm clouds gather.

'Happy! Happy! Happy!' says Malachy and hands me one small white pill. I don't even ask what it is, just swallow it like a good girl. Later I am given something else on top of my usual temazepam and I sleep heavily. The following day, though, is a desperate one. I regret telling the Boy to get out of my life, but I just can't watch him coping while I am not, can't be subjected to the pulling up of his emotional drawbridge, can't be what he wants me to be (even though it's what I want to be too). I can't do stoic and cheery any more. It's all gone.

My room is getting quite cosy. Some surprising people have sent flowers, while some of the more obvious people haven't sent any. I suppose if I'd broken my leg or had my appendix removed I would have been inundated, but there is so much stigma attached to being in a psychiatric hospital and so much ignorance about what it might mean that I guess lots of people are scared. It breaks down into two categories: the 'there but for the grace of...' faction, who send flowers; and the copers, to whom I was previously allied, who won't even acknowledge I'm here because they probably think: Padded cell, straitjacket, ECT, frontal lobotomy ... weird shit, all of it. Hopefully she'll just get better soon and we'll never have to mention it. But nobody could be more obsessed with mythologizing the minutiae of psychiatric illness than the Nutters in the Cuckoo's Nest. One night Carol, Giles and I bug Malachy to show us the straitjackets.

'There aren't any,' he sighs. 'We're trained to use arm-locks, that kind of thing.'

'Show us!'

'NO! Now, tell me you all want your pills. Tell me you want to go to sleep. Please.'

We pout and shake our heads, like small siblings refusing our greens.

'Do people top themselves very often here?' enquires Carol casually, as if checking on the Ovaltine supply.

'It happens.'

'If someone's going to do it, then they're always going to find a way – even in a hospital ...' observes Giles and we all nod sagely. Been there, nearly done it.

'When did it last happen?' Carol again.

'I'm not saying,' says Malachy, wearily.

'And what happens? Do you all get a bollocking?'

'There is, um, an Inquiry. *Now* would you please all take your pills and GO TO BED! . . .'

I remember that, earlier, when I went up to the first floor to use the shower I left my tweezers behind. A person could, I figure, do an awful lot of damage to themselves, or somebody else, with a pair of tweezers. What if a self-harmer got hold of them? I flush hot with guilt and slope upstairs. To my profound relief the tweezers are still on the window ledge, but I inspect them closely, forensically, nonetheless.

My bedside table is a kind of shrine to bonkersness. Debra lent me some big, smooth stones ('To make you feel at home. My home . . .'), gave me worry beads and, in her jewellery-making class last Saturday, she beat me a little metal heart, perhaps to replace the heavily corroded one I already own. She has also made me hummus and brought posh bread because the food here is so desperate. Caryn and her daughter Mateda brought me a little sandstone statuette of two abstract figures entwined in a hug, Jonathan Wilmot made me one of his Celtic knots and Emma has sent over exotic bath oil and body lotion.

My friend Claudia, who doesn't even know I am here, recently sent me a photograph she took of me when we were both about eighteen or nineteen, which has pride of place on the bedside doily, under the lamp that doesn't work.

I recall the occasion vividly. We were dressing up

to go dancing or, in my case, dressing down. In the picture I have a peroxide-blonde mop crowned with a paste diamond tiara (Courtney Love eat your heart out) and am wearing little else apart from red lips, a paste necklace, a lacy white underwired bra, a gold and white wedding sari tied low on my hips and my old tattoo. (The 1983 skull with the rose in its teeth, which was covered up by a dolphin, courtesy of the same tattooist, in 1988. I occasionally fantasize about covering the dolphin with a big black rectangle. Perhaps in 2001.) My smile says, 'I am young, I am fearless and anything is possible.' There is a mesmerizing (at least to me) amount of naked flesh. God but I was slim fifteen or so years ago: hips, ribcage, concave stomach. I can't stop looking at this picture. I thought I knew it all then. I had no bloody idea.

Perhaps inspired by this *memento vivere*, I start going to the yoga class held every morning at 9.30. After the first session I ache dreadfully. An external ache to match all the internal ones. Carol recommends a massage and of course I want one immediately, so I collar Sue-the-Masseuse in the corridor.

'I can't do you until next Tuesday, I'm afraid,' says Sue.

'Oh, I won't be in here by then!' I reply. It's Wednesday.

'Well, let's make the appointment and then if you're not here, you're not here . . .' says Sue. So I do and, come Tuesday, funnily enough I'm still here.

I'm in such a rush to get better because every day I wake up feeling guilty. Guilty for still being here and being ill. Guilty for taking up people's time and energy and being this monstrous burden. Guilty for not being at work. Guilty for not dealing with the Boy's rejection of me like a proper grown-up. Guilty for being such a self-absorbed wreck. Guilty for, oh, every bloody thing. Narcissistic guilt – could that be a psychiatric condition?

I think I know about massage – I must have had fifty in my life prior to this one – but Sue is in a different league. For a start she is a 'massage therapist', so she talks about much more than essential oils. She wants to know why I'm here, so I tell her, and then she starts work. I immediately recognize that this is not a normal massage because she ignores my legs and arms and literally hammers my solar plexus, before moving up around my heart and then to my head. My eyes are tight shut when she asks if I can see any colours.

'No, just a kind of grey . . .' And so she carries on beating me like a drum. The sensation is not unpleasant, merely new and unexpected.

'Can you feel the vibrations anywhere else in your body?'

'Yes. Through to my back and . . . in my fingers.'

'Good!' When she pauses my internal organs hum and throb and thrum and then she starts again, moving around my left breast. This feels not only slightly taboo but also as though it should hurt more than it does. *Hum, thrum, throb, tingle* ... and then flashes of green in front of my eyes, like a row of thin silk scarves hanging out to dry on a washing line.

'I can see green ...' I whisper, tentatively.

'Green? Excellent! Green is the colour of the heart chakra.' There is another pause. 'I can *feel* your broken heart, Kate,' she says, gently.

I desperately want to cry, but I hold back and save it for later (and when I do, I weep not loud but deep. I hadn't for one moment expected this kind of treatment in the Bin and it feels astringently emotional to be touched with extreme care and respect by another human being. I hadn't realized how very desperately, primally, I have missed it). I make another appointment for Friday. And then, on Saturday, I leave hospital.

'It is probably a week too soon,' says my consultant, but I want to go because my mother, having rather spookily intuited that something was very wrong, even from a distance of twelve thousand miles, finally tracked me down (I hadn't wanted to worry her, all that way away) and is now making a mercy dash to her daughter's bedside. She arrives on Sunday.

We had had a long and tearful telephone conversation the previous week.

'I know why you're in hospital,' she blurted, in between sobs. And indeed she did because, as I had told the Boy (the catalyst, after all, not the cause), this mess I found myself in was really the result of a much older, unresolved mess, of which both Eric and this latest desertion were simply echoes. My mother had understood without being told and so she was coming here in an attempt to bridge the gulf that had grown between the rational, grown-up thirty-four-year-old me and the needy, tiny, inarticulate me; the one that had been wounded the best part of a lifetime ago but had learned, as many of us do, to cope and to hide the scars. I was, finally, slowly coming to understand that this old pain was why, for me, every emotional rejection feels like a kind of death.

'You've been a model patient, Kathryn,' says one of the (nice) nurses as I prepare to leave.

'Really?!'

'Oh yes. No trouble at all.'

This is obviously meant to be a compliment so why does it feels like an insult – I'd been put in a psychiatric hospital and I'd been *no trouble at all*? Apparently I can't even 'fragment' without being a bloody control freak.

'Oh well, I'm sure all of us here aim to please,' I mutter, 'and thanks for your help.' And so they buzz me out into the world again, with their best wishes and a little bag containing six temazepam. *Six*. Is that it?

'The sun is shining,' I remark, embracing banality in an effort to stave off having to think about anything scarier, like tomorrow, and the day after, and the day after that.

'But – no, don't tell me – it's raining in your heart?' says George, with irony. She was with me right at the beginning of all this and now, having come to drive me home from hospital in the middle of a May day thirty-two months later, is therefore, quite by chance, also with me at the end of it. If indeed this is the end of it.

'Yeah, something like that.'

And we laugh.

from this day forward . . .

Out of the nine weddings that my friend Fiona went to in 1995, five of the marriages had failed within three years.

acknowledgements

With love and thanks to Tim Adams, Kamal Ahmed, Roger Alton, John Azopardi, Lindsay Baker, Peter Barnes, Bella Bathurst, John Battsek, David Bergin, Ian Birch, Moira Bogue, Mike Bradley, Mervyn Brady, Martin Bright, Lola Bubbosh, Carmel, Cate, Charles, Tim Clark, Nick Cohen, Stephanie Crean, B. J. Cunningham, Louise Coopman, Terence Trent D'Arby, Lucy Darwin, Fiona Dealey, Ian Denyer, Robin Derrick, Richard Dienst, Lucia Dolan, Dave Dorrell, Ursula Doyle, Dr Elza Eapen, Tony Elliott, Guy Evans, Euan Ferguson, Jane Ferguson, Ken Flanagan, Guy and Trina Fletcher, Caryn Franklin, Gideon, Raz Gold, Georgina Goodman, Hugh Hefner, Phil Hogan, Kathryn Holliday, Peter Howarth, Will Hutton, Dylan Jones, Terry Jones, Tricia Jones, Barry Kamen, Adam Kenwright, Lisa O'Kelly, Sherald Lamden, Harriet Lane, Fergus Lawlor, Kimberley Leston, Bel Littlejohn, Nick and Julie Logan, Sue Lyons, Neil and Liz Manson, Cynthia de Maria,

Mandi Martin, Jon Moss, John Mulholland, Anna Murphy, Dominic Murphy, Malachy Murphy, Claudia Nathan, Shirley and Jerrold Nathan, Ruaridh Nicoll, Dorota Nosowicz, Jade Parker, Emma Parry, Ian Penman, Oliver Peyton, Justine Picardie, Andrew Purvis, Quentin Radford, Jay Raynor, Brue Richardson, David Rosen, Mike and Suzy Schneideman, Seal, Avril Silk, Anne Smith, John Sobey, Neil Spencer, Ric Stell, Tatiana Strauss, John Sweeney, Jocelyn Targett, Gary Tarn, David Toop, Juliette Toop, David Vincent, Ollie Weait, Sarah Walter, Ian R. Webb, Paul Webster and Jonathan Wilmot. Also, special thanks to my extraordinary parents, Doug and Patsi, and my brother Jonathan – I love you very much.

BECKS LOVE YOU lots A. x x x

BABA YOU GAVE mo your heart it had no walls only a door don't lock me out with love me.

BMD I DON'T see you often but I still adore you love NKI

BEUERLEY BE MY valentine eighth in a series

BALDRICK, YOU'RE NEVER too far away, love Spacedust

BULULALOW, DREAMING OF you. My heart overflows , but empties itself completely each solitary dawn. ESNA

BABY YOU'RE THE best. love your chocolate button

BADGER DO WE have a date in june 831 always lady B.

BELNA ROAROAW! LOVE you always, Danda xxx

BK BLANCH MY runner beans. love Watermelon Man

BEV, I LOVE you lots. We do have a future together. It must be true. it's in the paper. M.

BUBBLES-THE MOUNTAINS and the sea are now behind us. We now look to tidal rivers and educational choice I love you very much-Capricorn

BOOZIE AND PEEPEE love Catchie and cady respectively.

BESTMAN DON'T EVER 'nop it love always bridesmaid

BACKGAMMON QUEEN. SNOTTY potty, dotty. and groty but you are still top totty.

BETH. IF LOVE returns.I'm here. Your best friend, whatever. Milo

BOWLESY IF I had a million dollars... Love Psycho.

BABY-BEACHED WHALE or 69 you're the expert-Scamp.

BEAR I LOVE your Steak Pud. Love ?

BUTCH VEGGIE ARTISTE, let me float your ducks in Bethnal Green.

BNBH Love you to the moon. Lnbh xxx

BEAN ADORE YOU and bellybutton fluffy, Bean.

BEAUTIFUL BECCA, BRIGHT as the moon, love from the man with a wooden spoon!

BEAVER THINKING OF you in your little lodge, knawing twigs and eating frogs. Badger

BISCUIT, thinking of you - blonde and blue - drinking, dancing, smoking too Pete.

BEAST, STILL CRAZY for you after all these years. Beauty

BOOZY, YOU'RE MY Broccoli and Nachos. Love has.

BUG EYED BEAUTY, you are my treasure forever, cuddles, kisses and much more, lots of love, Moronic Mighty Martian Monster.

BENJI, REMEMBER ME? I'm coming back to England in May, will you take me all the way? Maritza.x

forward to being Mrs Farrell - what do you think ? Marie xxx

DIVING MOOSE. LET me dry those big cuddly antlers.

DARLING HONEY I love you more and more want to make it offical? Wig

DARLING CAROL, FAMILIAR acts are beautiful through love. Bloggs

DETAIL OF MY heart love not renaissance man

DEMITRA- JE T'AIMES toujours, je t'envois des roses - S.

DANIELA I'VE LAID my dreams at your feet, please tread softly-your dreamer.

DANNY O' KIEFFE you complete me. Love always, Sharon Anderson.

DEAR NORAH ALL the very very best for 1998 and indeed the future from Nicol with love XXXX

DEAR RACHEL IT was always a risk going out with a scouser but it is only my heart you stole!

DEAREST MARK. APPORTE-MOI la tete de Nigel. Amities Guy xxxxxxxxx

DEAREST MUMMY DADDY RICHARD, and Toby miss you all lots of thinking of you, big cuddies. Boo Boo xxxx

DOCTOR DECLARES LOVE for naughty nurse. Sweet, sparkle-eyed Sue. sing your song with me.

DARLING S OUR love will endure beyond the magic of this brief shared breath.

DOVER MORE KISSES street amazing kisses kings road, burford, champagne, silk scarves. goats cheese, zematt, limes, promises kept, l'odeon, ear nibbling, charterhouse square! want you more.

DAVE, I NEED your love. God speed your love to me! Janice

"DRUNK AS DRUNK on turpentine". To M from D

DRAG QUEEN 1976 essay on love's auction overdue. see me!

DEAR, PET BAT, stay well. Everything improves at last!

DUCATI DARE DEVIL, have leathers will ride!! love Petal xxx

DAVID, I would give you my last Rolo any day. See you in Paris.

DOOKINS - Coocky Coocky Coo - I love my mummy munchkin. From your other big baby. Doh!!

DOM LOVE YOU always love Karla and Jay Jay xxx

DEBBIE I'M ON my knees buy me dinner, your number one fan D (reading)

DEAR KELLY. Love, hugs, hedgehogs and gorillas. Inarfanar?

DARLING W, NEED u, want u, love u, your M

DANIELLE MCDONALD See you tonight and I will treat you to a bite. Love always xxx $'s

DEAREST SYD, Happy Valentines. Lots of love Mutley.

DEAR KATE, I hope we have a wonderful valentines day. I love you lots Gareth xxxx

DUCATI DARE DEVIL, have leathers will ride!! love Petal xxx

DAVID, I would give you my last Rolo any day. See you in Paris.

DOOKINS - Coocky Coocky Coo - I love my mummy munchkin. From your other big baby. Doh!!

DANIELLE MCDONALD See you tonight and I will treat you to a bite. Love always xxx $'s

"DRUNK AS DRUNK on turpentine". To M from D

DAVID, I would give you my last Rolo any day. See you in Paris.

DAVE, I NEED your love. God speed your love to me! Janice

DEAR RACHEL IT was always a risk going out with a scouser but it is only my heart you stole!

DEAREST MARK. APPORTE-MOI la tete de Nigel. Amities Guy xxxxxxxx

---

FUR COATS AND fancy boots baby you drive me crazy.

FECK, ARSE, DRINK, now you've found the message Ian i want you always, days, years, eternities.

FOR ALL IN my mind, of all mankind, I love but you alone.

FATFREE HONESTLY YOUR chubbies are slimmer love the fox.

FIRST MATE TO crew-how about the mask tonight?

FLUFFY BUNNY, I love you, thankyou for everything

FATBELLY ON MY left! but as long as it's close to me.

FLOPPY LOVES BUBBLES, Bubbles loves Floppy, always and forever, home soon all my love, Craig

FINE WORDS BUTTER no parsnips but are cheaper than roses. Love M.

FROM ONE TOAD to another.

FOR ALL THE triple david's there's still cereal!

40 VALENTINES 40 birthdays. dear Mushie I'll love you for millions more. Scrumbie

FRIENDLY CHILD. DEAREST gentle one. Never truer love nor deeper sorrow. P

Frankie and Johnny Valentine Reunion 13th, 14th, 15th Angel Delight xxx be there.

FRUITY FROLIKER. balcony beauty, wanton wallower, love you flat out on the autobahn. moi!

FLOSSY SO NEAR so far but together forever. Brian.

FUNKY LOVEBUG Do you collect Butterflies? Love Helliecog.

G. MY WIFE. 21/09/1997 best day of my life. love always D.

GILLYWIFE SENDING YOU huge materia of love hub xxx

GILLIAN, NO ONE understood why he fell for mary? I still laugh out loud when I remember that night! love Jeremy

GILLIE CON CARNE. Hot in durobrivae or eboracum. May it ever continue!

GOD DID IT and you are handsome, clever and very special.

GUCH GIVES HEARTS strength hearts give guch thanks.

GIANNA B - " ITS all about you" - only you.

GENE, CAN'T WAIT for Tuscany, Love always, Helen.

GIVE ME A SNOG Scottie dog! Love from Posh Bird xxx

GERDY- PEDY PUDDING and pie. INI loves you.

GOOD MORNING MRS chip love, trouble at mill.

GRENDALDENE - Fancy room service again? Love Stoopid

GENTLE ELF STRONG, deep, healer love always Lucinda

Gold Heart Day is today, buy a Gold Heart and support The Variety Club.

Give Love. Buy a Gold Heart and show the world you care.

Gros Bisous A mes parents cheris et mes oiscaux. A bientot. Marlene

GARY, I THINK i'm in love with you. Silly fool? i hope not.

GODFRITH LOVES TISHA. Howl!

DAVID, I would give you my last Rolo any day. See you in Paris.

DAVE, I NEED your love. God speed your love to me! Janice

DEAR RACHEL IT was always a risk going out with a scouser but it is only my heart you stole!

DEAREST MARK. APPORTE-MOI la tete de Nigel. Amities Guy xxxxxxxxx

---

HIPPO COME AND wallow in the mud with me and we'll stick together for ever and ever with love frazzell.

HAPPY VALENTINES DAY to the most boringly good in bed man I know.

HOWEVER YOU SAY I love you, a Gold Heart says you care.. buy one today for sick, disabled and disadvantaged children.

HY NOTICE HERALDS angel travelling to October Nirvana

HI! BABE. SUPRISE! glad i've got you. smellbags.

HAPPY VALENTINE'S DAY gorgeous baby from the trainspotter

HB1 THE COOLEST bake in Leith, love Honey Bunny.

H. TOUCHY FEELY Huge Circles. Love you. Specky.

I LOVE YOU so very much HBB.

I LOVE YOU Ghashdi as long as sun shines, stars glitter, heartbeat.

I WOPILOPLOP LOPOVOPE yopou foporop evoperop soparopahop lopovope dopai.

I LOVE YOU Hazel. On we go with our journey, and FUZZI too.

IVYBEAR RENT CD1, track19 "I might do, definitely" all my love Bendy.

IN A DRAB, dark world your radiant beauty brings me light.

I LOVE MYSELF just like you and often forget to mention that I love you too. Axxx

INDEPENDENT CHISWICK GIRL, maybe you can take me up a grade at no extra cost.

I LOVE YOU ferret. Forever you and me

I WILL BE your celandine if you will be my valentine.

IAN GREYBOY ABBS wolf growl slobbery licks handcuff

JULIE MY SWAN you are the one may our love go on and on.

JANE DOVESTONES RESERVOIR, 180 busstop, burnedge fold road, room with a view, i remember forever 8.11.75 Mike

J, FLY WITH me my gorgeous butterfly. B.

JENNY MY DRAYLON sofa bed, love from porky.

J. GUESS WHAT? yes, I love you today too! T.

JANET BE MY Singapore chow mein on valentine day

J, FLY WITH me my gorgeous butterfly. B.

JENNY MY DRAYLON sofa bed, love from porky.

J. GUESS WHAT? yes, I love you today too! T.

JON, READ MY lips I Love You Beanface.

JANET the darling of darlings, thanks for everthing. Pete.

JASON MORGAN forever and always, your valentine. Miss Minga xxx

---

JIM - just because your birthday boy don't feel love you too! Madge

JON, READ MY lips I Love You Beanface.

JANET the darling of thanks for everthing. Pet

JASON MORGAN fore always, your valentin Minga xxx

JLW YOU BOONA Love xxxx

JANESK, WHAT WITH Death and nursery we find an evening for much love, Philbo.

Jules, my favourite bo Pierce aka agent pants

JIM - just because yo birthday boy don't fee love you too! Madge

JLW YOU BOONA Lo xxxx

JANE DOVESTONES RI 180 busstop, burnedge room with a view, i rer ever 8.11.75 Mike

J. GUESS WHAT? yes today too! T.

KISS FROM A ro have been loved on a line one book one en

KENNY DUST, I love y tale?

KATE MY LOVE for yo Eight months a short Paul

KAREN'S HAIKU 1998 you'll be 33

KAREN. THIRD TIME L lose you again. Andr

KIND HEARTED? Giv to the people who n Buy your Gold Hea help sick, disabled a taged children.

KIM-KIM YOUR BEAU the wonders of natu you

KARLA A VALENTINE Cancel the wedding moon too, we'll wait to say I do! Love yal

K. STILL BLOODY lov

K, LOVING YOU fro Holland — and be

KURTI: ICI LES rest brittanique-Autrich points. Austria twelv

KAREN PUT YOUR te gonna chase you re room, love John.

LIFE'S RICH PA weave around our l Romeo.

LISA IS IT enough Romeo.

LIEBCHEN. SCHOGGEN v aechzenden beine

LOOKING ARRANW darling M, with a' valentines day and

LOVE YOU ALWAY your suffolk sweet

LION MARY EVE lu love Kitten

L2X VSS001 THAT' for two?

LOR MON LE coeur monte mon. Chan